RITUAL
MAGIC
of the
GOLDEN
DAWN

RITUAL MAGIC

of the

GOLDEN DAWN

Works by
S.L. MacGregor Mathers
and Others

Francis King

Destiny Books
Rochester, Vermont

Destiny Books
One Park Street
Rochester, Vermont 05767
www.gotoit.com

Library of Congress Cataloging-in-Publication Data
Mathers, S. L. MacGregor (Samuel Liddell MacGregor), 1854–1918.
[Astral projection, ritual magic, and alchemy]
Ritual magic of the Golden Dawn : works / by S. L. MacGregor Mathers and others; edited by Francis King.
    p.   cm.
Originally published: Astral projection, ritual magic, and alchemy. London : Spearman, 1971.
Includes bibliographical references.
ISBN 0-89281-617-1 (alk. paper)
1. Hermetic Order of the Golden Dawn. 2. Magic. 3. Astral projection. 4. Rosicrucians. 5. Occultism. I. King, Francis. 1904– . II. Title.
BF1611.M378 1997
135'.43—dc21   97-1117
                                                           CIP

Printed and bound in the United States

10 9 8 7 6 5 4 3 2 1

Destiny Books is a division of Inner Traditions International

Distributed to the book trade in Canada by Publishers Group West (PGW), Toronto, Ontario

To the memories of Gerald Yorke and
Francis Israel Regardie

CONTENTS

CONTENTS

FOREWORD

New Golden Dawn Discoveries

In view of the current widespread interest in both the history of the Hermetic Order of the Golden Dawn and the magical system which was the basis of all the occult activities of its members, who included W. B. Yeats, Aleister Crowley, and Dion Fortune, it is surprising that today, in 1987, important Order-instructional documents dating from before 1900 should be published for the first time.

Yet, as readers of Appendix D of this book will discover for themselves, such is the case, and it would seem probable that *all* the Golden Dawn instructional documents, on which the Order's magical workings were based, are now available in printed form.

Only fifty years ago the position was very different, and the only people to have even heard of the Hermetic Order of the Golden Dawn, save for initiates of one or two obscure secret societies derived from it, were those comparatively few people who had read the *Autobiographies* of W. B. Yeats, and a handful of dedicated students of the writings of Aleister Crowley.

Somewhere around the middle of the 1930s the situation began to change. The fiction and non-fiction books and articles of Dion Fortune made available to the occult public a somewhat popularized version of some aspects of the Order's teachings: Israel Regardie's *Tree of Life* presented the Golden Dawn techniques of ritual magic in a readable and fairly easily comprehended manner; and, eventually, many of the Order's rituals and instructional documents were printed in *The Golden Dawn* (4 vols., Aries Press, Chicago, 1937-40).

Since then much more has been published and, as a result of all this, most western occultists of the present day are well aware of the general nature of the Golden Dawn system—although few of them have worked that system in its entirety. An awareness of the one-time existence of the Golden Dawn as a working magical order now extends well beyond the ranks of those who could consider themselves to be 'working occultists' or even serious students of the occult; most people who have, even cursorily, read such best sellers as Colin Wilson's excellent *The Occult* have heard the name 'Golden Dawn' and are vaguely conscious of the fact that such men as A. E. Waite, Aleister Crowley, Arthur Machen, and W. B. Yeats were, at one time or another, associated with the Order.

There is no doubt that some of the men and women who received Golden Dawn initiation found the Order's teachings and its syncretistic approach little to their taste. Thus, of the four names given above, A. E. Waite rejected all the specifically magical elements in the Order's system, while Arthur Machen seems to have eventually come to the conclusion that the Golden Dawn was no more than a bad joke—in some of his autobiographical writings he sarcastically referred to it as 'The Twilight Star'.

What undoubtedly repelled some of those who rejected the Order was the way in which they were, after their initiation as neophytes, given 'secret manuscripts' which contained no information which could not fairly easily have been obtained from printed sources—Crowley jibed that he had been, first, sworn to secrecy, and then 'had the Hebrew alphabet entrusted to his safe keeping'.

Some of the most prominent members of the Golden Dawn, amongst them J. W. Brodie Innes, were aware of this problem, which was particularly acute in relation to the instructional documents—known as 'Knowledge Lectures'—pertaining to the lower steps in the Order's grade system. Brodie Innes wrote, in reference to the first Knowledge Lecture, that given to neophytes:

> The newly initiated brother of our Order . . . experiences an involuntary feeling of disappointment—'Is this all', he will say to himself, 'After all the promises, the elaborate ritual, the pledges of inviolable secrecy. A few symbols to be found in scores of books.' But let him take heart. It is not to jest with him that this lecture is put forth in this way. Our curriculum is an elaborate system of occult education and training, designed many centuries ago, to lead men step by step to the highest advance they are capable in this life of attaining, and to the diligent student we can promise the unfoldment of the Spiritual Life, the development of all the faculties, and the power to fulfil the purpose of this present earth life and to enter with confidence on the future.
>
> I who write these few words have myself been a student of the Order for near on thirty years, and I can say with absolute truth and conviction I would not be without one atom of the teaching I have had. Let him

[i.e. the student of the Golden Dawn system] therefore not be discouraged at the outset. The First Knowledge Lecture indicates the plan and scope of his first studies, and gives him, as it were, the alphabet of the sciences he is to learn.[1]

It seems to me that the contention made in the last sentence quoted above is perfectly true; without the basic information given in the First Knowledge Lecture concerning such matters as the names and symbols of the signs of the zodiac it would have been difficult, perhaps impossible, for initiates of the higher grades of the Order—notably the grade known as Adeptus Minor—to fully understand the nature of the theoretical and practical teachings contained in the Order's official instructional documents and in the semi-official Flying Rolls which form, so to speak, a 'Golden Dawn apocrypha', a Coda to the 'Authorized Version' of the system developed by Mathers and his close associates.

The Flying Rolls contain much of interest to the student of the history, theory, and practice of what Dion Fortune called 'the Western Esoteric Tradition' and what is perhaps better termed as simply 'the Golden Dawn system'.

This new and enlarged edition of *Ritual Magic of the Golden Dawn* now contains *all* the Flying Rolls not included in the many editions of Regardie's *Golden Dawn*. Copies of those which were not included in the first edition have been traced by Mr R. A. Gilbert, and the full texts of them, together with Mr Gilbert's account of his discovery, appear as Appendix D of this book.

The long-missing 'fugitive' Flying Rolls, now, in 1987, printed for the first time are:

> Flying Roll XXII
> Flying Roll XXIV
> Flying Roll XXVIII
> Flying Roll XXIX
> Flying Roll XXXI
> Flying Roll XXXII

The first of these was generally known under the title of 'Free Will', but it does in fact contain two essays, only the first of which is on the subject of free will, written by a certain 'Frater *Quaestor Lucis*'. Of

[1] The full text of the paper from which this quotation is taken will be found in R. A. Gilbert's *The Sorcerer and His Apprentice* (Aquarian Press, 1983).

this occultist Mr Gilbert writes:

> *Quaestor Lucis* was Oswald Murray who entered the Golden Dawn in
> March 1891 . . . He entered the Second Order on 19 July 1892 and at some
> later date changed his motto from *In utrumque paratus* to *Quaestor Lucis*.
> He was not in the masonic *Societas Rosicruciana in Anglia* despite his
> reference to the Great Architect; I presume he was a member of the
> Theosophical Society and although probably a Freemason not overtly
> Christian and thus not able (if he had a conscience) to join the *Societas
> Rosicruciana in Anglia*.

Murray's knowledge of the nature of the work undertaken in the
Second Order is reflected in certain phrases used in Flying Roll XXII (for
example, 'Is not the Wheel of Life in the door of the Vault a key to this
question?'), but it seems to me that he had little real grasp of the nature
of the Order's teachings and that Free Will is little more than an ill-digested
mixture of Theosopy and the popular science of the 1880s.

Flying Roll XXIV is a derivation of a lecture, given by 'Frater Resurgam',
on the subject of horary astrology. 'Resurgam' was the occult pseudonym
of a homoeopathic physician named Berridge, a man who was not
only devoted to both the Golden Dawn magical system and the curious
quasi-tantric sexual teachings of Thomas Lake Harris, but was fanatically
loyal to S. L. MacGregor Mathers—Berridge, in fact, was the only senior
Golden Dawn adept who remained faithful to his Chief during the
1900 'Revolt of the Adepti'.

Horary astrology is that branch of this divinatory art which is
concerned with answering specific questions; a chart is drawn up for
the exact moment at which the question is asked, and an answer derived
from that chart according to fairly hard-and-fast rules. Contemporary
practitioners of horary astrology tend to argue that (a) the methods
used, however seemingly irrational, *work*, providing reasonably accurate
answers to the questions asked, and (b) horary astrology is, like the
I Ching, a special case of the general principle, enunciated by C. G.
Jung, that 'everything done at a particular time has the qualities of
that moment of time'.

Flying Roll XXIV admirably illustrates the approach of early Golden
Dawn initiates to astrology in general and horary astrology in particular.
For the benefit of those readers of this book who are inclined to matters
astrological it is perhaps worth adding that (a) I have quickly checked
the planetary zodiacal positions as given by Berridge and they are

accurate for the date in question, and (b) I have checked his interpretations for those positions, and the consequent planetary aspects, and they seem to be in accordance with the 'cook-book rules' of horary astrology as given in various seventeenth-century texts.

There is, however, one very curious anachronism in Berridge's working. It is clear from the House positions he gives that he had divided his chart into twelve 'Houses' on the basis of the time system of Placidus. But to those positions he had applied traditional rules which, in fact, pertain to the Houses as calculated by the system of Regiomontanus.

Flying Roll XXVIII, written by Mathers and Westcott jointly, is perhaps the 'fugitive Flying Roll' which will be of most interest and practical use to contemporary practitioners of ritual magic. The application of the methods it teaches should ensure that a solemn divination does not degenerate into vulgar fortune telling.

Flying Roll XXIX is concerned with an administrative matter—the appointment of four leading Golden Dawn initiates to be 'Lieutenants' of Wynn Westcott ('Non Omnis Moriar') in the governance of the Order in 'Great Britain with Ireland and its colonies.'

Flying Roll XXXI, written by 'V.N.R', i.e. the wife of MacGregor Mathers, is a very curious production in which an attempt is made to correlate the letters of the Ethiopic (i.e. Geez) alphabet with the 21 letters of the 'Enochian alphabet' which were revealed to the Elizabethan magus Dr Dee through the skrying of his associate Edward Kelley. While Mrs Mathers may have been, as she herself believed, an 'Adeptus Major', she was most certainly not an authority on such Ethiopian languages as Geez or Amharic. It is to be presumed, therefore, that the supposed correlation outlined in Flying Roll XXXI was based on some sort of revelation obtained through methods which are described in a document extracts from which are printed below as an addendum to this foreword.

Flying Roll XXXII is concerned with 'Theban letters', a magical alphabet which has intrigued many occultists. The contents of this document are self-explanatory, but it is worth adding that the Flying Roll referred to in the first paragraph is that numbered XII and it is to be found printed, in somewhat disjointed form, on p. 61 and pp. 62-72 of Volume IV of Regardie's *Golden Dawn*. Regardie does not include any reproduction of the image of Adonai ha-Aretz which is referred to in both Flying Roll XII and Flying Roll XXXII; however, a description of it is given on pp. 71-2 of *Golden Dawn*, Volume IV, and a rather fine drawing of it by J. F. C. Fuller was reproduced in one of the early numbers of Crowley's occult periodical *The Equinox*.

These, then, are the 'fugitive Flying Rolls', the Flying Rolls which really seemed to have taken flight, which have been discovered by Mr Gilbert and are now printed, for the first time, in Appendix D. Along with them, for the sake of completeness, I include some material which I had not thought worth including in the first edition of this book; this comprises Flying Rolls VIII, 'A Geometrical Way to Draw a Pentagram', and Flying Roll III, 'On Procedure.'

Whence came that system of the magical theory and technique which is embodied in both the Flying Rolls and the fully official instructional manuscripts of the Golden Dawn?

There is no doubt of the answer; the system was a synthetic one—which does not, in my opinion, devalue it—created very largely by MacGregor Mathers on the basis of, firstly, books and manuscripts he had studied, and, secondly, supposed revelations of which he and his wife had been the recipients as a result of their use of techniques generally known as 'Ring and Disc' and 'Table.'

The former involved the use of a disc divided into 32 sections, corresponding to the ten sephiroth and the twenty-two 'paths' of the qabalistic Tree of Life. These sections were coloured in accordance with their qabalistic correspondences and on them were inscribed the letters of the Hebrew and other alphabets, astrological sigils etc. The ring, which was the badge of a Golden Dawn sub-grade known as Theoricus Adeptus Minor, was usually made of thin, strong pasteboard; it was normally about an inch wide. Its hollow middle extended to about a third of the diameter of the whole ring; the remainder was divided into two distinct circles. On both sides of the ring the innermost circle was coloured white and lettered in black with, on one side, the 'magical motto' of the adept who had made the ring and, on the other, the words 'Pereclinus De Faustis.' The outermost circle, which was identical on both sides of the ring, was divided into four segments of which the topmost one was coloured yellow and inscribed with the Hebrew letter Aleph, the left hand one was coloured blue and inscribed with the Hebrew letter Hé, the right hand one was coloured red and inscribed with the Hebrew letter Yod, and the bottom one was coloured black and inscribed with the Hebrew letter Hé (final). In all cases the lettering was white.

In a Golden Dawn instructional document entitled Ritual Beth the mode of employing 'Ring and Disc' was described as follows:

> Now when the Theoricus Adept shall desire to employ the Disc and Ring for the purposes of Divination or of Consultation, let him—wearing the Insignia and having his necessary magical implements at hand—invoke in the ordinary manner the particular Spirit, Force or Elemental whom he wisheth to consult. (Note by N.O.M. 'By means of a Telesma if desired. Put names, seal and sigil of Force on one side, and the name of THMAH [spelled in Coptic] on the other.')
>
> Let him place the Disc flat upon the table before him, The Top thereof, i.e. the left hand line of the 'A' ray being always *opposite* to him. Then, leaning the elbow of the arm of the hand, by which he holds the thread attached to the Ring, upon the table for the sake of steadiness, let him so hold the Ring as to be suspended exactly above the White Centre of the Disc, directing his gaze to the same point.
>
> The thread by which the Ring is suspended should be passed immediately across the exact centre of the ball of the first joint of the thumb, (and this is most important) being there retained by the pressure thereon of the centre of the ball of the first joint of the finger selected to hold it with; (the first or the second finger will be found most convenient). The Ring will soon commence to oscillate and to vibrate.
>
> The mode of receiving a communication thereby is as follows. No notice is to be taken of a short oscillation that does not pass completely beyond the circle of coloured rays on to the circle of the letters. But if it goeth clearly on to the circle of letters, such letters are to be taken in order, as spelling out a word or a sentence. When the Ring circleth or oscillateth to the right hand (or with the Sun's course) it meaneth 'Yes'; but if it circleth to the left hand (against the course of the Sun) it meaneth 'No'; and if it continueth to oscillate vaguely it meaneth 'Doubtful'.
>
> The point of suspension of the Ring must be carefully maintained exactly above the *centre* of the Disc. To avoid self-deception, and until facility of action be attained, care should be taken that the hand should be kept as steady as possible; and every communication should be carefully tested (as in Skrying) to avoid either Automatic self-deception or Wilful deception, by either the Force invoked, or by a hostile Force endeavouring to cut between, and thus to vitiate the operation.
>
> Also, it should be clearly understood beforehand what language is being employed, and if a numerical value be intended instead of the Letter thereto belonging. And it is for the purpose of protecting against deception, and of identifying the Operator with the operation, that the Divine Names and the Motto of the Theoricus are placed upon the Disc and the Ring.

It will be obvious to most readers that the method described above is essentially identical with some of the techniques associated with what is now called radiesthesia. The authors of Ritual Beth were as well aware as any contemporary rediesthesist that it is very easy to deceive oneself—to get the answers one wishes to get—when employing such techniques, and warned of this possibility in the following passage:

> Let the Theoricus Adeptus Minor recall that which was said in the lecture on the Microcosm, under the headings of 'How the Spiritual Consciousness can act around and beyond the Sphere of Sensation', and 'Of Travelling in the Spirit Vision.'
>
> In the working by the Ring and Disc then, the Operator buildeth up partly from his own Nephesch and partly from the surrounding atmosphere a species of truncated cone of astral light. The Disc is its base, while the truncated summit thereof is at the point of suspension of the Ring where the thread thereof passeth between the thumb and finger of the Operator. The action of the Will of the Operator in formulating his desire of communication buildeth up the symbol of a receptacle of impressions. This will take the form of another inverted cone rising from the point of suspension of the Ring. So that upon the Disc as a base there will be built up in the astral light a form somewhat resembling an hourglass of which the centre will be the place of the finger and the thumb of the Operator, holding the thread of suspension of the Ring. And from the impressions received by the conical receptable, the hand will translate into action in the lower cone the expression of these ideas, in words and sentences spelled out by the movements of the Ring over the letters of the Disc.
>
> But were it an uninitiated person who attempted this form of Divination or of consultation, he or she, being ignorant of the formulas involved, would almost to a certainty open a conical receptacular funnel into the sphere of sensation (of him or her) thus preparing a ready path unto obsession. Therefore, it is not entirely the Force invoked which actually spells out the words, but to a great extent it is the Operator himself who translates his own impressions thereof. And for this reason it is that this form of Divination is not taught unto the Zelator Adept, self-deception therein being so extremely easy, and the hand being liable to translate that which the heart wisheth.
>
> Therefore it is also that the language wherein the communication is received need not *necessarily* be that in which the Force involved would speak, supposing it to be endowed with the human organs of speech, but the impression received by the Operator is translated *according to the understanding of the Operator.* And all this is in accordance with the degree

of the Force respectively exercised in the Upper or in the Lower cone . . .

Ritual Beth contains the following description of 'Table' workings, which it authors rather pompously referred to as 'Magical Consultation by Means of the Tripod.'

Now if the Theoricus Adeptus Minor shall wish to employ the Magical Consultation with the Tripod or table with three feet, let him know that the model thereof is the circular Altar of the Vault of Christian Rosenkreutz. One leg of the table should coincide with the Eastern point of the top which later should be coloured in exact representation of the Altar, and the legs should be black. (A table may have the regular painted top, and others, removable, painted for special purpose. N.O.M.) If desired, the magical Operator, the better to isolate him or herself, may trace any convenient magical circle of defence upon the floor (consonant with the force he desires to invoke) wherein to sit while employing the working of the Tripod. (Note: A circle may consist of a tape and on it at certain places, Telesma or pentacles may be placed. N.O.M.) The mode of Operation is as here followeth.

The table should be placed with the same orientation as the Altar in the Vault; one leg, which we will call the apex of the triangle formed by the legs, being placed at the Eastern point as regards the design upon the top thereof. The Operator will usually, if working alone, find it best to be seated either at the Western part of the table, or at the point immediately opposite to that of the Force to be evoked. Let him then place his hands on the top of the table towards each side thereof. After a certain time, the length of which will depend upon varying conditions, the Tripod will begin to tilt up and down; and in some cases even a species of explosive knocks may be heard, which ariseth from a more sudden transmission of astral force from the cone of reception to the table. Now remember that the movements of the table should be really the *combined product of the Operator and the communicating Force*, always supposing that the Operator be not obsessed by the Force invoked, nor voluntarily self-deceiving. And the philosophical explanation is of a similar principle to that of the Disc and Ring; only that in this instance self-deception is even yet more easy.

For the reception of communications by the Tripod some convenient preconceived plan of correspondences between the tilts of the table and the letters of the alphabet or simple words should be employed.

This form of magical operation is usually found to be more exhausting than the employment of the Ring and Disc, seeing that a greater amount of astral Force has to be employed in the operation. Not only one but several persons may take part in this operation by the Tripod, but in such

17

cases they should partition among them the points of the table corresponding either to their natures, or to the Forces with which each intendeth to ally himself, as if there be three persons, let them take Air, Fire and Water, leaving Earth vacant. If five persons, the Spirit and the four elements, the Spirit being at the point of the East. If six or seven persons the points of the hexagram and so on, according to the quarters that they occupy, so as always to form some intentionally and not accidentally equilibriated symbol. Now in the case of several persons taking part, each one will form his own cone. The synthesis will form together another Great Cone enclosing the whole, and so a large amount of force may be thus obtained. But also, careful watch should be kept against both obsession and self-deception.

The greatest harmony should prevail among the Operators for the least discordant feeling will produce some error or disruption. And remember that in working with the Tripod the cone of reception will attract any passing Intelligence or Force. Thus, without the greatest care, much deception could arise, and even against the intention of the communicated Intelligence deception may result through confused mistranslations by the Operator or Operators.

Results may be obtained from tables not circular in form, and having four or more legs. But the Tripod is the best form. Also the Ring and the Disc may be used in conjunction with the Tripod. In invocation, a flashing Tablet or Tablets of the nature of the Force to be invoked may be placed upon the table. Also by using the table as a physical basis of strength, and sitting thereat, even physical appearances and manifestations may be produced. In such a case it may be advantageous to have black drapery fastened around the edge of the table (not covering the table top, for this would hide the symbols. S.R.M.D.) and reaching to the ground, so as to form, as it were, a cynlindrical receptable of force extending from the top of the table to the floor. Such drapery should be in the divisions. Or three slits may be cut, one by each leg from the top of the table to the floor, so that the three are united only along the edge of the table top.

In all such operations let the greatest care be taken to combat obsession, for in case of this arriving, although occasionally striking physical results may ensue, yet there will be danger therewith. And the result of such obsession will always be to make the Operator personate and imitate the action of the Force evoked, even to the extent of attempting to deceive both himself and those who may be with him.

But the Theoricus Adeptus Minor hath sufficient knowledge to know what to do, and what to avoid herein, and when.

Now the Formula of this operation by the Tripod will be closely similar to that contained in the Pyramid and Sphynx Formula of the Enochian

Tablets. The truncated cone will answer to the Pyramid, with a cone of reception above opening therefrom to attract the Force which shall act through the top thereof. The surface of the table will answer to the place of the Sphynx.

And thus thou wilt easily see how particular the Operator must always be in discerning the Force which is acting through the vortex above.

It is clear from the above that 'Magical Consultation by Means of the Tripod' is, in essence, an elaboration of that standby of Victorian spiritualism referred to as 'table turning'.

Such, amazingly enough, were the techniques through the use of which Mathers and his associates were enabled to construct what it, in the opinion of myself and many others, that most effective (and intellectually impressive) synthetic structure, the Golden Dawn magical system.

The fact that many of the Golden Dawn's magical techniques were derived from teachings received through 'Tripod' and 'Ring and Disc' in no way invalidates them. If they work, and many occultists have found them to be efficacious, their source is unimportant. Equally unimportant are the literary merits or demerits of the Flying Rolls. What is significant is their content, not the clumsy forms which sometimes express it.

Take, for example, the Flying Rolls concerned with 'astral projection' and allied subjects. Sections of them are quite unquestionably badly written. Yet the processes they teach are, properly performed, capable of unlatching magic casements which look out on 'faery lands forlorn' and even stranger regions of 'inner space'. In this connection it is worth reminding those who have read Alan Richardson's fascinating *Dancers to the Gods* (Aquarian Press, 1985) that the remarkable experiences which were undergone by Colonel Seymour, the 'unknown magus', and his co-worker, Christine Campbell Thomson, were achieved as a result of using techniques derived from the Flying Rolls concerned with astral projection.

The Flying Rolls demand the attention of all serious occultists, not because of their source, not because of their literary merit, but because of their magical content.

FRANCIS KING

19

INTRODUCTION

I. The Survival of Magic

By the beginning of the last quarter of the seventeenth century ritual magic, alchemy, necromancy and the other mediaeval occult sciences were in a noticeable state of decline, seemingly doomed to extinction. There were, of course, many survivals of earlier ways of thinking, but nevertheless, the dominant intellectual trend of the period was rationalism; the belief that the unaided human reason was capable of solving all problems that were patent of resolution. In spite of this semi-deification of reason there was some resistance to the rising tide of scepticism and, against all expectation, the underground occult tradition managed to survive.

Both amateur astrologers and professional almanac makers played a part of some importance in this survival, for many of them also dealt in talismanic magic—the preparation and consecration of amulets designed to undo the effects of unfavourable planetary influences, find lost goods, gain the affection of another etc.—and it is clear that at least some of them dabbled in magic of a darker hue, occasionally with unfortunate results. Typical of these was Thomas Parkes, a more than ordinarily clever young man who met his death soon after (and possibly as a result of) the terrifying climax of his occult experiments. The story is best told in the pious words of the Reverend Arthur Bedford, a clergyman of the Temple parish in Bristol, who, on August 2nd 1703, wrote to Eduard, Bishop of Gloucester, as follows:

About thirteen years ago, whilst I was curate to Dr. Reid, rector of St. Nicholas, in this city, I began to be acquainted with one Thomas Parkes, a young man about twenty years of age, who lived with his father in Mangotsfield, in Gloucestershire, and by trade a gunsmith, with whom I contracted an intimate acquaintance; he being not only a good tempered man, but extremely well skilled in the mathematical studies, which was his constant delight—viz., arithmetic, geometry, gauging, surveying, astronomy, and algebra. He gave himself up to astronomy so far that he could not only calculate the motions of the planets, but an eclipse also, and demonstrate also every problem in spherical trigonometry from mathematical principles, in which he would discover a clear force of reason. When Mr. Bailey, minister of St. James, in the city, endeavoured to set up a mathematical academy, I advised him to this Thomas Parkes, as an acquaintance, in whom, as he told me, he found greater proficiency in those studies than he expected, or could imagine. After this he applied himself to astrology, and would sometimes calculate nativities, and resolve horary questions, which he told me oftentimes proved true; but he was not satisfied with it, because there was nothing in it which tended to mathematical demonstration.

When by the providence of God I was settled in Temple parish, and having not seen him for some time, he came to me, and we being in private, he asked my opinion very seriously concerning the lawfulness of conversing with spirits. After I had given my thoughts in the negative, and confirmed them with the best reasons I could, he told me he had considered all those arguments, and believed they only related to conjuration; but that there was an innocent society with them that a man might use, if he made no compact with them, did no harm by their means, and was not curious in prying into hidden things; and that he himself had discoursed with them, and heard them sing to his great satisfaction. He gave an offer to me at one time, to Mr. Bailey at another, that if we would go with him one night to Kingswood, we should see them, hear them talk and sing, and talk to them whatsoever we had a mind to, and we should return very safe; but neither of us had the courage to venture. I told him of the subtilty of the Devil to deceive mankind, and to transfer himself into an angel of light; but he could not believe it was the Devil. I proposed to try him a question in astronomy relating to the projection of a sphere, which he projected and resolved; and afterwards did so demonstrate from the mathematics, as to demonstrate that his brain was free from the least tincture of madness and distraction. I asked him several particulars concerning the method he used, and the discourse he had with the spirits he conversed with. He told me he had a book where there was the directions he followed.[1] Accordingly, in the dead time of night he went into a causeway with candle and lanthorn, which was consecrated for the purpose with incantations. He had also consecrated chalk, consisting of several mixtures, which he used to make a circle of what distance he thought fit, within which no spirit had power to enter. After he invoked the spirit by several forms of words, some of which he told me were taken from the Holy Scripture, and therefore he thought them lawful; without considering that they might, as the apostle saith, 'be wrested to his own destruction' (2 Pet. 3.16). The spirits for which he called appeared to him in the shape of little girls, about a foot and a half high, and played about the circle. At first he was affrighted, but after some small acquaintance this antipathy in nature wore off, and he became pleased with their company. He told me they spoke with a shrill voice, like an ancient woman.

He asked them if there was a God; they told him there was. He asked them if there was a Heaven and Hell; they said there was. He asked what sort of place Heaven was; which they described as a place of glory and happiness. He asked what place Hell was; and they bid him ask no questions of that nature, for it was a dreadful thing to relate. 'The devils believe and tremble'. He asked what method or order they had among themselves; they told him they were divided into three orders: that their chief had his residence in the air—that he had several counsellors, which were placed by him in form of a globe. Another order, they said, is employed in

[1] An eighteenth century note attached to a copy of the good clergyman's letter to the Bishop identifies Parkes' book: 'William Llewellyn had in his possession about twenty years ago the book T. Parkes made use of in raising spirits, for more than a half a year to peruse; it was the fourth book of Cornelius Agrippa's *Occult Philosophy*'.

going to and fro from thence to the earth to carry intelligence from those lower spirits. And a third order was in the earth, according to the directions they received from those in the air. This description was very surprising; but being contrary to the account we have in Scripture of the hierarchy of the blessed angels, made me conclude that they were devils; but I could not convince him thereof.[2] He told me that he had desired them to sing, and they went to some distance behind a bush, from whence he heard a perfect concert of such music, the like he never heard; and in the upper part he could hear something very harsh and shrill like a reed, but as it was managed it came with particular grace.

About a quarter of a year after he came to me again, and said he wished he had taken my advice; for he thought he had done that which would cost him his life, and which he did heartily repent of. He appeared to me as if he had been in great trouble, as his countenance was very much altered. I asked him what he had done: he told me that, being bewitched to his acquaintance, he resolved to proceed further in the art, and to have a familiar spirit at his command, according to the directions of his book; which was to have a book of virgin parchment, consecrated with several incantations; as also a particular ink-horn, ink, and pen. With those he was to go out as usual to a cross-way, and call up a spirit, and ask him his name, which he was to put in the first page of his book; and this was to be his familiar spirit. Thus he was to do by as many as he pleased, writing their names in distinct pages, only one in a leaf; and then, whenever he took the book and opened it, this spirit whose name appeared should appear also. The familiar spirit he had was called Malachi—*id est*, my king; an Hebrew name of an evil signification to him—*id est*, that an evil spirit was to become his king. After this they appeared faster than he wished them, and in most dreadful shapes—like serpents, lions, bears, etc., hissing at him, which did very much affright him; and the more so when he found it was not in his power to lay them,

[2] Most occultists would assume that the 'spirits' raised by Parkes were elementals.

expecting every moment to be torn in pieces. This was in December, about midnight, when he continued there in a great sweat; and from that time he was never well so long as he lived. In the course of his sickness he often came to the apothecary in Broad Street, concerning a cure; but I know not whether he told him the original cause or not. He also came to me at the same time and owned every matter as fact, which he had told before unto the last; and insisted that whenever he did anything of that nature, he was deluded in his conscience to think it lawful; but that he was since convinced to the contrary. But still he asserted that he made no compact with those spirits, never did harm to others by their means, nor ever pryed into the fortune of himself or others: he expressed a hearty repentance for, and detestation of, his sins; so that though these matters cost him his life, yet I have room to believe him happy in the other world.[3]

Thus ends Bedford's account (apart from some pious mutterings about the sobriety and respectability of Parkes' relations) but it is perhaps worth adding that Parkes died of 'a wasting distemper, without anything remarkable attending his death' and that it was only conjectured that this disease was 'occasioned by the fright he induced from the spirits the last time he raised them'.

Besides the astrologers (whether professional talisman manufacturers or incompetent amateur experimenters such as the unfortunate Parkes) there were the cunning-men—to use the common eighteenth-century term for the diviners, popular healers and white witches of the period—who clearly played an important part in the survival of magic at a more 'folksy' level. Not a great deal is known about the activities of these people, for they were usually discreet enough in their doings and, in any case, their clientele was largely drawn from a social class

[3] A brief and somewhat inaccurate version of these events was given by E. M. Butler in *Ritual Magic* (Cambridge University Press, 1949). Professor Butler seems to have relied exclusively upon *The Spectre, Or News of the Invisible World* (London, 1839) an unsatisfactory secondary source.

that made little impact on the periodical literature of the time. Nevertheless, it is clear that some of them specialised in the finding of missing property and persons; those familiar; with eighteenth-century legal history will remember the cunning-man who played such an odd part in the 'Canning Wonder', the mysterious vanishing and reappearance of young Elizabeth Canning. Others kept alive a knowledge of the use of love philtres, while a few of them may have been prepared to manufacture, at a price, philtres intended for other and darker purposes—it was not only in France that young wives afflicted with elderly husbands could obtain a 'powder of succession'. I am sure that at least one of these folk-magicians had either extraordinary hypnotic abilities or some other means of inducing collective hallucinations, for on no other hypothesis can I explain the following account (*circa* 1800) of the story told by a collier to a certain Stephen Penny, and relating to a conjuror (the word is, of course, used in its original sense of one who conjures spirits) named Coal.

——leaving work one winter evening about ten o'clock (about twenty-five years since), he went to refresh himself at a little public house he pointed out to us with his finger, not far from us. He sat down in company with the said Coal and six or seven other persons, amongst whom was the landlord of the house, who had been joking and laughing at Coal about his pretended art of conjuration, telling him he believed nothing of it, and that it was all mere imposition. Upon this Coal told the landlord and company that if they were willing to see a specimen of his art and would sit still and quiet whilst he was performing it, he would soon convince them by causing a tree to grow up before their faces, and men, too, to come in and cut it down. They promised to sit still; upon which Coal, retiring to a corner of the room with his back towards the company, seemed to take something out of his pocket; but immediately afterwards he and the whole company very distinctly saw by the light of the candle in the room a small tree, an inch or two thick, gradually rise out of the stone floor of the room, to the height, as he thinks, of three feet, with branches and leaves, and in all respects like a natural tree; that when it was thus grown up, this informant and all the rest of the company saw two little men, each about one foot high, dressed in short jackets, with caps on their heads, their complexions sunburnt, and bearing their axes, begin to cut it down with great celerity, the chips flying about at every stroke; that the tree seemed to fall with great force, and as soon as this was done, the tree, chips, and the little workmen went from their sight, they knew not how, leaving all the company in a great consternation, except this informant himself, who says he beheld the whole from beginning to end (which he thinks was about half an hour) without any sensible degree of fear, though at the same time he confessed he wished he had been elsewhere. That he observed one of the little workmen, during the gathering up of the chips, to look about very angrily, and that Coal observing the same also, said he was sure some of the company had taken away and concealed some chips of the tree, but whether it was so, this informant said he does not now well remember.

The great simplicity and seriousness with which this man delivered his whole narrative was so very remarkable, that there was not the least room to suspect his having any design to impose upon us, or that he himself did not really believe he saw what he related. He assured us he was in no way disordered by liquor at the time it happened, nor does he remember any of the company were so; and said Coal had the character of being a sober, serious man, much given to mathematical and other studies, that he died to all appearances of old age, and without anything extraordinary attending his death.

Parkes with his musical spirits and his unpleasant familiar, Coal with his wood-chopping gnomes, others of the same breed whose very names are now forgotten; such were the men who practised and kept alive the magical arts in the age of Locke and Voltaire.

II. The Revival of Magic

Other magicians beside Coal seem to have chosen to demonstrate their alleged occult powers in the public houses of England, and some three quarters of a century after Coal's curious
exhibition, Canon Wood the Rector of Newent in Gloucestershire, sent the following account to Father Lee of Lambeth, one
of the Bishops of the Order of the Corporate Reunion:

> A man named Hyett of Newent told me that he was in a
> public house many years ago, when a stranger came in. This
> stranger offered in return for some refreshment given him, to
> show the party assembled, three or four people, the following
> exhibition. He put a sixpence down in the centre of the
> apartment. The coin untouched moved along the floor to the
> wall, ascended it, and then traversed the ceiling until it
> arrived over the spot it started from, and then dropped down
> upon it. Hyett remarked that he was much relieved when
> the stranger departed.

Long before Hyett, however, there had been the first stirrings
of a revival of interest in the magical-mystical tradition. This
revival was at first closely associated with the late eighteenth-
century romantic movement and its admiration for all things
Gothic; thus the writings of Ebenezer Sibley, which presented
an ossified form of the magical tradition dressed up in a
romanticised mock-mediaeval costume, were clearly the product
of the same social forces that had been responsible for the
architecture of Walpole's Strawberry Hill, the literary success
of Monk Lewis, and the appearance of a high-grade and chivalric
free-masonry claiming descent from the Rosicrucians and the
Knights Templar.

The same Gothic influences can be discerned in Francis Barrett's *The Magus* (London, 1801)—the Gothic element is particularly noticeable in the illustrations—and in *Lives of the
Alchymistical Philosophers*, a piece of hack-work which has also
been attributed to Barrett but which, on stylistic grounds, I
think more likely to have been written by William Godwin,

whose *Caleb Williams* shows a considerable acquaintance with the occult literature of the period.

Without question, *The Magus* was one of the most curious literary effusions of its century; and, in spite of its inaccuracies (the formulae given were often woefully incomplete and misleading, the Hebrew was full of errors), in spite of the author's monotonous style and excessive credulity (he solemnly described one Adept as having lived on a diet of no more than a daily gooseberry), and in spite of the over-ambitiousness of attempting to produce 'a complete system of occult philosophy', from alchemy to talismanic magic, within the compass of a single volume, it was a genuine attempt to separate the wheat of the genuine Theurgic tradition from the chaff that had become so thoroughly mixed with it; a work of real importance in, and influence upon, the occult revival—indeed, it is still a potent influence upon some occultists at the present day.[4]

At the end of his book Francis Barrett advertised a school of ritual magic that he was engaged in establishing at his home in Marylebone:

> The author of this work respectfully informs those who are curious in the studies of Art and Nature, especially of Natural and Occult Philosophy, Chemistry, Astrology, etc. etc. that, having been indefatigable in his researches into those sublime Sciences, of which he has treated at large in this Book, that he gives private instructions and lectures upon any of the above-mentioned Sciences; in the course of which he will discover many curious and rare experiments.

[4] At the present time *The Magus* is available from four different publishers. The first of these modern editions, ludicrously re-entitled *Hindu Magic*, was originally published by the late L. W. de Lawrence who, with the impertinence and conceit that were so typical of him, claimed to be its author! There are two photolithographic reproductions of the original 1801 edition available, produced by, respectively, University Books of New York and Vance Harvey of Leicester. Finally, there is a roneo version produced by Helios Books of Toddington as part of its Rare Text series. On grounds of quality and price the Vance Harvey version is probably the best, but on no account should the serious student miss Timothy D'Arch Smith's learned and lucid introduction to the University Books edition.

Those who become Students will be Initiated into the choices operations of Natural Philosophy, Natural Magic, the Cabala, Chemistry, the Talismanic Art, Hermetic Philosophy, Astrology, Physiognomy etc. etc. Likewise they will acquire the knowledge of the RITES, MYSTERIES, CEREMONIES *and* PRINCIPLES *of the ancient Philosophers, Magi, Cabalists, Adepts, etc.—The purpose of this School (which will consist of no greater number than Twelve Students) being to investigate the hidden treasures of Nature; to mind to a contemplation of the* ETERNAL WISDOM; *to promote the discovery of whatever may conduce to the perfection of Man; thus alleviating the miseries and calamities of this life, both in respect of ourselves and others to secure to ourselves felicity hereafter; and finally the promulgation of whatever may conduce to the general happiness and welfare of mankind.—Those who feel themselves thoroughly disposed to enter upon such a course of studies, as is above recited, with the same principles of philanthropy with which the Author invites the lovers of philosophy and wisdom, to incorporate themselves in so select, permanent and desirable a society, may speak with the Author on the subject, at any time between the hours of Eleven and Two o'clock, at* 99, *Norton Street, Mary-le-Bonne.*

Letters (post paid) upon any subject treated in this Book, will be duly answered, with the necessary information.

I know that at least one student joined this school of magic, for I have seen his papers and diaries. It is likely that there were others, and Montague Summers, who, in spite of his more than ultramontane Roman Catholicism, real or assumed,[5] was

[5] With all due respect to such admirers of him as Father Brocard Sewell it seems to me that there was at least some element of affectation in Summers' ultra-Papalistic Catholicism. He was certainly a schismatic, for, although he invariably dressed as a Roman priest, his orders were derived from a highly irregular source, thus *ipso facto* bringing him under a major excommunication of the Latin Rite. Summers was probably ordained by Vernon Herford who was, of all things, a Syro-Chaldean bishop who was a Unitarian in theology! If this was the case Summers' orders were not only irregular but were probably invalid, for Herford's ordinations were almost certainly deficient in intention if not in form.

usually historically accurate, suggested that an occult association, derived from Barrett, was established in Cambridge. He wrote:

I have been told that Francis Barrett actually founded a small sodality of students of these dark and deep mysteries, and that under his tuition—for he was profoundly learned in these things—some advanced far upon the path of transcendental wisdom. One at least was a Cambridge man, of what status—whether an undergraduate or the Fellow of a College—I do not know, but there is reason to believe that he initiated others, and until quite recent years—it perhaps persists even today—the Barrett tradition was maintained at Cambridge, but very privately, and his teaching has been handed on to promising subjects.

Whatever may have been the extent of Barrett's influence in Cambridge it is certain that whole generations of occultists based their first tentative experiments in Ritual Magic and Ceremonial Skrying on information they extracted from *The Magus*. In the second half of the nineteenth century a group of occultists using Barrett's techniques gathered round the mystic and visionary Fred Hockley, who had himself been a pupil of a member of Barrett's school, and by the 'seventies demand for *The Magus* was such that a London publisher brought out a new edition.

Amongst Hockley's closest friends and associates was Kenneth Mackenzie who, while still a very young man, had become interested in the occult after a remarkable personal experience of the supernatural. This experience began, prosaically enough, with a conversation upon the subject of ghosts and apparitions between the Rev. T. A. Buckley[6] and Mackenzie himself. At the close of the conversation the two young men entered into a compact that whichever of them died first would return to

[6] Theodore Alois Buckley, born 27th July 1825, was one of the chaplains of Christ Church, Oxford. He died on the Festival of King Charles the Martyr, January 30th 1856. An obituary appeared in the *Gentleman's Magazine* for March 1856.

his friend 'to indicate the certainty and reality of the life beyond the grave'.

Three days later, just half an hour past midnight, Mackenzie, who was lying in bed, not thinking of Buckley, of whose death he was not yet aware, suddenly felt 'a cold clammy hand very gently placed upon his forehead'. Not surprisingly, Mackenzie turned round in order to see what had caused this odd and frightening sensation. He saw 'the spirit of Buckley, in his usual dress, standing at his bedside with a portfolio under his arm, exactly as he had so often seen him in life'. Mackenzie claimed that after he had recognised the figure it 'retreated towards the window, but after remaining there most distinctly visible both in form and feature for more than two minutes, it slowly faded away'.

This apparition, which Mackenzie saw twice more, seems to have had a profound effect upon his intellectual development. He began to attend seances and to make a study of spiritualism, already becoming fashionable since the commencement of D. D. Home's spectacular mediumistic career in the previous year. More significantly, he became almost the first English student of the works of Eliphas Levi—*Dogme de la Haute Magie* had been published in 1854 and its companion volume, the *Rituel*, in 1856—and I suspect that he fell completely under the spell of that writer's limpid French style and ingenious romanticisation of the magical tradition, for by 1861, when he had two long interviews with Levi, his attitude towards the French mage was one of veneration. I am certain that Levi found his English visitor's solemnity difficult to cope with—Mackenzie actually mistook his host's tobacco-jar for a valuable statuette of the goddess Isis—and reading between the lines of Mackenzie's lengthy account[7] of these visits it is clear that Levi indulged in a good deal of leg-pulling.

There is no doubt that Mackenzie developed into what is sometimes called 'an advanced occultist'; he claimed a continental Rosicrucian initiation from a mysterious Count Apponyi, he became an important figure in a masonic Rosi-

[7] This account is reprinted in full in my *Ritual Magic in England* (Neville Spearman Ltd. 1970).

crucian organisation, the *Societas Rosicruciana in Anglia*, he studied magic (whch he defined as 'a psychological branch of science, dealing with the sympathetic effects of stones, drugs, herbs, and living substances upon the imaginative and reflective faculties') and, when he died, he left behind him notebooks dealing with the extraordinary Enochian magical system of the Elizabethan occultists Dee and Kelley.

III. The Golden Dawn

Mackenzie spent a good deal of time in Europe—both his French and his German were excellent—and I am inclined to believe that working-notes made by him of rituals he had witnessed in some German Rosicrucian temple were the basis of the odd cipher manuscripts that were found by the Rev. A. F. A. Woodford amongst the papers of Fred Hockley, who had died in 1885. It was the discovery (and transcription) of these manuscripts that was the immediate cause of the foundation of the Hermetic Order of the Golden Dawn, the organisation whose activities and teaching were largely responsible for the survival of the so-called 'Western Esoteric Tradition' and whose members, although few in number, exerted an enormous, while sometimes hidden, influence on their own time and times since.

These manuscripts are of such importance that I feel it worth spending a short time upon an examination of their contents. Early in 1970 shortly after the completion of my *Ritual Magic in England*, Mr. Ellic Howe, a distinguished historian of the printing industry, showed me a xerox copy of what I am now convinced was A. E. Waite's own transcription of the original manuscript. At first I thought that there was a faint possibility that the Waite manuscript was not a copy of the original document but was simply a cipher manuscript concocted by Waite himself in order to validate the rituals he had written (*circa* 1910) for the *Holy* Order of the Golden Dawn—a splinter-group controlled by Waite and one of his friends. Later, however, with the permission of the London collector who owns the original, Mr. Howe allowed me to make a detailed examination of the photocopy and to complete its decoding into English, a task which had been begun by Mr. Howe himself. It soon became clear to me that my suspicions were quite unjustified; for although the manuscript was full of errors, they were not the errors of someone transcribing an English text into an alphabetic code; rather were they the mistakes of someone (presumably a professional scribe) mechanically copying symbols of whose real significance he was quite unaware.

I am sure that the ordinary reader of this introduction would be bored if I went into a lengthy technical examination of the contents of the cipher manuscript; I shall therefore confine myself to simply stating my observations and conclusions in tabulated form:

(a) The manuscripts give an outline of five allegedly Rosicrucian grade rituals—Neophyte, Zelator, Theoricus, Practicus, and Philosophus—all except the first of which are attributed to various stations on the Qabalistic Tree of Life. I found these rituals to be in a form far less skeletonic than I had expected, for even such minor points of detail of the design of the sash worn by initiates are given. As I compared the manuscript rituals with those actually used in the Golden Dawn I realised that the latter owed far more to the former than they did to the synthetic genius of S. L. MacGregor Mathers.

(b) Those—they include Crowley, Regardie and myself—who have condemned Mathers for introducing an excessively complicated and, to some extent, antagonistic symbolism into the 'Grades of the Elements' have been quite wrong to do so. Our criticisms may have been justified, but, if so, they were aimed at the wrong target; for the confusion of symbols (even to the appearance of the Samothracian gods known as the Kabiri) comes from the manuscript, not from Mathers.

(c) The manuscripts originated in the latter half of the nineteenth century, for their eclectic approach makes an earlier date inherently improbable; the high-grade masonic rituals of the eighteenth century are often boring and always technically inferior to the manuscript rituals, but their symbolism is usually consistent. If, for example, a ceremony is centred around the tomb of some obscure Old Testament figure one is not suddenly dragged off to the coffin of Mahomet or the Vault of Christian Rosycross!

(d) While the basic structure of the rituals was probably based on someone's (Mackenzie's?) observation of a Rosicrucian temple in Europe (Germany? There is some resemblance to 1777 rituals of the Golden Rosicrucians) a good deal had been added from English sources—for example, the 'Enochian words of power' given in the elemental grades.

(e) Whoever prepared these manuscripts had a profound knowledge of even the most obscure of English occult writings; there are phrases that seem to come from such almost unknown sources as the works of the seventeenth-century mystic Jane Lead and the slightly later group of her followers known as the Philadelphians.

(f) Those—they include that distinguished Yeats Scholar Kathleen Raine—who have stated that Yeats had a hand in 'working up' the Golden Dawn rituals are incorrect. There are two sentences in the later Golden Dawn rituals that are identical with lines of Yeats poetry; both are in the original manuscripts. In other words, Yeats was quoting the rituals, not vice versa.

(g) Either the author of the manuscripts drew upon the writings of Eliphas Levi or, more probably, they both drew upon the same unknown sources. Thus both a diagram of 'Daniel's Man' and a diagram of the 'Altar of Incense' that appear in the manuscripts are identical with diagrams appearing in the supplement to the French edition of Levi's *Key of the Greater Mysteries.*

The London temple of the Golden Dawn, named Isis-Urania and working the rituals given in the cipher manuscripts, was founded on March 1st, 1888, its three chiefs being Dr. Woodman, an elderly physician, W. Wynn Westcott, the Queen's Coroner for North-East London, and that flamboyant character G. S. L. MacGregor Mathers. While the newly initiated Neophyte was assured that 'the Order of the Golden Dawn, of which you have now become a member can show you the way to much secret knowledge and spiritual progress, it can ... lead ... students ... to the Summum Bonum, True Wisdom, and Perfect Happiness',[8] there does not seem to have been much teaching of magical practice (as distinct from magical theory) until 1892 when a new grade (Adeptus Minor) and a Second Order (Roseae et Aureae Crucis) were established.

Both the ritual—based on the legend of the mediaeval adept named Christian Rosycross—of the Adeptus Minor grade and the magical techniques taught to its members were derived from MacGregor Mathers, who had allegedly obtained the former from a continental adept, named Frater Lux e Tenebres, and the latter from the 'Secret Chiefs of the Order', superhuman beings of the same type as the Masters who were supposed to have given Madame Blavatsky her mission. Mathers has left his own description of how these new teachings were received; a brief extract reads as follows:

> Almost the whole of the Second Order Knowledge has been obtained by me from them in various ways, by clairvoyance ... by astral projection on their part or mine ... by the table, by the ring and disk ... at times by Direct Voice audible to my external ears ... at times copied from books brought before me I know not how ... at times by an appointment *astrally* at a certain place ...[9]

For some years all went well with the Golden Dawn and much magical work was done, but in course of time personality clashes and other factors—I have told the story in full elsewhere—led to quarrels, revolts and schisms. By 1903 the Order was split into various warring schisms. Some of these worked the Golden Dawn system in its entirety, others, such as the group led by A. E. Waite and M. W. Blackden, threw the magical tradition overboard, rewrote the rituals to suit their own prejudices, and took refuge in an exclusively Christian mysticism. Still another

[8] From the Order's official history lecture, reprinted in full as an appendix to my *Ritual Magic in England*.

[9] The 'ring and disk' referred to are the mediaeval equivalents of the ouija board and of the pendulum used in modern radiesthesia. The 'table' referred to is a table of letter—part of the Enochian magical system. The full text of Mathers' 1896 manifesto to the Second Order, from which the above extract is taken, may be found in my *Ritual Magic in England*.

group, the Stella Matutina, became obsessed with astral projection and many of its members wasted their time buried in the murky depths of their own unconscious minds.

In spite of this unhappy end to the original Order there is no doubt that the authentic Golden Dawn system demands respect; it is a coherent, logical system of practical occultism. No one who has used the system to 'evoke' a spirit from the dark realms of the unconscious to 'charge' a talisman, to travel astrally through the Enochian 'Aires', can deny its effectiveness or doubt that it achieves what it sets out to achieve.

IV. The Magic of the Golden Dawn

With one important exception there was, as I have pointed out in the previous section of this introduction, very little practical magical work taught in the five grades of the Outer, or First, Order of the Golden Dawn. The exception was a ceremony known as the Lesser Ritual of the Pentagram, a rite simple enough in itself but capable of a considerable extension into what is known as the Exercise of the Middle Pillar.

The existence of this ritual, or of something very like it, was hinted at by Eliphas Levi who wrote:

The Sign of the Cross used by Christians does not belong to them exclusively. It is also Qabalistic and there are two ways of making it, the one reserved for priests and initiates, the other set apart for neophytes and the profane. Thus, for example, the initiate, raising his hand to his brow, said: 'Thine is', then brought his hand to his Breast, 'the Kingdom', then transferred his hand to the left shoulder, 'the Power', finally to the right shoulder, 'and the Glory'; then, joining his hands, he added 'Tibi sunt Malkuth et Geburah et Chesed per aeonas'—a sign of the Cross which is absolutely and splendidly Qabalistic, and which the profanation of the Gnosis has completely lost to the official Church Militant. The sign made in this manner should precede and conclude the conjuration of the Four.

By the 'conjuration of the Four' Levi seems to have meant the invocation of the four Archangels of the Elements—Earth, Air, Fire and Water—and the full rubric of the Golden Dawn ceremony was as follows:

1. Take a dagger into the right hand and face East.
2. Touching the forehead say Ateh (unto Thee)
3. Touching the breast, say Malkuth (the Kingdom)
4. Touching the right shoulder, say ve—Geburah (and the Power)
5. Touching the left shoulder, say ve—Gedulah (and the Glory)
6. Clasping both hands upon the breast, say le—Olahm Amen (Unto the Age of the Ages, Amen)
7. Make an Earth Pentagram with the dagger and vibrate JHVH.
8. Turning to the South do the same, but vibrate ADNI
9. Turning to the West do the same but vibrate AHIH
10. Returning to the East do the same but vibrate AGLA.
11. Extending the arms in the form of a cross say 'Before me Raphael, behind me Gabriel, on my right hand Michael, on my left hand Auriel, for about me flames the Pentagram and in the column stands the six rayed Star.
12. Repeat 2—6, the Quabalistic Cross.

This ritual, at first sight almost trite in its simplicity, is capable of being transformed into a potent method of spiritual development; as Aleister Crowley said, 'properly understood it is the Medicine of Metals and the Stone of the Wise'. I would advise those who doubt this statement to (a) make a detailed study of Regardie's book *The Middle Pillar* and (b) to do the lesser Pentagram Ritual daily for a period of three months; they will soon come to realise that Crowley was not exaggerating.

When the member of the Golden Dawn had undergone the Adeptus Minor initiation ceremony—a magnificent rite, its symbolism based on the discovery of a seven-sided Vault containing the uncorrupted body of Christian Rosycross—he entered the Second Order and began to undertake occult work of a more complex nature. His first task was the manufacture and consecration of his own magical insignia and weapons.

These were seven in number; a Rose Cross, worn on the breast of the initiate, a Lotus Wand, symbolising the twelve zodiacal signs and the triumph of spirit over matter, a Sword, signifying the force and power of Mars, and the four Elemental Weapons —a Cup for Water, a Pantacle for Earth, a Dagger for Air, and a Wand for Fire.

After this making and consecration—the latter had to be carried out in the presence of a Chief of the Temple or some other qualified Adept—and the completion of certain advanced theoretical studies the Adept moved on to such matter as Talismanic and Enochian magic. In the former he was instructed to 'gather names, sigils etc. for a Talisman for a special purpose. Make a design for both sides of it ... make up a special ritual for consecrating to the purpose you have in mind and arrange a time with the Chief for the Ceremony of Consecration', while in the latter he had to 'make and colour a pyramid for a selected square, and to make the God-form and Sphinx suitable to it ... prepare a Ritual for practical use with this square, and in the presence of a Chief ... build it up astrally and describe the vision produced'.

It is almost needless to say the initiate was not confined to a mechanical copying of magical rituals devised by others; he was expected to use his own theoretical knowledge of occult principles in the construction of ceremonies to suit his own particular circumstances. Thus Aleister Crowley, while still a member of the Golden Dawn, wrote his own complex ritual for the consecration of a Jupiterian talisman designed to heal the mother of a friend. Many of the rituals improvised by other initiates were much simpler, but, it would seem, still remarkably effective. Here is an example of such a simple ceremony, dating from about 1895: [10]

---

[10] The document I now reproduce (known as Flying Roll XXXIV —the term Flying Roll is explained at a later stage of this introduction) was written by J. W. Brodie-Innes, a Scottish lawyer and novelist, under his Order motto of *Sub Spe*. The notes, signed N.O.M., D.D.C.F., and *Resurgam*, which appear in the text, are by Wynn Westcott (N.O.M.), S. L. McGregor Mathers (D.D.C.F.) and Dr. Berridge (*Resurgam*).

Flying Roll XXXIV—An Exorcism by Frater Sub Spe

My wife had suffered a severe attack of influenza; her recovery was followed by great exhaustion, an exhaustion which ultimately I came to share. I considered this exhaustion, which seemed more than natural and it came to me that this was the obsession of some vampirising elemental. I seemed to hear a voice say 'cast it out'. I contemplated consulting an Adept of our Order, but during intense concentration I heard an almost audible voice say 'You must do it yourself under my instruction'. Thereupon I became conscious of the presence in the room of a stately figure in a black robe, wearing some shining insignia—I did not see or hear it speak physically, but, nevertheless, I saluted it with the Portal and $5°=6°$[11] signs. The figure first responded by saluting me gravely and then appeared to merge with me, to take possession of my body. It gave me, partly signs and partly by words, the following instructions: —

1. Lower the gas. (I did.)
2. Burn Incense (I used Incense on a live coal from the fire).
3. Trace invoking Pentagram of Fire towards East.
4. Trace the sigil of Leo in the centre of pentagram.
5. Vibrate the Name of Power ADNI ha ARETZ.
6. Return the coal to the fire.
7. Face East and make Qabalistic Cross.

[11] This, and similar equations, represent various grades of the Order. As the reader will frequently come across them in the course of this book I take the opportunity to give them in tabulated form: —

Neophyte $0°=0°$)
Zelator $1°=10°$) } attributed to Elemental Earth
Theoricus $2°=9°$ attributed to Elemental Air and the Moon
Practicus $3°=8°$ attributed to Elemental Water and Mercury
Philosophus $4°=7°$ attributed to Elemental Fire and Venus
Portal Grade. No Numerical Equation, attributed to Akasha, Spirit
Adeptus Minor $5°=6°$ attributed to Air and the Sun

8. Trace invoking Pentagram of Earth.

I carried out these instructions to the letter but in default of any magical implement traced the Pentagrams with my hand. As I drew the Earth Pentagram I called up the foul thing that had troubled me to manifest visibly before me. As I did so a vague blot, like a scrap of London fog, materialised before me. At the same time I sensed my guide, standing close to my right hand, raising his hand in the attitude of the 1°=10° sign. I felt him (my guide) mentally order me to command the appearance of the obsessing entity, using the Names JHVH, ADNI, AGLA, AHIH. I did so and the mist thickened and formed a kind of nucleus. My guide then instructed me, 'Use the Name of the Lord Jesus'. I did so, commanding in that name a fuller manifestation. I saw, at first dimly, 'as in a glass darkly', and then with complete clarity, a most foul shape, between a bloated big-bellied toad and a malicious ape. My guide spoke to me in an *audible* voice, saying 'Now smite it with all your force, using the Name of the Lord Jesus'. I did so gathering all the force I possessed into, as it were, a glowing ball of electric fire and then projecting it like a lightning flash upon the foul image before me.

There was a slight feeling of shock, a foul smell, a momentary dimness, and then the thing was gone; simultaneously my Guide disappeared. The effect of this experience upon me was to create a great tension of nerves and a disposition to start at almost anything. (You ought to have brought back to yourself the ray you projected. N.O.M. And you should also have closed up the opening you made to admit it, Resurgam). Afterwards, when going upstairs, I saw floating balls of fire; this may have been hallucination. (No. D.D.C.F.)

Both my wife and myself rapidly recovered our full health. Afterwards, a message came to me that 'the unclean spirit is gone out, but it remains to purge away his traces from the house of life'. (The effect was first upon the Ruach and later upon the Nephesch. N.O.M.)

A *Final Note by D.D.C.F.* It is not always permissible to completely destroy an Elemental; you must not do it on your own responsibility—but what you did was to disinte-

41

grate a collective built-up form, not one Elemental, but *many*, built up into one. Always invoke the Higher Forces first, Angelic as well as Divine.

Some idea of the complexity of the magical studies and work of the Golden Dawn initiate can be gained from the following catalogue of manuscripts circulated to each member of the grade of Adeptus Minor:

(A) General orders and curriculum of prescribed work

(B) Full Pentagram Rituals

(C) Full Hexagram Rituals

(D) Instructions for the Construction and Consecration of the Lotus Wand of the Adept

(E) Description of the Rose Cross Lamen together with Ritual for its consecration

(F) Sigils from the Rose, being a description of the way in which the Sigils of Angels, Spirits etc. are derived from the Rose Cross Lamen.

(G) Description of the sword and the Four Elemental Weapons together with consecration ritual

(H) Clavicula Tabularum Enochi (a treatise on the Elizabethan Enochian magical system)

(I) Notes on the Obligation of the Adeptus Minor

(K) Consecration Ritual of the Vault of the Adepti and Corpus Christi ceremony

(L) The official history lecture

(M) The description of the Hermes Vision together with Coloured Delineations of the geometrical figures attributed to the Sephiroth of the Qabalistic Tree of Life

(N, O, P, Q, R) Complete treatise of the Tarot with attributions to Star Maps of both hemispheres and instructions for projecting the Tree of Life in a sphere; i.e. the so-called globular Sephiroth

(S, T) The Book of the Concourse of Forces and the Book of the Angelical Calls: another two treatises on the Enochian magical system

(U) A treatise on Man, the microcosm (little universe)

(V) A treatise on the four colour-scales of the Tree of Life

(X) Ancient Egyptian god-forms applied to the letter squares of the Enochian magical system

(Y) Rosicrucian Chess: yet another aspect of the Enochian system

(Z 1, 2, 3) Three documents giving the symbolism of the Temple and Ritual of the Neophyte grade of the Order. Z2 is particularly important and applies the formulae of the Neophyte to such seemingly diverse magical operations as invisibility, alchemical transmutation and spiritual development

Most of the material catalogued above was published in the four volumes of Israel Regardie's monumental *Golden Dawn* (Aries Press, Chicago 1937/40). However, in addition to these fully official documents there were thirty-six side-lectures known as Flying Rolls, dealing in depth with various aspects of the magical-alchemical tradition, that circulated among the Adepti of the pre-1900 Golden Dawn. Only a few of these were included in Regardie's compilation. The rest of this material, hitherto unprinted, is included in this volume.

At first I intended to present the Flying Rolls in simple numerical order (which would also have been their chronological order)—i.e. 1-36, but excluding, of course, all material already printed by Regardie I soon realised that this would be confusing for the ordinary reader, and I have therefore chosen to divide the material into sections, each dealing with one aspect of occult theory and/or practice.[12]

[12] See also my *Exegetical Note on the Flying Rolls*, published as an appendix to this volume.

PART ONE

Imagination and Will-Power

being

Flying Roll No. V
Some Thoughts on the Imagination
By V. H. Fra. *Resurgam*[1]

The uninitiated interpret Imagination as something 'imaginary' in the popular sense of the word; i.e. something unreal. But imagination is a reality.

When a man imagines he actually creates a form on the Astral or even on some higher plane; and this form is as real and objective to intelligent beings on that plane, as our earthly surroundings are to us.

This form which Imagination creates may have only a transient existence, productive of no important results; or it may be vitalised and then used for good or evil.

To practice magic, both the Imagination and the Will must be called into action, they are co-equal in the work. Nay more, the Imagination must precede the Will in order to produce the greatest possible effect.

The Will unaided can send forth a current, and that current cannot be wholly inoperative; yet its effect is vague and indefinite, because the Will unaided sends forth nothing but the current or force.

The Imagination unaided can create an image and this image must have an existence of varying duration; yet it can do nothing of importance, unless vitalised and directed by the Will.

When, however, the two are conjoined—when the Imagination creates an image—and the Will directs and uses that image, marvellous magical effects may be obtained.

The following instances may serve to illustrate the operation of magical projection, which I have practised myself, and partly taught.

But here a caution is necessary—though this method became known to me by study and reflection before I was initiated

---

[1] *Resurgam* was the Order name—the so-called magical motto—of Dr. Berridge. (Editorial Note.)

into the G.D., so I only deemed it safe to entrust the process to two others, who I knew could be trusted.

It must never be forgotten that an occult process which may be used for good may also be used for evil. A black magician possessed of this knowledge might strengthen himself thereby, and protect himself from the danger of the recoil of his own evil actions on the occult plane, and so become energised for further evil. Added to which—one knowledge leads to another, and a single clue may lead to further important discoveries.

The more I reflect on the matter, the more I feel convinced that this knowledge should not pass beyond our Order.

First Illustration

A few years ago, I noticed that invariably after a prolonged interview with a certain person, I felt exhausted.

At first, I thought it only the natural result of a long conversation with a prosy, fidgetty, old gentleman; but later it dawned upon me, that being a man of exhausted nervous vitality, he was really preying upon me. I don't suppose that he was at all externally conscious that he possessed a vampire organisation, for he was a benevolent kind-hearted man, who would have shrunk in horror from such a suggestion.

Nevertheless, he was, in his inner personality an intentional vampire, for he acknowledged that he was about to marry a young wife in order, if possible, to recuperate his exhausted system.

The next time, therefore, that he was announced, I closed myself to him, before he was admitted. I imagined that I had formed myself a complete investiture of odic fluid, surrounding me on all sides, but not touching me, and impenetrable to any hostile currents.

This magical process was immediately and permanently successful—I never had to repeat it.

Second Illustration

A lady, hoping to develop herself spiritually had allowed

herself to become passively mediumistic, and her health began to fail.

On one occasion, feeling very weak, she asked me to mesmerise her. I availed myself of this opportunity, and while apparently only making mesmeric passes over her I occultly surrounded her with a protective aura as in my own case. The result was successful, she improved in strength, and, as a well-known student of occultism observed to me, 'she looked more human'; and with all this, her mediumistic experiences ceased. Had she followed my advice, and held herself positive; I believe she would have fully recovered her health and strength; but she again drifted back into her former condition of passive mediumship, her health broke down, and after a lingering illness, she died.

I had not been initiated into the G.D. then, or should have afterwards used the Banishing Pentagram for my own protection. About two weeks after, I had a vivid dream that I was endeavouring to evoke an elemental, which attacked me, causing a sudden choking in the throat, and an electric shock in the body. The dream had an astrological meaning; and at the same time I believe it had a physical basis and that same vampirising spirit which had been preying on its victim, determined to attack me, in revenge for having thwarted its designs.

Third Illustration

A lady asked my occult aid against a man whom she often met, whose presence invariably made her exhausted and ill.

He had bad health, and I judged it to be another case of vampirising.

I obtained a description of this man, but without telling the process, or when I would undertake it.

First, I imagined they stood facing each other; then I interposed a shield of defence. I then formed round her a complete investiture of odic fluid.[2] I also made the ordinary Invoking Pentagram upon her for protection. The injurious effects which

[2] The phrase 'odic fluid' is derived from nineteenth-century mesmerism. It is roughly equivalent to the Astral Light of Levi and the Akasha of the Theosophists. (Editorial Note.)

she had formerly experienced never returned and she remained ever completely passive to him.

Fourth Illustration

A lady told me of a man who exercised a peculiar fascination over her; she was always thinking of him, although she did not care for him.

As I had received some intimation that he had some acquaintance with Voodoo magic I determined to sever the chain.

I imagined they stood facing each other and that he had thrown out currents of odic fluid, which had entangled her in their meshes. Then I imagined a sword in my hand with which I severed them, and then with a torch burnt up the ends of the filaments still floating round her.

The unnatural fascination soon ceased and in a few months, their acquaintance came to an end.

Fifth Illustration

A man complained to me, that some years ago, he was constantly having another man make use of a peculiarly profane expression, which ever after haunted him, obtruding itself into his mind at the most inopportune times.

It seemed to me that the words constituted what the Oriental occultists call a mantram; that is, a word or phrase which can produce occult effects by setting up vibrations in the akasa.

I judged that some elemental had been vitalised thereby, and had attached itself to a sensitive. I advised him the next time the phrase troubled him—first to imagine he saw before him some horrible creature as the embodiment of the profanity itself —next to hold this creature firmly before him, and then to send forth an occult dynamite shell, penetrating into the elemental, and then exploding and blowing it to atoms.

When I next saw him he said that he had not succeeded in disintegrating the elemental, but that he had driven it away, and was now very little troubled by it.

One further caution may be made in conclusion.

While it is always lawful, and often advisable, to consult with some higher Adept before commencing any important magical work; yet, in every other direction, absolute secrecy must be maintained until the work be done. If it be talked about to others it tends to decentralise it, and so dissipate the force, besides running the risk of meeting with inharmonious currents from their minds.

If it be mentioned to the one on whose behalf the work is done, it tends to disturb his equilibrium by causing a state of nervous expectancy, which is unfavourable for the reception of the Occult good intended.

Supplementary Remarks
By G. H. Fra. N.O.M.[3]

The paper now read by our V. H. Frater Resurgam seems to me to require a preliminary chapter of introductory and more simple matter.

His remarks are valuable, and his instances are such as you may yet each possibly attain to the performance of; they are a credit to himself.

I can only add a few notes.

Imagination must be distinguished from Fancy—from mere roving thoughts, or empty visions: By it we now mean an orderly and intentional mental process, and result.

Imagination is the Creative Faculty of the human mind, the plastic energy—the Formative Power.

In the language of Esoteric Theosophists, the power of the Imagination to create thought forms is called KRIYA SAKTI, that is the mysterious power of thought which enables it to produce external phenomenal, perceptible results by its own inherent energy when fertilised by the Will.

It is an ancient Hermetic dogma that any idea can be made to manifest externally if only, by culture, the art of concentration be obtained; just similarly is an external result produced by a current of Will Force.

The Qabalah taught that man, by his creative power through

[3] The initials are short for *Non Omnis Moriar*, one of the magical mottoes of Wynn Westcott. (Editorial Note.)

Will and Thought—was more Divine than Angels; for he *can* create—they cannot. He is a step nearer the Demiurgos, the Creative Deity—even now that he is encased in matter—nearer than the Angelic Hosts although each Angel is a Spirit only— and not tainted with matter.

Even the orthodox conception of an Angel is that of a being who executes commands and not of one who originates, creates, and acts 'de novo'.

Flying Roll No. I, Part II
A Subject for Contemplation
By G. H. Frater N.O.M.

To obtain magical power, one must strengthen the will. Let there be no confusion between will and desire. You cannot will too strongly, so do not attempt to will two things at once, and while willing one thing do not desire others.

Example

You may at times have passed a person in the street, and as soon as passed may have felt some attraction, and the will to see him again; turning round (you) may have found that he also turned to you.

The will, although untrained, may have alone done this. But if you, untrained, walk out again, and decide to make the experiment of Willing that he who passes you shall turn round, and try it, you will fail. Because the desire of gratifying your curiosity has weakened the force of your will.

Flying Roll No. II, Part I
A Subject for Contemplation
By G. H. Frater N.O.M.

Before even strength of will, you must have purity of body, mind, intellect and of emotion if you hope for magical power.

The spiritual powers will flourish only as you starve the animal soul, and the animal soul is largely dependent on the state and treatment of the animal body. The animal man is to be cared for and protected, kept in health and strength, but not petted.

Be moderate in all things human. Extreme ascetic habits, are to you here, a source of another danger, they may lead only to a contemplation of your own Heroism, in being abstinent. To be truly ascetic is indeed to submit to discipline and to curb unruly emotions, thoughts and actions. But, who is a slave to his animal soul, will practice vice even in a Forest; while he who restrains himself among the crowds of a city, and passes through a busy life—unpolluted, shows more resistance and suffers a severer discipline, and shall obtain a greater reward.

Flying Roll No. II, Part II
Remarks upon Subject for Contemplation
By V. H. Fra *Levavi Oculos*[4]

Spiritual power results from the *transmutation* of the gross animal nature. The various centres of sensation in the human body can be harmonised by the equipose or circulation of the contrary forces of attraction and repulsion—or, on the other hand, the vehicle of excess.

If 'Our God is superlative in His unity', analogy must follow between the greater and lesser worlds.

One of Danton's clairvoyants once described a lake of gold in the centre of the earth, and we have the injunction 'visita interiora terrae, etc.' The primum mobile of even a commonplace vessel is placed in the centre of the ship. Now, the place of power and seat of equipoise is in numbers; the number 5 as has been pointed out: —

$$1\ 2\ 3\ 4\ 5\ 6\ 7\ 8\ 9.$$

That is the Sephira Geburah 'Where there is Gold', whose lineal figures traced with the single point uppermost is the most powerful continuous symbol there is.[5]

By the sign of the Microcosm is symbolized the athanor of the Alchemists—at everybody's hand without their knowing it.

'A strong and decided will', says Levi, 'can in a short space of time arrive at absolute independence'.

This condition of equipoise is therefore necessary before the manipulation of the will is even possible; and will is something more than the ascending of our higher desires over the lower, being a kind of electric force, the executive of desire.

In this light it is the creative power, which fashions according to the ideal forms or subsisting types. It is therefore through the agency of the will that the hidden becomes manifest, whether in the Universe or Man.

[4] *Levavi Oculos* was the magical motto of P. W. Bullock (Editorial Note).

[5] I.e.—the Pentagram. (Editorial Note.)

The student has to learn to arouse those forces within him or her self.

This masterly indifference is the great theme of the Bhagavada Gita and the Indian Yogis—in fact both East and West unite in teaching us to preserve that equal mean between two extremes, which is the law of immortality.

Flying Roll No. II, Part III
Three Suggestions on Will Power
By
S.S.D.D.

Head 1.   In studying the nature of the will force we are aided by our Minutum Mundi scheme. Mars, Geburah, Fire, Aries, each expressive of the will force on different planes, are all red in colour. The Red Lion was used as a symbol by the Alchemists to express the highest powers of the Adept. The whiteness of purity having been attained, the heat must be violently increased, until the redness of perfect strength manifests itself.
Head 2.   Now the danger which attends our labours arises from attempting to exercise this will power, before we have purged ourselves of ignorance and darkness.

Until we *know* we must refrain from *doing*. This sounds as if the case was pretty hopeless; but we have each in our own persons all the materials for experiment, and as long as we desire light, and do all we know to obtain it, we are not likely to do ourselves permanent harm; but at the same time we cannot be too careful in applying the very superficial magical knowledge we have at present to others, especially to those who are uninitiated. The danger I have found is that though the first step is most difficult, I mean it is extremely difficult to gain control over another's will so as to alter their natural tendencies; yet this once done the force you have set in motion becomes almost uncontrollable, the other individual seems sometimes to only live in your presence, and the last state of that person is worse than the first. This is a noticeable feature in the cases of those who have been cured by faith healers; or professional hypnotists.
Head 3.   Having explained these dangers, the method I advise for cultivation of will is, to imagine your head as centre of attraction with thoughts like rays radiating out in a vast globe. To want or desire a thing is the first step in the exercise of Will; get a distinct image of the thing you desire placed, as it

[6] The initials stand for *Sapientia Sapienti Dona Data,* the magical motto of Florence Farr. (Editorial Note.)

were, in your heart, concentrate all your wandering rays of thought upon this image until you feel it to be one glowing scarlet ball of compacted force. Then project this concentrated force on the subject you wish to affect.

Flying Roll No. VI
Concerning Flying Roll No. II
A Note by G. H. Frater
D.D.C.F.[7]—$7°=4°$

With regard to the admirable note by V. H. Soror S.S.D.D. on Will Power and Use—I would suggest that:—

Before bringing the scarlet ray into such intense action in the *Heart*, as is explained by her, that the Adept should elevate his thought and idea to the contemplation of the Divine Light in Kether, and considering Kether as the crown of the head, to endeavour to bring a ray from thence, into *his* heart—*his* Tiphereth through his path of Gimel and *then* to send the scarlet ray into action; the effect will be powerful and the process safer: otherwise there is a risk to the heart, and a risk of fever, if it be frequently done.

[7] These are the initials of the *Deo Duce Comite Ferro*, one of the magical mottoes of S. L. MacGregor Mathers. (Editorial Note.)

PART TWO

Astral Projection

being

Prefatory Note

I feel it advisable to preface the following material with a short note on the Golden Dawn technique of using symbols as a means of obtaining controlled astral visions; that is to say, meaningful, extremely vivid, and completely coherent day-dreams in which the dreamer retains all his normal powers of choice, will-power and judgment. In these dreams, so it is believed, the seer is enabled to come into contact with deepest levels of what Jungian depth-analysts call the Collective Unconscious and the mediaeval Hermetic philosophers called *Anima Mundi*—the Soul of the World.

The process used is best described as auto-hypnosis by means of a symbol. The seer begins by holding before his mind a symbol—it may be physically present, painted on a card, or, more difficult, formulated in the imagination only—and persists in this until no other factor is consciously present in his thinking. He then, in his mind's eye, deliberately transforms the symbol into a vast door (or sometimes a curtain, ornamented with the symbol), wills the door to swing open, passes through it in imagination, and allows the day-dream to commence. It is perhaps worth saying that most experimenters with this technique have found that the dream experienced bears a real relationship to the symbol used. Thus if the seer uses a symbol equating with Elemental Fire he may find himself near a volcano or observing the self-immolation of a Phoenix, but never will he find himself bathing in a lake or flying through the air.[1]

The symbols normally used by the beginner in this practice were, and are, the Tattvas and sub-Tattvas, coloured symbols of the Elements and sub-Elements. These simple geometric forms, which Mathers and his fellow Chiefs seem to have derived from an early Theosophical treatise, *Nature's Finer Forces*, by Rama

---

[1] This congruence between symbol used and vision experienced was described by W. B. Yeats in *The Trembling of the Veil*, Book III, Section II-VI inclusive. Yeats claimed that he had made York Powell talk of a burning house at a dinner party by imagining Tejas, the Fire Tattva.

Prasad, are five in number and from them are obtained a further twenty sub-symbols. The five mother-symbols are Tejas, a red equilateral triangle representing Elemental Fire, Prithivi, a yellow square representing Elemental Earth, Apas, a silver horizontal lunar crescent representing Elemental Water, Vayu, a blue circle representing Elemental Water, and Akas, a violet-black egg shape representing Elemental Spirit. The twenty sub-Tattvas are formed by taking a mother-symbol and placing in the midst of it a small-scale representation of any of the four symbols. The various sub-symbols must not be confused with one another. For example Tejas of Prithivi, Fire of Earth, represented by a small red triangle on a yellow square, is a very different thing from Prithivi of Tejas, Earth of Fire, represented by a small yellow square on a red triangle.

After Tattva-vision had been thoroughly mastered the Golden Dawn initiate went on to the use of more complex symbols, for example the Tarot trumps and the strange sigils of Phaleg, Ophiel and the other Olympic Planetary Spirits. The really advanced students used the so-called Enochian Pyramids[2] as their doors to the Unseen.

It may be that some of my readers may wish to undertake personal experimentation with this method of astral exploration. If so, they should bear in mind that any traditional symbol may be used to induce the required state of auto-hypnosis. Thus some contemporary occultists use the sixty-four Hexagrams of the Chinese Yi King, simple black and white symbols, made up of whole and broken lines, which are held much more easily in the imagination than more complex glyphs such as the Tarot trumps. If the Yi King is used in this way there seems to be, once again, a real causative link between the symbol used and the visions experienced. This connection is splendidly illustrated by an experience undergone by W. B. Seabrook, the American journalist and traveller.

[2] The last Flying Roll printed in this section is concerned with visions obtained in this way. I have therefore felt it advisable to give a brief explanation of the Enochian magical system, its letter-squares, and the Sphinxes and Pyramids derived from these letter-squares, in Appendix B of this book.

Seabrook had been experimenting for a year or so with 'travelling through the door'—he had probably learnt the technique from Aleister Crowley, with whom he had at one time been friendly, using a Yi King Hexagram, chosen at random by throwing tortoise-shell sticks in the air, as the symbol on the door. Seabrook himself does not seem to have had any particularly interesting experiences beyond the door, and he usually found himself looking for a mysterious lost object, the exact nature of which he remained unaware. His friends seem to have been more fortunate; one was transformed from a staid Professor of Greek into a wanton female Corybant, another found himself in the body of a mediaeval Benedictine monk. The really exciting and significant experience was undergone by an ex-singer named Nastatia Filipovna, a White Russian refugee.

Nastatia had been experimenting with astral projection for some time, obtaining the required disassociation of consciousness by gazing fixedly into a crystal ball. No symbol was used, and the experiences she underwent were unpleasant, monotonous, and completely outside her conscious control; almost always she found herself in a primitive nomadic camp, engaged in skinning and gutting a dead bear with a stone knife.

In the summer of 1923 Nastatia re-met Seabrook, an old acquaintance whom she had not seen for some years, and told him of her crystal gazing and its unsatisfactory results. In return Seabrook told her of the use of the Yi King Hexagrams in astral travel; inevitably Nastatia wanted to try the experiment and asked her friend to arrange it. Seabrook agreed and took her along to the scarlet draped studio of John Bannister, a wealthy occult dilettante, where they were joined by a young Englishman, the British vice-consul in New York, who was anxious to witness anything that might happen.

The experiment began with the tortoise-shell sticks—notched on one side, smooth on the other—being thrown into the air. They fell in a pattern which formed Ko, the forty-ninth Hexagram.

Nastatia knelt in the centre of the semi-dark studio, her eyes closed, formulating the Hexagram in her imagination. For three hours there was silence, save for a complaint from Nastatia about her aching knees. Then she spoke:

'The door is moving. The door is opening. But it's opening into the outdoors! I supposed it would open into another room. Its beautiful out there ... and yes ... I'm going.

'Snow ... everything's white ... everywhere snow, and the moon ... the moon on the white snow ... and black trees there against the sky. Yes, I'm outside now, I am lying in the snow ... pressed against the snow ... I am not cold ... I am wearing a fur coat ... and I am warm in the snow ... flat with my belly and chin on the snow I lie. It is good to lie warm in the snow. I am moving now ... but I am not walking I am crawling on my hands and knees ... why am I crawling? I'm not crawling now, I'm running, on my hands and feet, lightly ... now! now! now! ... I'm running lightly like the wind ... how good the snow smells! I have never smelled the snow before. And there's another good smell. Ah! Ah! Faster ... faster. ...'

Seabrook said that by this time Nastatia 'was breathing heavily, panting. Her big handsome mouth was open, drooling. And when she next broke silence, it was with sounds that were not human. There were yelps, slaverings, panting, and then a deep baying such as only two sorts of animals on earth emit when they are running—hounds and wolves.'

All three observers were alarmed by the girl's condition and the Englishman attempted to bring her round by slapping her cheeks. Nastatia's reaction was astonishing; she snarled and leapt, fortunately unsuccessfully, at the vice-consul's throat. Falling back to the ground she crawled, snarling, into a corner of the studio. Seabrook described how he and his companions dealt with the crisis:

'We had the lights on, snared her in big blankets, wrapped her tight as she struggled like a maniac, put ammonia under her nose, and she came out of it.

'We helped her to a couch. We brought a towel and a basin. We didn't talk much. We brought her brandy. In a few minutes she made us find her handbag with powder and makeup. She went into the bathroom. She came out and sank into an arm-chair and lighted a cigarette and said "What time is it?"'

It might be thought that Nastatia's experience was simply a

rather nasty case of wish fulfilment, that beneath her placid Slav exterior she nursed a bestial desire to rip, tear, kill and revel in blood—such unpleasant fantasies are not uncommon. I think that this was probably so, and I have no doubt that the particular form the girl's animal transformation took was conditioned by her own unconscious desires; but the really interesting thing is that there *was* an animal transformation. For Ko, the name of the Hexagram used, literally means skin, hide, fur, an animal pelt, moulting. Even more significant are the traditional Chinese commentaries on the lines of this Hexagram. One of them reads 'wrapped in the hide of a yellow cow', another reads 'the great man changes like a tiger', still another reads 'the superior man is transformed into a panther'. All of them express the idea of transformation in one form or another—so there was a link between Nastatia's experience and the symbol she used; a link of which she herself was unaware, for her personal knowledge of the Yi King was limited to what little Seabrook had told her of the subject.

I do not think that the average astral experimenter is likely to undergo such odd experiences as the one I have related—even if he or she is using the forty-ninth Hexagram of the Yi King— but I would advise those who are worried by the possibility to confine themselves to the Golden Dawn symbols and their use as taught in the Flying Rolls printed in the following section.

Flying Roll No. IV
An Example of Mode of Attaining to Spirit
Vision and What was seen by Two Adepti—
S.S.D.D. and F.[3] on November 10th 1892.

Secure for an hour or for longer absolute freedom from interruption. Then alone, or with one or two other Adepti, enter the vault, or a private chamber. Remain in silence and contemplation for several minutes.

Rise, and perform the Qabalistic Cross and prayer. Then proceed to contemplation of some object, say a Tarot Trump: either by placing it before you and gazing at it, until you seem to see *into* it; or by placing it against your forehead or elsewhere, and then keeping the eyes closed; in this case you should have given previous study to the Card, as to its symbolism, colouring, analogies, etc.

In either case you should then deeply sink into the abstract ideal of the card; being in entire indifference to your surroundings. If the mind wanders to anything disconnected with the card, no beginner will succeed in seeing anything spiritually.

Consider all the symbolism of the Tarot Card, then all that is implied by its letters, number, and situation, and the paths connected therewith.

The vision may begin by the concentration passing into a state of reverie; or with a distinct sense of change, something allied in sensation to a faint, with a feeling urging you to resist, but if you are highly inspired, fear not, do not resist, let yourself go; and then the vision may pass over you.

If you have anything occur or disturb you, you will come to readily enough—or as from a doze; otherwise the vision ends of itself, or some can check it by will, at any stage, others can not, at first, at any rate.

Example

[3] The meaning of S.S.D.D. has already been explained; F. was *Fidelis*, the magical motto of Elaine Simpson, who later became the mistress of Aleister Crowley. (Editorial Note.)

The Tarot Trump, the Empress[4] was taken; placed before the persons and contemplated upon, spiritualised, heightened in colouring, purified in design and idealised.

In vibratory manner pronounced Daleth. Then, in spirit, saw a greenish blue distant landscape, suggestive of mediaeval tapestry. Effort to ascend was then made; rising on the planes; seemed to pass up through clouds and then appeared a pale green landscape and in its midst a Gothic Temple of ghostly outlines marked with light. Approached it and found the temple gained in definiteness and was concrete, and seemed a solid structure. Giving the signs of the Netzach Grade (because of Venus) was able to enter; giving also Portal signs and $5° = 6°$ signs in thought form. Opposite the entrance perceived a Cross with three bars and a dove upon it; and beside this, were steps leading downwards into the dark, by a dark passage. Here was met a beautiful green dragon, who moved aside, meaning no harm, and the spirit vision passed on. Turning a corner and still passing on in the dark emerged from the darkness on to a marble terrace brilliantly white, and a garden beyond, with flowers, whose foliage was of a delicate green kind and the leaves seemed to have a white velvety surface beneath. Here, there appeared a woman of heroic proportions, clothed in green with a jewelled girdle, a crown of stars on her head, in her hand a sceptre of gold, having at one apex a lustrously white closed lotus flower; in her left hand an orb bearing a cross.[5]

She smiled proudly, and as the human spirit sought her name, replied:

'I am the mighty Mother Isis; most powerful of all the world, I am she who fights not, but is always victorious, I am that Sleeping Beauty who men have sought, for all time; and the paths which lead to my castle are beset with dangers and illusions. Such as fail to find me sleep;—or may ever rush after the Fata Morgana leading astray all who feel that illusory influence —I am lifted up on high, and do draw men unto me, I am the

---

[4] Corresponding to the Hebrew letter Daleth according to the G.D. system. (Editorial Note.)
[5] She has a shield with a dove upon it—S.A. (Wynn Westcott.)

worlds' desire, but few there be who find me. When my secret is told, it is the secret of the Holy Grail.' Asking to learn it, (she) replied : —

'Come with me, but first clothe in white garments, put on your insignia, and with bared feet follow where I shall lead.'

Arriving at length at a Marble Wall, pressed a secret spring, and entered a small compartment, where the spirit seemed to ascend through a dense vapour, and emerged upon a turret of a building. Perceived some object in the midst of the place, but was forbidden to look at it until permission was accorded. Stretched out the arms and bowed the head to the Sun which was rising a golden orb in the East. Then turning, knelt with the face towards the centre, and being permitted to raise the eyes beheld a cup with a heart and the sun shining upon these; there seemed a clear ruby coloured fluid in the cup. Then 'Lady Venus' said 'This is love, I have plucked out my heart and have given it to the world; that is my strength. Love is the mother of the Man—God, giving the Quintessence of her life to save mankind from destruction, and to show forth the path to life eternal. Love is the mother of the Christ—

'Spirit, and this Christ is the highest love—Christ is the heart of love, the heart of the Great Mother Isis—the Isis of Nature. He is the expression of her power—she is the Holy Grail, and He is the life blood of spirit, that is found in this cup.'

After this, being told that man's hope lay in following her example, we solemnly gave our hearts to the keeping of the Grail; then, instead of feeling death, as our human imagination led us to expect, we felt an influx of the highest courage and power, for our own hearts were to be henceforth in touch with hers—the strongest force in all the world.

So then we went away, feeling glad that we had learned that 'He who gives away his life, will gain it'. For *that* love which is power, is given unto him,—who hath given away his all for the good of others.

Flying Roll No. XI
Clairvoyance
By G. H. Frater D.D.C.F.

In order to obtain a clear idea of the relation of Man to the Universe, and to the spiritual planes, it is necessary to understand and perceive that the scheme of the Ten Sephiroth, and their symbolic representation as the Tree of Life is to be applied both to the Macrocosm and to the Microcosm; to the Celestial Heavens to Stars, Planets, the World, and to Man. One aspect of this assertion that has been recently pointed out to you, and has been demonstrated to you on the globe, is in reference to the scheme of Divination; you must further extend this idea when considering the rationale of Clairvoyance and must recognise a Sephirotic arrangement in the constitution of every Star, and of every atom, of Man and his principles.

We look above us into heaven, and see the Stars, and it is commonly supposed that we see the material globes, their Malkuth, but they are complex in constitution and we see but their luminous aura or atmospheres, containing the rest of the Sephiroth, etc., or a reflection of them.

Then as to ourselves, we must never forget our own complex Sephirotic symbolism, and that our bodies that we feed and clothe are but our Malkuth on its lowest plane, and that the higher nine Sephiroth hover around us in our auras, or atmosphere.

We pass through life affecting others, and being affected by others through these akashic envelopes that closely surround us— so that when we close the eyes of the body and senses upon the material world, we first apprehend by interior vision the essences of our own and contiguous natures. This perception of our own environment is a source of error to the beginner in Clairvoyance; for he believes himself to have gone away and to see elsewhere, and may be but among the confused images of his own aura.

An old name of Clairvoyance, in our ancient MSS was 'Skrying in the Spirit Vision'; becoming a 'Skryer' was not simply becoming a Seer, but one who descries what he *seeks*, not only

75

the impassive receiver of visions beyond control or definition.

When one stands in common life in the kingdom of Malkuth, there is but little confusion of sight, but when one voluntarily leaves the dead level of materialism and passes up the Path of Tau towards Yesod, then there is a confusion of lights; one comes within the scope of the crossing, and reflected, and coloured, rays of the Qesheth, the Rainbow of colours spread over the earth, and here then we require instruction and guidance to avoid confusion and folly. And yet this stage must be passed through—to go higher.

Beyond Yesod you enter the path of Samekh, the strait and narrow path which leads to truly spiritual regions of perception, this is attained by the process called Rising in the Planes.

Our subject falls most conveniently into three heads, which are however, closely related, and the three forms or stages pass one into the other.

1. Clairvoyance. Descrying in the Spirit Vision.
2. Astral projection. Travelling in the Spirit Vision.
3. Rising in the Planes.

Begin with simple Clairvoyance, and then pass to the other states.

It is well to commence this form of practical occultism by means of a Symbol, such as a drawing, or coloured diagram, related in design, form and colour to the subject chosen for study. The simple and compound Tattva emblems are suitable for this process. It is better for them not to be in the complementary 'flashing' colours for this purpose as though more powerful, they are also more exhausting to the student. The Symbol should be of convenient size, for the eye to take it in at a glance, and large enough not to require too close an application of sight to realise the details.

There are several scales of colour, but for our present purpose we need only note two. Firstly, the scale of the King, that of the G.D.; and that of the Adept Minor. Scarlet is Fire, Yellow is Air, Blue is Water, Four dull colours are Earth and White is Spirit. Secondly, the Tattva scheme, which is nearly the same as our scale of the Queen, which is applied also to the Sephirotic colours in the Minutum Mundum Diagram. Red is Fire, greyish White is Water, Golden Yellow is Earth, Blue (greenish) is Air, Violet Black is Akasha or Spirit.

Tablets and Telesmas are described as being made in Flashing Colours, when in one tablet, a certain colour and its direct complementary are shown in opposition and shine by contrast. In such tablets do the elemental forces manifest most readily, and most students can perceive their flashes of radiance, which are, however, partly subjective and partly objective. They attract and reflect the rays of light from the akashic plane enveloping them.

These tablets when formed by an Adept of high spiritual attainments receive from him a charge of akashic force of a magnetic character; as line by line and colour by colour is added, the Telesma grows in virtue as well as progresses to completion. But the beginner fails, thus, to impregnate his work with his vital astral force and his finished Telesma needs a ceremony of consecration, after which the figure should remain sacred to his touch alone. All Telesma, however, are better consecrated ceremonially, for they then hold more firmly the 'charge' of force, and if carefully preserved, apart from contamination, and from influence by other Telesma, will retain force for an indefinite period. All powerful Occult work, such as this, exhausts the Vital force, especially from beginners, and you will feel at first distinct exhaustion from loss of akasha, which however is not lost but transferred to the symbol and there preserved, fading away from thence, only slowly into the ocean of energies.

To use the Symbol for Clairvoyance, place it before you, as on a table, place the hands beside it, or hold it up with both hands, then, with the utmost concentration, gaze at it, comprehend it, formulate its meaning and relations. When the mind is steady upon it: close the eyes and continue the meditation, and let the conception still remain before you, keep up the design, form, and colour in the akashic aura, as clearly as they appeared in material form to the outward seeing. Transfer the Vital effort from the optic nerve to the mental perception, or *thought seeing* as distinct from seeing with the eye; let one form of apprehension glide on with the other—produce the reality of the dream vision, by positive will in the waking state. All this will be only possible if the mind is steady, clear and undisturbed and the will powerful. It cannot lead to success if you are in an unsuitable state of anxiety, fear, indignation, trouble or anticipation. You must procure peace, solitude and leisure and you must banish all disturbing influences.

But, above all, never attempt these Magic Arts if there be any resentment in the mind, anger, or any evil passion; for if you do, the more you succeed, the greater will be the evil that will follow—for yourself.

With the condition favourable, the process may be continued, and this, by means of introducing into the Consciousness and by formulating into sound, the highest Divine Names connected therewith; this invocation produces and harmonises currents of spiritual force in sympathy with your object. Then follow with the sacred names of Archangelic and Angelic import, producing them mentally, visually and by voice.

Then, maintaining your abstraction from your surroundings, and still concentrating upon the symbol and its correlated ideas, you are to seek a perception of a scene, panorama, or view of a place. This may also be brought on by a sense of tearing open, as a curtain is drawn aside and seeing the 'within' of the symbol before you. As the scene dawns upon you, particularise the details, and seek around for objects, and then for beings, entities and persons—attract their attention, call mentally to them by suitable titles and courtesies, and by proper and appropriate signs and symbols, such as the signs of the Grades, Pentagrams, etc. Test them by divine and angelic names, observing their attitude and responses thereto. Thus losing sight of the symbol, you see its inwardness, perceive things as in a mirror by Reflection. In this form of Descrying, note, that you see objects reversed, as to right and left, for which suitable allowance must be made. You project, in this process, part of your own nerve and spirit force upon the symbol, and by this you attract and attach to it more akashic force from the environment, hence the results obtained. If, instead of this Simple Spirit Vision, a ray of yourself is sent and actually goes to a place (astral projection) there is not necessarily the sense of reversal of objects.

In using Symbols it is necessary to avoid Self hypnotisation, for this occurrence would dispose you to mediumship, and to be the playground of forces you must control, and not permit to control you. For this reason, partly, it is well not to have the Symbol too small. It is of advantage to pursue these researches with the aid of the presence before you of the four Magical Implements, and even to hold the one suitable to the investigation. If you enter upon the Spirit Vision without a Symbol you proceed by a mental symbol, imagined in the Astral Light: this is not a wise proceeding for learners because it opens the door to other Astral effects; you create a vortex, into which other astral influences are drawn and hence confusion and mischief may result.

The process of working by a small symbol placed upon the forehead, or elsewhere, is not wholly good; it is more liable to derange the Brain circulation and cause mental illusion and disturbance, headache, and nervous exhaustion than the first method.

In using symbols, placed before you—it is a useful addition to provide a large circular (or square) tablet, around which are placed Divine Names etc. related to the Elements, and to the cardinal points; then after arranging this duly, with respect to the compass, place your symbol upon and within this frame.

Astral Projection, although from one point of thought a development of Clairvoyance, yet is from another distinct: in Astral Projection, the Adept emits from his Ego a perceptible ray of his identity, and by cultured and instructed Will, sends it to travel to the place desired, focusses it there, sees there—directly and not by reflection—perceives its bodily home, and re-enters it.

In this Travelling of the Spirit the process may be caused to start also by the Symbol, as before, or by Will alone; but anyway the Divine names should be used and relied upon. If the ray be emitted, and you succeed in this travelling to the place—you perceive a different result to that of the clairvoyant, mirror-like vision—scenes and things instead of being like a picture, have the third dimension, solidity, they stand out first like bas relief, then you see as from a Balloon, as it is said, by a bird's eye view. You feel free to go to the place, to descend upon it, to step out upon the scene, and to be an actor there.

Having attained success in projection you should practice the method when opportunity offers, and having passed to any place, should make efforts—and if you Will—success will follow —to pass through all elements, Water and Earth as well as through Air—practice will enable you to fly through air either quickly or slowly as willed, and to swim through water, or pass through earth and through fire fearlessly with the aid of the Divine Names, in this Astral Projection.

Seek then the forms and persons of the place or of the Plane you reach to, seek converse with them, by voice, word, letter and symbol and claim admission etc. by signs, and by invocation. Every figure is to be tried and tested, whether he be as he appears or whether a delusive and deluding embodied power. It may be, too, that your travel is not real, and that you are wandering in your own environment, and are misled by memory etc.; hence you might be self-deceiving by your own reminiscences.

Try all beings, and if offered favours or initiation by any, try and test them by Divine names and forces; and ever remember your own Adept Obligation and your allegiance to it, to your own Higher Self, and to the Great Angel HVA, before whom you stood fastened to the Cross of Suffering, and to whom you pledged your obedience.

This old Proverb enshrines a great truth, as many of them do: 'Believe thyself *there* and thou art *there.*'

Rising in the Planes is a spiritual process after spiritual conceptions, and higher aims; by concentration and contemplation of the Divine, you formulate a Tree of Life passing from you to the spiritual realms above and beyond you. Picture to yourself that you stand in Malkuth—then by the use of the Divine Names and aspirations you strive upward by the Path of Tau toward Yesod, neglecting the crossing rays which attract you as you pass up. Look upwards to the Divine Light shining down from Kether upon you. From Yesod leads up the Path of Temperance, Samekh, the arrow cleaving upward leads the way to Tiphereth, the Great central Sun of Sacred Power.

Invoke the Great Angel HUA, and conceive of yourself as standing fastened to the Cross of Suffering, carefully vibrating the Holy Names allied to your position, and so may the mental Vision attain unto Higher Planes.

There are three special tendencies to error and illusion which assail the Adept in these studies. They are, *Memory, Imagination* and *actual Sight*. These elements of doubt are to be avoided, by the Vibration of Divine Names, and by the Letters and Titles of the 'Lords Who Wander'—the Planetary Forces, represented by the Seven double letters of the Hebrew alphabet.

If the Memory entice thee astray, apply for help to Saturn whose Tarot Title is the 'Great One of the Night of Time'.

Formulate the Hebrew letter Tau in Whiteness.

If the Vision change or disappear, your memory has falsified your efforts. If Imagination cheat thee, use the Hebrew letter Kaph for the Forces of Jupiter, named 'Lord of the Forces of Life'. If the Deception be of Lying—intellectual untruth, appeal to the Force of Mercury by the Hebrew letter Beth. If the trouble be of Wavering of Mind, use the Hebrew letter Gimel for the Moon. If the enticement of pleasure be the error, then use the Hebrew letter Daleth as an aid.[6]

Never attempt any of these Divine processes when at all influenced by Passion or Anger or Fear—leave off if desire of sleep approach, never force a mind disinclined. Balance the Mem and the Shin of your nature and mind, so as to leave Aleph like a gentle flame rising softly between them.

You must do all these things by yourself alone. No one can make you nor take you. Do not try to make, or take others. You may only point out the Path, and guide but must not help others.

A strong person can galvanise a weak one, but its effect is only a temporary folly, doing good neither to the strong nor to the weak. Only offer guidance to those who are making necessary efforts of themselves: don't assist a negligent pupil, nor encourage one whose desire is not in the work.

[6] Use the Hebrew letter Peh for Mars to coerce sense of anger and violence. Use the Hebrew letter Resh for the Sun to coerce sense of haughtiness, vanity. (Note in original.)

This rule is open to some alteration when, passing from our Mystic studies, you refer to the worldly guidance of childhood —a parent is in a special position, and has a natural duty incumbent upon him or her to train, guide, and protect a child.

Still, even here, do protect and lead, but don't 'obsess' a child, don't override by your peculiar personal predilections all the personal aims of the offspring. A man's ideal of true propriety is often *himself*, and his idea of doing good to a child is to make it like himself. Now, although this father may be a good man, his form of goodness is not to be made a universal type, and there are many other forms equally existing, and equally fit to exist, and any attempt to dictate too closely a child's 'thought life' may, while failing of success, yet warp aside from the truth what would otherwise pass into a Good Path, through its own peculiar avenue.

It is well to make all symbols for Clairvoyant use yourself, otherwise, to obtain a purely individual result, you have to banish the influence of him who made them.

It is best to do high Clairvoyance alone, or only with others of the utmost purity, and in whom you have the utmost confidence.

If more than one, is attempting in concert the same process, there is the source of error that there becomes formed in the Astral Light a complex symbol, and a struggle ensues as to who shall lead the direction of the currents. When two sit together, as in the Vault, they should be balanced: and so with three. For two; one each side of Pastos or one at each end; for three assume the position of the angles of a triangle, say one at head of Pastos, one at the Right and at the Left hand of the form of Christian Rosycross.

Example

The V.H. Soror V.N.R. $6° = 5°$, sat at a table, robed, and took a Tattva card coloured symbol (Tejas—akasha)—an erect red triangle, upon which is a dark violet black egg shaped centre. She placed her hands beside her side, or held it in turns before the eyes (held the Magic Fire Wand). Gazed and contemplated and considered as the Symbol grew before her, so enlarged and filled the place, that she seemed to pass into it, or into a vast triangle of flame. She realises that she is in the presence of a desert of sand, harsh, dry and hot.

Thinks of and vibrates—Elohim. Action seems set up, increase of heat and light. Passing through the symbol and scene: seems to arrive and descend there, feels the hot dry sand—perceives a small pyramid in the distance—Wills to rise up and fly through air to it, descends beside it, passes around, sees a small square door on each side. Vibrates—- 'Elohim—Michael—Erel—Seraph, Darom. Ash.'

Stamps five times—figure appears at an entrance, stamps again five times and vibrates Seraphiel. A Warrior figure leads out a procession of Guards, she asks for his Seal—he shows a complex Symbol of four triangles around a central emblem—? deceptive. Draw Beth before him—he appears terrified. Withdraw Symbol—he is courteous—ask him about pyramid: he says they conduct ceremonies there—she seeks admission—gives sign of $0°=0°$—there is a sense of opposition—gives sign $1°=10°$, this appears to suffice—But he gives signs of Adeptship —Guards kneel before her and she passes in—dazzling light, as in a Temple. An Altar in the midst—kneeling figures surround it, there is a dais beyond, and many figures upon it—they seem to be Elementals of Fiery nature—she sees a Pentagram, puts a Leo into it, thanks the figure who conducts her—Wills to pass through the pyramid, finds herself out amid the sand. Wills her return—returns—perceiving her body in Robes seated in the Second Order Hall.

Flying Roll No. XXV
Essay on Clairvoyance and Travelling in the Spirit Vision[7] By *Sub.Spe*—Zelator Adeptus Minor

The best theory of the phenomenon of Clairvoyance seems to be founded on the relation between Man as the Microcosm and the Universe as the Macrocosm; regarding the former as a reflection in miniature of the latter, as in a grass field full of dewdrops each drop might present a perfect tiny image of trees and mountains, the sky, clouds, the sun and the stars.

If, then, everything in the Cosmos is somehow reflected or pictured on each man's own sphere of sensation, or Akashic envelope, it follows that if he could but be conscious of the pictures so reflected or imprinted he would at once be possessed of all actual or potential knowledge of everything in the Cosmos, and further assuming that time itself is merely an illusion, and that the reality of things is, as it were, one vast picture along which we travel seeing point after point in succession and producing the idea of lapse of time, then it further follows that the full and complete knowledge of all that is reflected in our sphere of sensation includes all knowledge past, present and future.

The reason, then, why we have not such knowledge *consciously* to *ourselves* must be from the obtuseness of the Sensorium, the actual physical brain, which cannot perceive the images on the sphere of sensation. If, then, all knowledge lies *within* each man's own sphere, it is by looking within, or *intuition*, that such knowledge is made available.

Know thyself and thou wilt know everything. But seeing that the brain and sensorium are physical, it is necessary at first to use physical means to produce the sensitiveness necessary to consciously perceive the images on the Sphere of Sensation. And the readiest and safest means is the use of a symbol. This is familiar in everyday life, but so much so as to escape notice.

For example—to a depraved and debauched person an obscene

[7] A totally different version of this Flying Roll is given in Appendix C of this book. (Editorial Note.)

85

word or figure—carelessly drawn and seen by chance, is a symbol calling up a host of unclean images and ideas. To a lover the name of his mistress spoken by chance in his hearing—the sight of a colour she usually wears, or the scent of a familiar perfume will suffice to raise the image of the beloved form almost visibly before him and to produce quickened pulse, heightened colour, etc.

To the soldier the sight of the flag of his country or his regiment, produces visions of martial glory, ideas of devotion, loyalty, patriotism and unflinching courage.

In all these cases ideas and visions are produced in the brain by the symbol, and if the above theory be accepted it follows that the effect of the symbol is to render one portion of the physical brain more sensitive, or it may be more translucent, so that the images lying within the corresponding region of the Sphere of Sensation may be dimly perceived (such sensitiveness of brain may be produced in other ways, such as by Hypnotism or self-induced Trance, by Obsession, Disease, etc.—but the method by symbol seems to remain the surest and the best).

This theory is made use of in the practice of inducing Clairvoyance.

A large number of well known and recognised symbols have a definite relation to certain portions of the Sphere of Sensation and the corresponding regions of the Cosmos, and also to the regions related thereto of the physical brain.

The experimenter should know thoroughly the attributions and meanings of the symbol employed, as this knowledge produces an immediate concentration of thought, of vital energy, of nerve force, and of actual physical blood on the tract of brain related thereto, and thus materially aids the establishment of a special sensitiveness there.

Thus if the Tejas Tattva card be taken, the knowledge that it belongs to fire will at once charge with nerve force and with blood all the centres of the brain relating to fire, and will involuntarily recall the various Divine and Spirit names which the experimenter has learnt connected therewith. The actual speaking of these with the solemnity and impressiveness of the Vibration will increase the effect—gazing fixedly at the symbol and touching the appropriate implement which is also a symbol of the same brain tract, momentarily increases the force—vires acquiret eundo—until every other brain cell is shut down, muted and inhibited; the whole consciousness is concentrated on the perception of fire.

The physical brains thus become sensitive and translucent in this respect and able to perceive dimly in the Sphere of sensation the reflection of the Macrocosmic idea of fire, with all its connotations.

The sensation is as though one stepped out through a window into a new world.

The reality probably is that the new sensitiveness enables the actual physical brain to become conscious of ideas and pictures hitherto unknown.

At first it seems as though everything thus perceived were just the product of one's own imagination—i.e. that one simply took scraps of memory, scraps of other men's ideas gleaned from books, pictures, etc. and built them up at will into a composite picture. But a little further experience generally convinces one that the new country one has become conscious of has its inviolable natural laws just as the physical world has: that one cannot make or unmake at will, that the same causes produce the same results, that one is in fact merely a spectator and in no sense a creator. The conviction then dawns on one that one is actually perceiving a new and much extended range of phenomena; that, in fact, which is known as the Astral World or Astral Plane.

Here, then, comes an experimental confirmation of the theory above set forth, which will probably be deepened and intensified with every experiment which is carefully made.

Personal experience confirms the foregoing: On taking any symbol whereof I know the meaning, such as a Tattva—or Tarot card, the abstract idea of the meaning of the symbol comes first —as fire, or water in the abstract—and a pose of mind cognate and sympathetic thereto, a desire for that particular element— not keen but perceptible—gradually the feeling of the physical effects of the element—as of warmth—moisture—etc.—and especially the sound as of the roaring or crackling of fire, the rush—or patter, or ripple of water. Gradually the attention is withdrawn from all surrounding sights and sounds, a grey mist seems to swathe everything, on which, as though thrown from a magic lantern on steam, the form of the symbol is projected.

(This I conceive is due to the withdrawal of blood and nerve force from other centres of the brain and their consequent inhibition.)

The Consciousness then seems to pass through the symbol to realms beyond but, as above-said, I think it more probable that visions and pictures from beyond come on to the hypersensitive brain centres and, as these have been sensitised by the symbol and the first effect has been the vision of the symbol itself on the grey mist, so they seem to take the form of the symbol and to pass through it. At all events the sensation is as if one looked at a series of moving pictures, although there are beings in this new world with whom one can converse, animals that one can dominate, or that attract one, yet to me personally it is all no more *solid* than the pictures of a Kinetoscope or the sound of a phonograph.

Yet when this sensitiveness of brain and power of perception is once established there seems to grow out of it a power of actually going to the scenes so visionary and seeing them as solid, indeed, of actually *doing things* and producing effects there.

This is what I imagine is termed Travelling in the Spirit Vision.

Whether it is more than an extension of the power of perceiving the pictures on the Sphere of Sensation or Akashic envelope is very difficult to determine. The sensation, however, to me personally is first to become, as it were, dimly conscious of a figure walking among the scenes of the new country—or the Astral Plane—gradually to become conscious that it is my own figure I am looking at—gradually, as it were, to be able to look through the eyes—and feel with the sensations of this *doppel ganger*. Further to be able consciously to direct its motions, to control it, to inhabit it, and in this body to be able to visit the scenes and persons I had previously only looked at, as it were, through a telescope.

It is as though my Consciousness had extruded from my own body to take possession of a body which I had either created for the purpose, or invoked out of the Astral Sphere as a vehicle for myself.

It seems, however, almost more probable that as the Sphere of Sensation reflects everything that is in the material Universe so it must needs contain a reflection also of the material body of the percipient and if this be so it is not hard to suppose that such reflection can be made to travel about within the Sphere of Sensation and visit all things therein reflected with as much ease (or more) as the will of the man can make his physical body travel to material places on the earth.

The Perception of the Astral plane seems to be peculiarly liable to delusions, arising probably from defects in the sensorium or physical brain—as an object seen through faulty glass is distorted, that is to say the personal element, or what scientists call the 'personal equation', becomes so strong as to produce actual error.

As the brain can be rendered sensitive in a particular direction by symbol—so can these errors also be corrected by symbol. The various qualities in each man's nature are symbolised by the planets—hence when this symbology is well known the planetary symbols may be used to correct errors arising from the particular quality attributed to each. Thus the error could be that the visions are merely compounded from memory.

In this case build up in brilliant white light in front of any image which you suspect to be merely a product of memory the letter Tau, the symbol of the Path of Saturn, 'The Great One of the Night of Time'—whose sober and steadying influence will cause a memory picture to disappear. Similarly Beth for Mercury formulated in the same way will cause to vanish any product of lying intellectual delusion—or Daleth for Venus is used for the result of intellectual vanity—Gimel for Luna for a wavering mind—Resh for the Sun for delusions of haughtiness, vanity, etc. and Kaph for the path of Jupiter against imagination, and Peh for the path of Mars against revenge, hatred etc.

Flying Roll No. XXX
Tattva Cards and Tattvic Clairvoyance
and Hierophant rising 0°=0° signs
By G. H. Fra. D.D.C.F

1. *Concerning Tattva Cards and Tattvic Clairvoyance or Skrying*

The Cards used should be of a convenient size. The Tattvas thereon should be as uniform as possible, that is the full sized Apas should be as nearly as possible of the same area as the full sized Tejas—that is if it can conveniently be done.

The Tattvas should be placed on the card so that their perpendicular coincides with the card's length rather than its breadth if the card be oblong i.e.

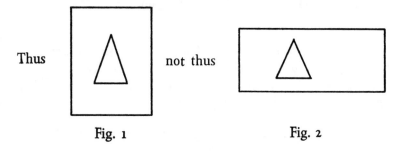

Thus   not thus

Fig. 1   Fig. 2

This is not of great importance, but the horizontal method is apt to increase the negative side too much.

The Sub-Tattva should occupy about one fifth of the area of the main Tattva—one quarter is rather too large, and makes the Sub-Tattva nearly as important to the eye of the operator as the main Tattva when the former is superimposed upon the latter.

The cards should be *clean* and the colours correct when first made; not dirty cards whose uncleanliness is covered over to the physical eye by the Tattva pasted thereon. For if the cards are thus made they are apt, without the intention of the maker, to attract evil and delusive Elemental Influences from the fact that their formulae necessarily imply hidden iniquity.

2. Of Tattvic Skrying

The Skryer, using the proper Names, Implements etc. should endeavour to attain the following results for passing the C. Examination in Tattvic Clairvoyance.

He should test everything in the vision, that is to say, everything at all doubtful to him. He should describe carefully and in detail the landscape etc. of the vision, and discover, if possible : —

The special attributes and varying natures of the Plane.

Its Elemental Nature.

The Inhabitants (Elemental, Spiritual etc., etc.).

The Plants, Animals, Minerals etc., which would be correspondent to the Nature of the Plane.

The Operation of its Influence in the Universe or Macrocosm upon (a) this particular Planet (b) animals, plants and minerals.

The Operation of its Influence upon the Microcosm, i.e. Man.

He or she who is operating should avoid carefully any self-hypnotisation by the Tattva, for this will simply lead to foolish and hysteric visions, the offspring of the intoxication of the Operator's astral sphere by the Tattva.

Of the Mode of delivering the Signs of the 0°=0° in a Temple of the Outer Order

The Initiated Hierophant, or any other member of the Second Order present in a Temple of the Outer Order, should give the Signs in the manner laid down in the Z Ritual, and should teach them to be given thus; but he must *on no account* describe their secret formulae, confining himself to the explanation usually given in the Ritual of the 0°=0° Grade of the First Order. It does not matter so much whether the First Order members give them quite properly, but the Second Order initiated members should *always* do so.

Flying Roll No. XXVI
By G. H. Fra. D.D.C.F

In Flying Roll XII there appears Venus (Daleth) as Water of Earth.[8]

The Planets are not Tattvas but have a sympathy with them.

The Planets are not Elements but have a great sympathy with them.

Planets represent, for the most part, the compound action of the Elements *with* the Spirit. For the Spirit enters into their composition from their attributions not only to the Paths, but also to the Sephiroth. Here follows a Table of Attributions and correlations between Planets, Elements and Tattvas. The Elements may be in any proportion, but chiefly and better with the Element first mentioned preponderating in each case. Save in the case of Luna, the Akasha Tattvic symbol is not to be expressed, but Akasha represents the darkening aspect of the Spirit, that is, in a too neutral and negative sense.

Saturn	Spirit	Air	Earth		Earth of Air
Jupiter	Spirit	Fire	Water		Water of Fire
Mars	Spirit	Fire	Earth		Earth of Fire
Sun	Spirit	Fire	Air		Air of Fire
Venus	Spirit	Earth	Water		Water of Earth
Mercury	Spirit	Air	Water		Water of Air
Luna	Spirit	Water	Earth and Alchemic	Earth of Water
			Mercury	

The Tattvas however, are not exactly the Aspects of the Spirits with the Four Elements, as we treat them. They almost coincide with these five forces in our Hermetic and Rosicrucian Scale of the Queen—the complete understanding of which comes later. They are powerful as representing the Natural Passive condition

[8] Flying Roll XII is not included in this volume as it was printed by Regardie on pages 66-73 of the fourth volume of his *Golden Dawn* where the attribution of Venus to Water of Earth can be found on page 67, line 4. (Editorial Note.)

of the Forces and are, in a sense, dangerous; because, if ill understood and directed, their operation induces too passive a condition and one too subject to fatality.

Their roots are in the material reflections of the five forces in the Scale of the Queen in the Earth's atmosphere; and they are more nearly material in their nature than those of the more active Scale of the King. Wherefore their forces are more easily perceivable materially, though less powerful in reality, than ours in the Scale of the King; because there is a certain *mode* of combination wanting in them which is present in our Scale of the King.

Used with the full knowledge of a Zelator Adeptus Minor, they are perfectly safe, because his knowledge supplies what is wanting in their teaching. Used by the uninitiated, they are dangerous, as quickly leading to a dangerously passive condition.

Flying Roll No. XXXIII
Visions of Squares upon the Enochian Tablets[9]

A Vision of the Square A of the Airy Lesser Angle of the Tablet of Water.

The Pyramid God is Ahephi 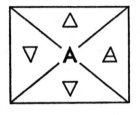 A.x.p.a.

Fig. 3

After vibrating the names of Airy Angle of Water and reading the Call, I seemed to be in the Air, ascending in a current of tiny drops of water which darted upward and in every direction, and were of every colour of the rainbow, very minute and light. On looking about for the cause, I saw below a tremendous volume of Water falling to a great depth, and this atmosphere in which I was, was the spray rising from it. I called on Ahephi to appear and gradually got the God form, as before, but standing above a pyramid composed of the *living* Elements. The Water sides of the Square were like two greenish-blue waves, always rising and falling and on all sides were in continual motion, and gave the idea of intense restlessness. I gave the $5°=6°$ Signs, tested it, and asked to be shown the Sphynx. This appeared in a greenish yellow mist behind Ahephi in a crouching position,

[9] In all this Flying Roll contains seven visions. Only four of them are printed here as the other three (the first, sixth and seventh) are reproduced on pages 318-22 of the fourth volume of Regardie's *Golden Dawn*. Regardie does not state whose visions he is reproducing—so I have given the correct attributions in Appendix A of this book. (Editorial Note.)

with the human arms stretched out in front. A silver crown on the Lion head set with sapphires. I saluted with the Signs which were returned. I asked for the explanation of the force of the Square, but could not get it clearly. It seemed an ever-moving subtle force, which working imperceptibly brought purification and cleaning with it.

The elementals I got were something like those of the 'n' Square, but smaller and in Rainbow colours, and they moved more quickly. They carried cups in their hands, shaped like lotuses in which they caught drops of water and darted into the Air with them. On the Earth their work seemed to be the purifying of the magnetism. I could not get anything clearer although I tried for a long time.

Vigilate.

A vision of the 'x' Square in the Watery Lesser Angle of the

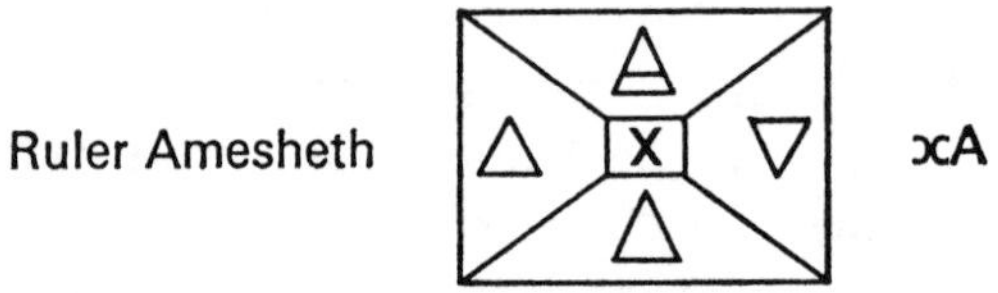

Ruler Amesheth xA

Fig. 4

Fire Tablet. I rose through the pyramid with the White Light, which streamed down from the Apex, and came into the Sky, where the same colours are repeated like sunrise etc. The colossal pyramid and Amesheth on it, a mummified figure in white, bands of colour like the pyramid and a *blue* human face (the same blue as I have seen in Egyptian paintings). I made the Signs and called on the Names and begged to be allowed to see the Angel. She appeared with a blue lunar crescent on her head and brown hair which was very long. Her robe was pale blue with a black border, and a pentagram in red on her breast: her wings were blue also, and so was the Cup in her left hand, in her right hand she bore a red torch. Around her was a diamond of red yods. She told me her office was 'Change and purification through suffering such as spiritualises the material nature'. I told her that her pale face and blue eyes had a sad and tender expression as she spoke. The subs were similar but smaller and not all of them winged. The elementals were like blue maids, bearing flames and their robes were black bordered. Some wore blue winged helmets and cloaks, red breast-plates and Swords and black leg-armour. I was told that only through my Knowledge of Amesheth was all this shown unto me.

Then I saw the Sphynx. The head was that of a Blue Eagle, and so were the back and wings, the tail and hind legs were black like a Bull and the fore legs and chest that of a Red Lion. The creature lay on a black marble pedestal. I saluted it and called on it by the Names to tell me its nature and office, its universal quality; it said 'It is change and development, not apparently harmonious, but growing stable after the first efforts'.

In the Elements (weather) floods of rain and lightning refreshing the Earth. The elementals and angels are above described. The general effect of this Square upon the Earth is the partly unbalanced efforts of the material universe towards perfection—which efforts are all towards spirit and are all necessary—as taken all together they *are* balanced. In the Tablets there are equal numbers of triangles of each element.

On this World the effect is that of the floods of water mingling with submarine volcanoes and so disturbing the Earth under the Sea. The animal life is that represented by the fish who rest hidden among the rocks in warm climates. I seemed to see them, blue with black or red specks. The plants are water-lilies, a root in the black mud, the leaves resting on the surface of the water, loving the Sun. In regard to minerals I saw a great blueish opal with red lights playing in it: it rested in a black marble basin, and from all sides radiated a lovely light.

On man the effect of the Square is restlessness, like waves of the sea, carrying him on with enthusiasm to some completed work. I seemed to see a nervous (highly strung) person with a pale face, dark deep-set eyes, and thin white hands, making a great effort, willing to pass through fire to reach his goal, a solid black pedestal from which I knew that he could begin to rise to the Higher. But hot clouds of steam and great water tried to hinder him from even reaching the fire. The lesson seemed to me that severe criticism, social difficulties, and heredity must all be overcome before we can reach the purifying fire of Initiation and, through that, the solid ground of spiritual knowledge.

F.E.R. (i.e. Miss Horniman)

A vision of the 'n' Square of the Airy Lesser Angle of the Fire

Ruler Ahephi 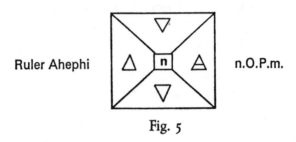 n.O.P.m.

Fig. 5

Tablet. Formed pyramid[10] over me. Went through it, looked for pyramid of the plane and saw it immediately with its yellow face towards me, and a large glowing white brilliance on the top. Approached and saw Ahelphi in the centre of the brilliance, and himself light and white. On calling on him he turned his head and in answer to $5° = 6°$ Signs he inclined it. I said I wanted to interview the Sphynx of the pyramid, he consented to my doing and I descended thereunto.

I saw him easily and at once, but his colours were not brilliant. I asked him to explain to me the forces to which he corresponded, beginning with the universal force he represented. *Answer* (By expression, I am deaf to words) 'I represent active forces acting between the waters above and the waters below the firmament dividing the waters and energised by Fire. Two active forces operating in the midst of a polarised passive force. You personally cannot see a universal application of this cor-

---

[10] Remember that the pyramid is only the symbolic *Formula* of the plane, and not a solid material pyramid (This is only a *symbolic* aid). (Original Note.)

respondence; but you may see it in nature in the weather, where the Fire and the Air keep the upper and nether Waters apart. It represents a cloudy atmosphere with a sea below, but the air between is dry and in active motion: there is no chance of rain, nor is there much evaporation from the surface. It is a very stable weather with plenty of circling clouds high in the atmosphere.' Later on he said—'In creation I represent the separation of the Waters; the expression of physical form out of the all-containing Astral; and also the reverse, the restoration to the physical of that which keeps it in that condition; hence the return of the physical to the Astral. I am but one of the forces through which Fire would act.[11] In Man's figure you have a type with round face and full lower parts and legs, with active and strong, but perhaps less clumsy, back and arms; the type of mind, however, is a very good one, it will be meditative, and its meditation will be accompanied by subtle and keen reasoning and energetic thinking. It will lead him to compare the lower with the higher and the higher with the lower. Just the sort of mind to find out for itself that 'as above so below' is a great truth in nature. Because he directs his attention to the upper and to the lower equally he is hence a philosopher combining religion and science into a sublime union.'

Among animals, I caught nothing but the Elephant, and from the nature of the Elephant's mind, which may be considered meditative from an animal point of view, his intelligence, physical force, bulky watery build, and warm blood I am inclined to think this attribution correct, although it seemed incongruous at first. Furthermore the use of Tau did not alter the vision.

Among vegetables I received the impression of the banana. Among minerals I saw an orange crystal column with pyramidal ends (I think hexagonal).

I asked him (the Sphynx) to show me the Angel and to accompany me outside to see her. She appeared as follows: face

[11] This seems to me to be a force spoken of in Alchemy as that which 'fixes the volatile' and 'volatilises the fixed', according to which way it is directed. (Original Note.)

roundish, short curly hair, light brown brilliant halo, and a small golden crown. Robe blue at the neck and bottom, girt with a white and gold belt, with the name in gold, and the robe white in the centre. Wings small and bluish-white. In her right hand she held a small wand of wood like cedar, with a gold top nearly cubical in shape, and in her left hand a peculiarly shaped, dark maroon coloured base.

Then, from the summit of the pyramid, I surveyed the surrounding country. On the yellow side at some distance was a sea, passing round to the right there was a dark thick wood, the land gradually rising till opposite, the red side of it (the pyramid) rose apparently as a sandy desert hill until it encountered a fogbank which hid all behind it; passing round to the fourth side the country was very flat. There were lakes and marshes and beyond them some slightly wooded land. The lakes and marshes seemed as if partly salt and partly fresh water. As if the pyramid stood at a spot where the waters from the land came in contact with the waters from the sea, though I could not see where or how either the one or the other, the salt or the fresh, got there. There was no inlet from the sea, nor was there a river from the land.

Anima Pura Sit (i.e. Dr. Pullen-Berry)
A Vision of the Square 'c' of the Earthy Lesser Angle of the Tablet of Air

Ruler Kabexnuf 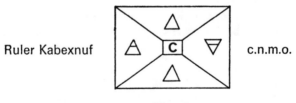 c.n.m.o.

Fig. 6

Having rehearsed the 8th Angelical Call and enclosed myself within a pyramid as above, vibrating the Names, I followed the ray and found myself in a hot, very dry atmosphere; I therefore invoked the God Kabexnuf by the power c.n.m.o. on whose appearance I used all the tests I knew, whereby he was strengthened. At my request he then made manifest the Sphynx of his power, who became visible to me. He was resting upon a black cube. Having once more used the Signs and applied the tests I asked for information respecting the Square, when my repeated invocations brought before me the Angel, a powerful virile figure of exquisite proportion and strength. He then showed me the action in the Macrocosm, which appeared to be the solidifying of Nebulae into Worlds by mutual attraction of the particles. Then, on this planet, we rested in the mouth of a volcano in active eruption, so much so that we were surrounded by flying lava. It was intensely hot, and almost mechanically I formulated in myself the idea of wrapping myself in an Apas, but a stern voice said: 'You must not, if you want to learn you must bear the discomfort.' Embedded in the sides of the volcano were crystallised jets and drops of fire which, I was told, was living gold; I asked for another scene and was taken on to a higher plane where there was a luxuriant forest of tropical plants of gorgeous scarlet and orange waving to and fro in an imperceptible breeze. The earth in which they grew was of a rich black colour, but there poured on them such fierce rays from the Sun that I looked to see them wither, but was told that they were on a higher plane than our flowers, and defied the scorching rays by virtue of their own internal heat which sustained their life. This Square being akin to our tropics, we went there, and saw a beautiful scene smiling in the heat of the Sun; suddenly a hot wind arose, bearing with it stones and dust with which it devastated the whole landscape. Here I was shown many tigers, and for flowers tiger lilies and Japanese red lilies in abundance. The type of human being I was shown was such a man as Chopin playing madly on a piano in a large empty room. The elemental is a bird like creature which hops rapidly over the ground; its influence on human nature gives the desire for violent sensation.

Resurgam (i.e. Dr. Berridge).

PART THREE

Rosicrucian Adeptship

being

Flying Roll No. XVI
The History of the Rosicrucian Order
By
G. H. Frater N.O.M.

The opening words of that part of the $5° = 6°$ Ritual which deals with the History of the Order of R.C. are as follows: 'Know them O Aspirant, that the Order of the Rose and Cross hath existed from time immemorial and that its mystic rites were practised and its hidden knowledge communicated in the initiations of the various races of Antiquity, Egypt, Eleusis, Samothrace, Persia, Chaldea and India alike cherished these mysteries, and thus handed down to posterity the Secret Wisdom of the Ancient Ages....'

This statement is one which comes home to every member of the $5° = 6°$ Grade, for although, in a sense, one in that position, is but on the threshold of really serious Occult study and development it is still easy enough to trace the masterful manner in which our mystic knowledges has been consolidated; and the essential unity of the system speaks eloquently of the Wisdom which formulated it.

'Albeit the manner of its introduction into mediaeval Europe' is chiefly interesting to us. C.R. is the great figure-head around which has clustered the most romantic traditions of mediaeval Occultism. History has not passed down the real name of this unique character: for C.R. is obviously a fictitious or assumed name chosen for mystic purposes.

Born in 1378 and dying in 1484 a life of 106 years was apparently the term of his physical manifestation: and to his exertions and efforts, it is that we may ascribe the great reformation of Occultism in the West. Fired by a noble purpose and ensouled by divine energies, his was the beau ideal of a life of Occult usefulness: it recks little if the world knew nought of that obscure personality, but it was a matter of supreme importance to the progress of Western Occultism and the full significance of this observation will probably be only appreciated by you in proportion as you may advance hereafter. The first years of his eventful life were spent in study, both intellectual and occult, to be eventually followed by a series of initiations at several places (out of Europe) 'Where there existed Temples of our Order.' Thus were laid foundations 'whereon to erect a more extended superstructure of practical application' and, having chosen three other Fratres to share with him the heat and burthen of the day, the establishment of the Order was effected in Europe. With the principal features of their subsequent activity you are already familiar and it suffices to say that when our Founder 'entered into his chamber' his work was accomplished, and every member among us thereby placed under a lasting debt of gratitude.

It is to be observed that there are three important epochs in the history of the Rosicrucian Order: the first being the life period of Christian Rosycross, who died before the time of the Protestant Reformation—the second, the 120 years of silence and secrecy, being the period from 1484 to 1604—and, the third, the period subsequent thereto, and subsequent to the Reformation. It was during the latter period that the opening of the Vault formed the historical basis for the subsequent publication of the *Frama Fraternitatis; or a Discovery of the most laudable Order of the Rosy Cross* the publication of which took place at Cassel in 1614, though this tract is dated 1610. This event called forth most intense curiosity and excitement and the enormous effect which it had upon the learned world of that time may be better understood when it is stated that no less than 600 tractates exist at the Museum at Berlin, all criticising —either favourably or otherwise—the mysterious association revealed by the 'Fama'. In 1614, then, public attention was for the first time directed to the Order and many thousands are said to have responded to the invitation proffered by the 'Fama': those who were admitted being bound over to keep the matter secret, and that larger proportion who received no response to their overtures believing the whole thing to be an illusion.[1]

[1] The sudden publication by a secret Lodge of Students of a Manifesto, and semi-public initiation to Occultism—such as then occurred has been recently repeated, for similar reasons by the Eastern School—which in 1875 sent from India the learned woman H.P.B.—

It will be obvious upon reflection that the ceremonial and *allotment* of Rituals and *instruction* in the Second Order as now existing, cannot be identical with that which obtained prior to the opening of the Vault because the principal symbolism of the $5° = 6°$ Grade chiefly centres around the discovery and opening of the Vault: this being so, it may be noted in passing that the two preceding epochs, already referred to, may be attributed by sequence of comparison to the Grades of $6° = 5°$ and $7° = 4°$ respectively: the former—a degree of death and solmnity—referring to the precedent stage of obscuration, during which silent study and meditation may be considered as the typical condition—the latter—the Grade of Adeptus Exemptus—being referred to the higher and more exalted rank and attainments of him who founded the Rosicrucian Order, as a new formulation of that Occult philosophy or Wisdom Religion which, we cannot doubt, has never been entirely absent since the manifestation of human intellect with a capacity for the apprehension of things Divine.

On comparing the Esoteric historical account given in the *Fama* with that contained in our $5° = 6°$ Ritual, several important divergencies and discrepancies become apparent: for the *Fama* was written for the public and is therefore not absolutely correct. Instances of the 'blinds' introduced into the *Fama* occur where in the description of the Vault it is stated 'This is all clear and bright, as also the seventh (the Seven Sides—the 7th was not different) side and the two heptagons ...' And again later on—'Every Side or Wall is parted into ten squares every one with their several figures and sentences ...' 'Every Side or Wall' is moreover represented as having a door for a chest wherein many things and books lay—including the vocabularium of Paracelsus who lived from 1493 to 1541—or during the 120 years of closure before referred to. This was an obvious inconsistency—and was in fact an intentional blind inserted for the purpose of disappointing the critics of that day: (the

an initiate to make a semi-public Propaganda—and also to admit a few selected persons to Esoteric teaching issued from a lodge of concealed instructors—whose published names are probably substitutes, mottoes, or symbols. (Original Note.)

critic is rarely or never an Occultist: the Society, to ensure the exclusion of such men, did cunningly when it authorised the publication of a tract, with a blot which would condemn it straight off in their eyes—and so kept such men from clamouring for admission). For, be it remembered, the *Fama* was an official manifesto, the publication of which was authorised by the Fratres then empowered. Subsequently, on account of the great stir roused by its publication, and especially on the assertion of some that the principles of the Order were subversive of the simple orthodox faith of Christianity, its publication by Valentine Andreas was authorised (in 1615) with a Supplement under the Title *Confessio Fraternitatis R.C. ad Erudotos Europa*. This was prefaced by an advertisement to the effect that the 'gentle reader' should find 'incorporated in our Confession thirty-seven reasons of our purpose and intention, the which according to they pleasure thou mayest seek out and compare together, considering within thyself if they be sufficient to allure thee'. The point of this, however, is that examination of the contents does not reveal the thirty-seven reasons, nor do the Hebrew Letters representing that number form any Word which might seem to be the secret meaning, but by Temurah, two pregnant words are shown forth, thus LHB $= 30 + 5 + 2 =$ Flame, Lux. Light. Illumination and LGD $= 30 + 3 + 4 =$ 'For the Society', or army.

There is another reference to Paracelsus in the *Fama* which has a curious interest: it runs 'although he was none of our fraternity, yet, nevertheless hath he diligently read over the Book M., whereby his sharp ingenium was exalted.' Now Paracelsus was taught by Johann Trithemius of Spanheim, Abbot of Wurtzburg, and Solomon Trismosin: he also travelled in the East, and being taken captive in *Tartary* (Compare with H.P.B's initiation in Thibet.—Paracelsus was not a Rosicrucian yet after initiation taught very similar tenets—he found another allied Temple in the East) was initiated there; he is moreover said to have received the Stone in Constantinople from one Sigismund Fugger.

Although the *Fama* is in some cases deficient in its historical account, it contains here and there redundant description, which affords food for reflection: — thus, it is said 'In another chest were looking-glasses of divers virtues, as also in other places were little bells, burning lamps, and chiefly wonderful artificial songs....'—The latter are of course, the Mantrams of the Easterns, Carmina or incantations,—instructions on the vibratory mode of pronouncing divine ames.

The only other important Rosicrucian publication was a very curious work entitled the *Hermetic Romance*, or the *Chymical Wedding*, which likewise excited much controversy: — it is full of perplexities (for the casual reader) though the meaning is entirely allegorical and only to be seized by violence. Of this class of study, all that can be said is 'Sometimes a light surprises the student on his way.' The date of publication was 1616, the year following the appearance of the 'Confessio Fraternitatis'.

I should mention that an English translation of the *Fama* was done in London by Eugenius Philalthes. (Thomas Vaughan) in 1652;—he was at that time Supreme Magus in Anglia, or Chief Adept in charge in our phraseology.—

In conclusion it only remains for me to point out that while the historical element has a unique interest for every member of the $5° = 6°$ Grade of the Second Order; this in itself is a minor consideration as compared with the mystic symbolism involved therein. The 120 years has other references, as the $5° = 6°$ Ritual itself testifies. This was the number of Princes, which Darius set over his Kingdom,—and Daniel was a Magus among the Chaldees;—while another hint as to its meaning lies in the suggestion as to how that number was arrived at.

In the $5° = 6°$ Grade the symbolism of the Rainbow Colours is especially exemplified,—a range of Colour which may be said to be the most apparent and obvious: — while the $6° = 5°$ Grade is of interest to many of us, especially because the colouring is different. The $7° = 4°$ refers still further back and possesses an even more arcane symbolism.

Supplementary Notes

It is especially desirable that when our brethren meet, the ancient form of salutation should be preserved: — thus on meeting they should salute each other in the following manner 'Ave Frater'. The second shall answer 'Roseae Rubeae', whereupon the first shall conclude with 'et Aureae Crucis'.

It was also the ancient custom after having thus discovered their position, for one to say to the other *Benedictus Dominus Deus noster qui Dedit nobis signum*—(uncovering Cross or Seal). This latter form should also be observed on all *formal* occasions and especially when Fratres meet who are little acquainted with each other.

Members are moreover further requested to endeavour upon all occasions when taking leave of each other to use the old formula Vale, adding 'Sub umbra alarum tuarum, Jehovah!'[2]

The effect of the foregoing observance is to directly maintain the psychic link which has ever served to bind the Members of this Ancient and Honourable Order one to the other;—in this light it is something more than a mere form.

The following beautiful sentences were inscribed upon the Tablet. At the head was written.

'Granum Pectaris IH SH VH insitum'—

A grain—or seed, sown or planted—in the heart of Jehoshua (The worn out physical body—laid aside—from whence has escaped the Spiritual entity which shall function in a spiritual body—as Paul said; until—if ever—it be again required to clothe itself with skin, and come down—again to teach and guide others) in commemoration of Frater C.R.C. our prototype.

Pater dilectissimies = Most loved father!

Frater Suavissimus = Most courteous brother!

Preceptor fidelissimus = Most faithful instructor!

Amicus integerrimus = Strongest friend!

Well indeed shall your life have been spent in helping the world, and teaching others, if you can earn such an Epigraph.

[2] A wand to guide you and protect you in the ascent of the Mountain is the Staff of Hermes, about which the twin Serpents of Egypt twine: above the wings of Binah and Chokmah—shrouding the sacred Diamond lying on the Crown of Kether—the Supernal. *Sub umbra alarum tuarum*; beneath the rays of spiritual *Understanding* emanating from Divine *Wisdom*, you may indeed be safe, trusting to the protection and aid of the High and Holy Powers summed up in the great Name JHVH. (Original Note.)

Flying Roll No. XVIII
Progress in the Order
By F.e.R.[3]

A few words on the natural wish to make progress in our Order may interest some of those who have just joined us and also whose efforts seem to lead to little or no result.

Of course the experience of each one is unique, and must be so; no one could have been led into the path of serious occult study without a certain determination of character, and in most cases the necessity of overcoming opposition at the outset, is a test in itself, which shows individuality and fixity of purpose. Naturally, when first asked to join and told that he is considered suitable, the Candidate feels strongly that he must be rather a remarkable person to be so chosen. That was the first stage with me, and it lasted until I was actually admitted into the Order nearly two years later. Of course some spiritual gifts are necessary to make true progress, but it is very hard to judge which person has them or even to tell our own power until time and training have developed the tendencies hidden in our innermost natures. At first it is probable that the Neophyte will exaggerate every little astral incident that happens and the only way to fight against that temptation is to force the mind to serious study so as to gain strength; and by the power which will come gradually to the earnest student, to learn to distinguish the false from the real, the Astral from the Spiritual.

The uncongenial spiritual surroundings in which most of us are obliged to live out our lives have their uses; we learn to concentrate our minds amidst the distractions which are the more dangerous to our progress when they are not in active opposition to it.

For the first few weeks the secrecy enforced on us by our Obligation is a novelty, but when the Knowledge in the first lecture is learned and found to be information easily gained

[3] These initials are those of Annie Horniman's motto of *Fortiter et Recte*—but see my note on this Flying Roll in Appendix A. (Editorial Note.)

from other sources, a questioning feeling arises as to the need of so much fuss about labels for MSS, mottoes to be used instead of names etc. etc. If we look a little closer, however, it will appear only reasonable; we must be trained to be silent and perfectly discreet, so that secrecy will be no effort to us, when after much labour and many struggles we are gradually entrusted with the hidden knowledge belonging to the higher Grades of our Order.

Some of the obstacles which keep the Fratres and Sorores in the lower Grades are quite trivial in themselves and might be easily overcome by an effort of Will; but they do not realise that the fault lies in themselves and put down the fact of their standstill to many other causes. If our Order be anything deeper and higher than a mere club for the dissemination of archaeological and literary knowledge, the obstacles to be overcome must be more subtle than those which come between us and success in the ordinary aims of life.

Acts which were meaningless trivialities before are serious matters to a Frater or Soror who is truly striving to rise as high as possible during this life. Habits of indecision and caprice in the minor matters of conduct have a great cumulative force and weaken the will and leave us open to astral influences which must be conquered as completely as our present strength allows. A strong feeling of disinclination for study at convenient times, once given way to, grows into indolence, and then when each succeeding lecture if found to be more difficult, the thought that perhaps it is not worthwhile after all, creeps in and gradually the student loses interest and occult study becomes tedious to him. On the contrary, great opposition and difficulty spur us on in this, as in any other, course, and when the opportunities for study have to be *made* they are seldom neglected. Do not accept the excuses you feel inclined to make to yourselves—that you have to live alone amongst people who are only hindrances, that no one takes particular interest in your progress, or that you will have more time bye and bye.

Not one of us has any time to lose; youth and strength do not last us very long, and the present opportunities may never arise again. Work done to please or gain approbation from another is not what we want, but that real enthusiasm which overcomes difficulties and grows the stronger because of them. Naturally, members of higher Grades take a personal interest in those with whom they are connected by social ties, but sometimes that is a source of disappointment. Each must strive upwards by himself, for himself, no help can take away the real difficulties, for they are the tests which must be passed, and by which our spiritual fitness for Higher Things is shown. Uncongenial surroundings are an obstacle, because they seem to waste the strength, but is it truly as difficult to work when unhappy after the performance of burdensome duties, as to overcome the far more insinuating influences that come into play when all seems smooth before us? Sometimes in those painful surroundings there are others also struggling towards the light which we are longing to reach ourselves; we may not as yet be able to help except by sympathy and kindliness; but when the time comes, then we can stretch forth a helping hand with a full understanding of the need for assistance.

To those who have made some little progress the true prosperity of our Order is very dear, and we look back with real gratitude to those who watched us until they thought fit, and then brought us in to what has become a great and important part of our lives. In some cases it was an intimate friend, in others a comparative stranger whose acquaintance at first seemed to be of very little importance.

Of course, we are often disappointed; when beginners ourselves we were most anxious for those dear to us to come in also, but as time goes on we see how rare are the qualities required and we find that we must have great patience and hope in regard to our friends, who as yet do not want to sympathise with our Hermetic aims.

Those who expect worldly or social gain for themselves through this Order will be disappointed, yet none of us who have made sacrifices for it in a right spirit are disappointed with the result.

To some natures ceremonies are repulsive, to others they are most attractive. They are part of the necessary discipline which insists upon us all being treated exactly alike, which seems arbitrary to some minds, yet without it, we could be trained to understand those causes which lie behind the ordinary events of life and form our characters for good or evil.

We must all take courage and look our difficulties full in the face, neither magnifying them nor avoiding them; and we shall find in many cases that a little self-denial, a little exertion of Will, or even a little commonplace prudence will vanquish them completely. Nothing impossible will ever be asked of any of you, but what will be possible to each of you is in the Future, none can say exactly what. With knowledge will come strength, and then experience will follow and the power and the wish to use that Knowledge rightly.

It is a gradual process, and often a painful one to experience, but well worth the sorrows to be borne and the difficulties to be overcome by the earnest student.

Trondhjeim. June 1893.

Flying Roll No. XIX
The Aims and Means of Adeptship
By N.O.M.

Among the objects for which you have joined the Second Order some are specially named by the Obligation which you have taken, and others are indicated by the documents which you have received on loan.

Speaking generally however, we may say that the main object is what is called the Higher Magic or the development of the Spiritual sides of our natures in contradistinction to the purely intellectual.

As regards Spiritual Development you promised in the Obligation to use every effort to purify and exalt the Spiritual Nature so that you may be able to unity yourselves with what the Hermetist calls his 'Higher Genius'.

A second aim we may say is the extension of our powers of perception so that we can perceive entities, events and forces upon the super-sensuous planes.

Thirdly, and in connection with the other two, you are encouraged to practice the system of divination of which there are several but which are only aids to your intuition and methods by which the intuition may be developed and encouraged.

Fourthly, there is what may be called the procuring of the influence of Divine Powers through the peculiar modes taught in our Order and Vibrating of Divine Names.

There are then these four aims—Spiritual Development— extension of the powers of perception; learning the modes of Divination and becoming familiar with the vibratory mode of pronouncing Divine Names. To these may be added the practical study of the particular influences of colour and thus we are called Lords of the Path of the Chameleon.

Now as regards this Spiritual Development in the first place we mean by it that you perform or endeavour to perform the transmutation of the vital forces of life into higher currents of life or rather their transmutation out of the lower into the higher so that you can use them for the purposes of Theurgia. Transmutation of physical force is what is discussed in many of the old alchemical books. A large proportion of these books which have come down to us refer to purely physical processes. But there was an opposite pole of thought of which the language referred entirely to man and by transmutation was meant the directing of physical life and force into the channels of spiritual perception and the higher magical powers generally.

Secondly, as to the extension of our powers of perception beyond the plane of matter into the super-sensuous world, you must remember that the Theosophical view is the correct one and that our Thinking Personalities are incarnated into these material bodies and are acting therefore under the consequent disadvantages. It is because the mind is immersed in matter that its powers are so limited, and we can readily understand that a mind freed from constraints of the body would enjoy vastly enlarged powers. Thus, although our senses are the means by which we perceive; yet at the same time they necessarily limit the extent of our perception. It is therefore our material bodily organs which circumscribe as well as bestow. All of our five senses are capable of enlargement and development. It is however the sense of sight which we most commonly seek thus to develop. Having intellectually learned the laws which relate to sight and colour we are encouraged to practice Clairvoyance and to seek to see beyond material things into the plane most adjacent to us—the Astral, and then we seek to travel in the Spirit Vision through the confusions and the uncertainties of the Astral into the planes beyond.

One of the first of your experiences when practising in the Vault in the dark will be the appreciation of the minuter graduations of light and darkness.

You will find it very difficult to get perfect darkness, but you will often find that there are certain days when you can get the Vault quite dark.

The cultivation of your sight will enable you to perceive the variations of colour and especially to note, observe, and fix in your minds, the contrasts of colour on which our Rituals place so much importance, and the flashing colours. Allied to this is the cultivation of View in the Mirror.

The ears also require to be cultivated until you obtain some success in what is called Clairaudience. This is sometimes easier than Clairvoyance but development in either direction implies great perseverance and must be carried out with energy and enthusiasm.

Among Theosophists the phenomenon which you hear most commonly mentioned in connection with Clairaudience is that known as the Astral Bell. This is almost entirely Eastern: if you find a Hermetist who can hear sounds that others cannot hear, they very rarely take the form of a bell.

Those who get a certain amount of Clairvoyance also often get the power of hearing sounds which the world cannot hear and it is often a definite sound sent for a definite purpose. Touch, also is a sense which should be cultivated. I will mention some examples of the way in which this sense may be trained, and by touch I do not mean simply the touch which comes through the fingers. One of the most elementary methods is the perception of magnetism. You will find that, with closed eyes, you can detect the presence of a magnet held near the skin, and that with continued practice you will be able to appreciate the difference between the North and South Poles of the Magnet.

You will find that the forehead is the best point upon which to experiment. We need not dwell upon the senses of taste and smell, but these can also be developed.

Theosophy tells us that corresponding with all other Septenaries in Nature there are also two more senses. I may say that the sixth can be called that of Astral perception, or the power of perceiving forces and entities on the plane next to the earth; and the seventh, of which, no doubt, some of you will get glimpses in due time is the faculty of receiving Knowledge from spiritual sources. There is no organ corresponding to these senses, so that, where necessary, we must utilise the organs which we already possess. Now by what means do the Adepts suggest that these powers may be obtained? It has been urged against us that, as a society, we do not preach the necessity for such strict purity of life as do the Theosophists. It may be true that we are not always preaching it, and as we do not hold public meetings, the same opportunities for doing so do not exist. If, however, there is one thing more than another which I would impress upon you as a social sin, it is that of hypocrisy. As to asceticism, the Hermetists have always taught that this necessary purity of mind should and can be combined with the absence of all ostentatious morality and of un-natural habits of life.

The Western Teachers have always recognised the fact that for so long human life has been so painful, that to most people these studies would be denied if they were to insist upon asceticism, and they have found by experience that a very considerable amount of success without attendant danger may be obtained by those who are willing to make strenuous efforts, without the aid of positive asceticism. It seems to me that the chief danger of asceticism in a city like this and at the present time is that even if we succeed, the extra advantage which we shall derive from totally abstaining from these things of the sense, will be counterweighed by a distinct and added danger of falling, on the other hand, into the Scylla of hypocrisy which I have mentioned. What is apt to happen is this,—that a man is liable to compare himself with his neighbours, and say how much better he is than others. Now self congratulation is second only to open hypocrisy, and we hold that it is just as harmful to spiritual progress. On the other hand if you make strenuous efforts to lead a moral life, if you do this while leading a pure life in the city, if you succeed in doing these things, you may depend upon it that your reward will be greater than his who removes himself from his fellows and shuts himself up in a forest. The reward of a man who can remain pure and yet live in the midst of a crowded city is greater than his who avoids the responsibilities of life by burying himself in a wilderness.

It is possible even there to commit many sins which you would not like to confess!

The next principle which we formulate is the necessity for studying and doing all Hermetic exercises from a positive point of view. We look upon the negative attitude of simple abstinence from sin and exertion and effort, in which are comprised to a great extent the methods of the East, and we think that this is an error of judgment and of practice.

I am sure that any attempt at a negative attitude is a mistake. Many persons are, I am sure, deterred from taking up Theosophical studies more closely by the sense of coldness, and an apparent want of human sympathy, which is sometimes exhibited and felt in Theosophical Lodges. Theosophy itself teaches that we should give ourselves up to humanity, and yet their private lodges are often marked by the absence of that enthusiasm for their work which should distinguish them.

The Hermetists have always been noted for their social relations, and this is, I believe, in every way compatible with the strictest purity of life. We believe that a harmonious whole is thereby produced and one likely to lead to success in practical magic.

The next point of importance which is insisted upon in our Obligation and Rituals and put forward with great solemnity in the Vault itself is the extreme necessity for refraining from judging other people. This does not mean that you are not to condemn sin, but it means that you are not to go out of your way in condemning the sinner. It does not imply that you are to condone faults, but it does imply that you are not to endeavour to seek grievances against your fellows, or seek to rule or supervise them, unless you happen to be in authority over them. Very few people are in this position of being rulers. Such have to bear the Karma of occasionally judging their fellow members. It is at any rate a duty which falls upon some of us. You must however, avoid the opportunity of thus judging others until the obligation is thrust upon you.

The opportunity and the act should both be avoided as far as possible. Thus the Ritual says 'therefore art though inexcusable, whoever thou art, who judgest another'.

Let me now say a word about the risks of negativity. It seems to me that the negative attitude and the negative constitution required to be checked and controlled. Firstly because we do not progress under these conditions, and secondly because they carry with them definite risks to ourselves are those from elemental forces which may attack us.

So long as you lead an ordinary life you are safe from the assaults of influences beyond the material world of your brother men; but as soon as you get outside of that world and put yourself in a position to seek out occult mysteries, you bring yourself under the action of forces of which you know very little or nothing. The only way to avoid being controlled by such forces, to which you have rendered yourself liable, is to preserve what we call the positive attitude, which is the extreme contrast to what is called mediumship. A medium is one who cultivates negativity and such a person is therefore one to be avoided. The condition we want you to cultivate is that of positivity. I could give you a very good example of a person who is negative and who has got into trouble almost entirely through that.

The next thing which we are taught and enabled to practice is Divination. There are at least three distinct systems suggested to you, but they are all of them methods whose routine may be superseded, when you get on far enough. The first of these systems is that of Geomancy and there is also that of Astrology. It will be noticed that the lectures of the First Order give brief outlines of these systems, but there is no direct encouragement to perfect yourself in them.

The third system which is virtually introduced and taught in the Second Order is that of the Tarot.

This goes very much deeper than either of the other two and gives results which are more true because its points of contact with the world, with man, and the influences which surround him, are more numerous. The fact that this is more complicated gives you more of such points of contact than either of the other two systems. With a properly conducted Tarot process and with a cultivated intuition you can obtain almost anything you wish for, but as the process is so complex it is a most difficult system to learn, but having once grasped it you can get results which are most amazing. When you have mastered the first six manuscripts of the Order and are familiar with the Rituals of the Pentagram and Hexagram, and have made your Implements, the Tarot is then suggested to you as a desirable system to learn. Moreover its study is so enticing that you would be apt to neglect those things which should precede its practice.

By these systems of divination you are really inducing and cultivating the intuitive power. Now in order to get success in Divination it is necessary to cultivate the Will. First you want an intellectual knowledge of the subject. Then a cultivation of the intuitive power is necessary, and finally you must develop the Will. You must have a steady will or else your intuition will be of little avail. Now this cultivation of the Will should be a process which is continually going on. There are fallacies which exist in connection with the Will. A person may say to you, I am extremely interested in all these studies and I am always willing and endeavouring to succeed in them, and he will say to you that he is thinking of the Tree of Life or of some other occult subject while he is doing his accounts or interviewing his wife. Now I am sorry to say that I have to tell such a person that he is on the wrong tack. If you want success you must will only one thing at a time. The habit of doing two or three things at once is fatal to the Occultist. The Will which is necessary is an undivided Will and its cultivation must be continued at all times.

It is therefore necessary to get into the habit of never Willing more than one thing at a time. Never allow your Will to be mixed up with any desire. The Will which is divided is not the Will which can be of any use to you. It is quite impossible to Will strongly to see an elemental, for instance, unless you are able to think only for that moment.

A fixed concentration of mind must be encouraged if you want to have success. We often get strange demonstrations of the strength of the Will. I will give you an example. We continually find that if we turn round in the street to look after someone whom we have just passed, that person is also turning round to look after us. If however, you deliberately try to do this you will probably fail, and the point is that in this latter case your mind is divided between the will to succeed, and the desire to show your power, and the Will is thereby weakened.

The other two principal items are the Vibration of the Divine Names and the properties of colour, but as these ought to be demonstrated in the Vault, I will not go into them today.

PART FOUR

Man, God and the Rosicrucian Initiation

being

Flying Roll No. XV
Flying Roll No. X

Flying Roll No. XV
Man and God
By N.O.M.

The circle of Members of the Adeptus Grade of the Order R.R. et A.C. is a fraternity of students of the Hermetic Sciences and of the Hermetic Art.

The chain which unites us in the acceptance of the doctrines and wisdom contained in the Rituals of our Order. The same assertion is true of the Order of the G.D., that preliminary course of instruction through which all must have passed. The common ground of brotherhood is the sincere acceptance of the Hermetic ancient philosophy, as expressed in the Ritual, and Pictorial and Symbolic representations which have been tendered to us at each stage of our progress.

The G.D. teaching has reference mainly to Religion and to Philosophy; but it is of course obvious that our Rituals are but outlines and landmarks in the world of thought.

The vacant spaces each member fills for himself or leaves blank.

A little consideration will assure us that these vacant spaces are filled by individual members in very different manners. Every shade of unorthodoxy is represented among us; and some of us are almost orthodox, yet we are all sensible of a mighty tie which binds us together: this is our Ritual Wisdom.

Whence these rituals come, through whom they come, and even who are our present Temple Chiefs are all matters of secondary interest. The personal element of rule is but a question of the arrangements of time, place and finance, and there is no claim of authority by any beyond the accepted Ritual. You who are here today to listen to this lecture (or you who read it hereafter), have come to this Hall only to seek from my words further suggestions of thought on Occult teachings, you are well aware that I represent myself alone, in what I say, and that you are each perfectly free to take what seemeth good unto you and to reject the refuse. In my honour to the Order in which I bear a part, I have always made the clearest distinction between the Ancient Ritual and our modern comments, and this distinction you must always bear in mind, for it must not be considered that the doctrines of any single elder or ruler are necessarily all true to the Hermetic faith. All individuals go astray even if some go farther than others. The Order here then has no Pope nor Popess and our Bible at every stage is imperfect; we are fellow students, still crying for the Light; and every lecture given here is but the expression of personal opinion, from some one who has far longer than most trod the path of Hermetic progress, and the proportion of doctrine or fact which you accept must be estimated by yourselves, for yourselves—it is a duty you owe to yourselves to work out your own transmutation—to change the powers of physical sensuous life into the refined spiritual faculties of Adeptship, in truth as well as in name. As senior Adept among you, just now, my duties are to keep you to the doctrines of our Rituals, as far as they go,—to leave you quite free where they do not lead, but to stimulate your efforts in the search for the Philosophic Gold by occasional short essays of my own, which although quite without authority, will suggest subjects and lines of thought which those who have gone before you have found fruitful of high ideals.

I am about to take, today, a leaf from the clerics and say something on two texts, from the Hebrew Bible; and so you are all free to think as you please about the subject.

My opinion is that a part is historical, and a part of the history is allegorical and that while it was intended as a text book for the populace, yet there are in it many references to an esoteric creed held by the priests of the Nation.

It seems to me that the Divine Names of the Hebrew Volume especially hide and yet reveal a glimpse of the secrets of Divine power, majesty and governance. Occult Science has in every age seen mighty mysteries in the name Jehovah. Now the two texts I am about to refer to, alike, allude to the great name 'Elohim'.

The first text is found in Exodus XXXII, Verse I, and was as I will remember, used as a text by my G. H. Fra. D.D.C.F. in a lecture he gave ten years ago to the Hermetic Society of my dear Friend Anna Kingsford—it is the words of the Israelites to Aaron, when Moses had gone up to seek God.

'Make us Elohim which shall go before us', or, let us make Gods to help us, to form our ideals. The other text is in Genesis I, 26, Veamar Elohim Nosher Adam Be Azelinunu Re demuthun. 'And the Elohim said let us make *man*'—'in our image and after our likeness'. Note the contrast, and alternation of expression. The men cried let us make gods—The Gods said let us make men—We are *here* seeking gods, or divine ideals;—and we are making men; for men make themselves and they make their own gods—The Poet sings—

The Ethiop gods have Ethiop eyes
Thick lips, and woolly hair;
The gods of Greece were like the Greeks
As keen, as cold, as Fair

A modern philosopher has written 'The Gods may have made man, but men have made their own Gods, and a pretty mess they have made of it'. Let us be careful what gods we make for ourselves, and on what pedestals we place them.

The great Jehovah may have made man in the Garden of Eden, it matters not to me; but I know I make myself, and I know you are hourly making yourselves—the child is father to the man indeed, quite as surely as that the man is father of the child—a mighty mystery. Now Moses had gone up into the holy mountain to seek divine help: — this Sinai was the Mountain of God—the Mountain of the Caverns, the Mountain of Abiegnus, the mystic Mountain of Initiation—that is of divine instruction. Even so do we seek inspiration in the mystic Mountain, passing through the wilderness of Horeb, that period life which is *at first* a desert to us, as we cast aside worldly joys, and seek to pass through the Caverns—our Vault, to union with the spiritual powers above us, which send a ray of light to illumine our minds and to fire our hearts, the spiritual centre, with an enthusiasm for the higher life of greater self sacrifice, more self-control—by which means alone can man reach up to the Divine and become one with the All self—the great One-All.

Our V.H. Sor.-S.S.D.D. has in an earlier Roll pointed out this passing through the desert, and that volume of beautiful thoughts, the *Voice of the Silence* alludes to the same period of trial, which must precede success in the attainment of the Higher Life—*Light on the Path* too, well portrays the period of transition, when by the energy of enthusiasm the inspired pupil casts aside wordly ambition and the joys of life, the pride of the eye, the lust of the flesh, and stands seeking the foothold of the first step of the mystical ladder, whose ascent can fill the heart with such sublime aspirations that the way is no longer steep, nor the path dreary, and when the dawning Sun of Tiphereth, shedding a ray of splendour upon the Path, encourages the toiler to the consummation devoutly to be desired. I have said that we make our own gods, and this is a great secret truth. Moses made his God, and impressed his ideal upon the people he led—Mohomet formulated his own idea of God, and of post mortem union with God, and of a Heaven where men are visitors to a vast Supernal Harem. Jesus taught his idea of his Father, and his suggestions have tinctured the God ideal of millions; but the mere adherence of the millions to any doctrine is but slender evidence of its truth, for as Carlyle has said, the majority of men are fools—Man does not alone formulate a Deity, but designs also a contrast to our notion of Supernal greatness, knowledge and power. So does Genesis, for there we find Jehovah thwarted by the Serpent; we find in the book of Job that the Supreme One was lead into folly or ingratitude or worse, by Satan who came before him among the 'Sons of God' and by dint of applying to Job every earthly suffering, sought to degrade him before his Master. We find the Evangelists describing a Satan only second to Jesus, who had power to promise, and, we must suppose, to confer upon Jesus, either Lordship of the World or a divine supremacy over matter, —if he would but tender a nominal submission.

We find the mediaeval European priest formulating the grotesque horned and tailed human demon, and lastly we are instructed concerning the Qabalistic enumeration of the Evil and Averse Sephiroth. Are not these all human ideals, and if we were but philosophic at heart, should we not confess that these notions are but futile attempts to express the unknown and unknowable? No man can go beyond his own powers, and if we do but formulate as divine our own highest ideal not much harm may be done, so long as we grant equal powers of formulation to our brothers.

But in respect to Evil Beings, let us forbear, and beware of speculating or designing forces contrasted to our high ideals; for the mind has a creative force we but little know of, or understand, and in our ignorance we may create in our own auras evil personalities in spaces that might have remained vacant.

Never risk the creation of Evil forces, let us avoid and repel all the evil promptings that attack us with firmness, courage and decision—but avoid arrogance and impertinence, for even the so-called evil forces, the contrasted powers have functions to perform, and even the evil forces may help forward the good, as is so beautifully alluded to in our Adeptus Ritual. Suffice it to say, that every man has a dual nature, or every man has dual forces—Yetza ha Ra—Yetzer ha Job—attendant upon him; or as the Theosophist prefers to put the matter, man has a higher and a lower manas, and the destiny of any individual is within limits under his own control.

The general result of this present life may be upward or downward, for Man has Free Will, within limits, and very expansible limits too. God, or the Divine Powers, did indeed design and constitute the plan of Man's constitution, origin and destiny, and it is but of slight moment, whether in philosophy we view Man as a Termary, a Septenary or as a Decad, but it is of vital importance to remember that with Free Will comes personal responsibility, and that every thought and act; that we are daily and hourly making the future history of ourselves, and piling up destiny whose realisation cannot be baulked by divine interposition nor changed by a maudlin sentimental repentance, nor by the surreptitious substituted sufferings of others. The type of man may indeed be viewed as emanating from the Elohim of Life, from the High Septenary of Powers, and his constitution may be in elementary form allotted to the Sun as the Giver of Vital Fire,—to the Moon for the Astral

Mould of Form, to the Earth for the Material body: the Planets and Stars may influence man's form, stature and tendencies, but the destiny of the Thinker will depend upon the Thoughts. This is all true of man as a type of Creation,—Man as an Individual hourly makes himself—One life makes another. There may be a final Heaven, a final rest, a re-absorption into Deity, but this is not yet. The ladder of progression from earth to heaven must be climbed, before the foot can attain the summit. Some egos may go up rapidly, some may pass slowly, self exertion is the measure of success.

Let us then make Man—make the Divine Man out of the Human Man. Let us create the Hermetic ideal man from the material sensual man. It is our bounden duty to rend the Veil 'Paroketh' and to let our human intellect attain to the perception of the Holy of Holies which shines within us from above. For now we see us in a Glass darkly, but with the Veil rended, we shall see God face to face.

How have the Alchemists of old, when passing from the physical, drawn the picture of the Souls transmutation or translation to eternity from time,—how have they also figured this Soul Growth and Development.

They wrote in beautiful allegory:—

The Heart of man is as the Sun, the reception organ for the Divine Ray of spiritual intuition descending unto Man. The Brain of Man is as the Moon,—the source of human intellect. The Body of Man is the Earthy vehicle.

Let the sun impregnate the Moon, or let Spiritual Fire prompt the human intellect—and let the result fructify in the womb of a purified Body, and you will develop the Son of the Sun, the Quintessence, the Stone of the Wise, True Wisdom and Perfect Happiness.

Flying Roll No. X
Concerning the Sybolism of Self-Sacrifice, and Crucifixion contained in the 5°=6° Grade
By G. H. Frater D.D.C.F.

This lecture was delivered on Good Friday, March 31st, 1893, to the Adepti in College Assembled.[1]

Dealing first of all with the diagrams in the First Order and proceeding upwards, it will be noticed that in the lowest Grade in the Outer (0°=0°) there are no diagrams properly so called, but that on the two Pillars is depicted the symbolism of the passage of the Soul from the Egyptian Ritual of the Dead; this being as it were a synthetical aspect to be developed and explained with the advance of the candidate through the various stages.

After the first Grade comes the 1°=10°, where we find the first form of the Sephiroth in the Tree of Life;—this is the representation of the Flaming Sword descending, but it is not until the 2°=9° comes that we begin to find the actual symbolism of self sacrifice.

The 2°=9° Altar Diagram, then, represents the Serpent of Wisdom twined through the Paths. In the 4°=7° Grade, however, you are shown the same Serpent, its representation being that of the Serpent Nechushtan. This was the Serpent of Brass that Moses made in the Wilderness, and which was turned around the central Pillar of Mildness,—having three cross bars upon it,—representing a species of triple cross.

Dealing now with the Altar Diagram of the 3°=8° Grade, it will be seen that Adam is the Tiphereth part: wherein he is extended. That is to say that the form of the man is projected from there.

The figure of Eve stands in Malkuth in the form of the Supporter.

[1] Those readers who are unacquainted with the technical terminology of the Qabalah would be well advised to read the Prefatory Note to Part Five of this book before tackling this Flying Roll. (Editorial Note.)

The first ideal form of the Man is in Adam Kadmon—behind the Kether form and, as it were, the prototype of the Tiphereth form. This Tiphereth answers to the letter Vau of the Holy Name, as representing the Prince. The letter Vau also represents the number Six and Adam was created on the Sixth Day, for Tiphereth is the symbol of the Creation. Furthermore, the Hexagram consists of the two forms Fire and Water;—i.e. the ideal Fire and the ideal Water; the Spirit and the Water of Creation,—the spiritual Ether and the Ethereal Fire (the Fire of the Holy Spirit). Thus, in the Creation the Man is extended from Tiphereth i.e. the moment Adam is created, that is the beginning of the reflection of the lower Triad, and, finally, of Malkuth. Eve is the synthesis of Creation and represents the Mother of Life, as the name ChaVaH is. The $3° = 8°$ diagram thus represents the establishment of life, i.e., created life, and the Good and Evil is represented in Malkuth, and it is the Tree of Knowledge of Good and Evil because it is the balance point between Good and Evil: for in the material body we are placed to give the victory to which we will. Hence the significance of the words of the Serpent, 'Ye shall be as Gods, knowing Good and Evil'. But the knowledge of Evil brought with it the descent into the Qlipoth, and although Malkuth is directly involved in the 'fall', the Sephiroth immediately above cannot be said to have actually entered into the knowledge of Evil. Therefore in the allegorical account of the Creation in Genesis, it is said that Man is checked from putting forth his hand to take of the Tree of Life, so as not to involve the higher Sephiroth in the 'Fall', which, (he being unbalanced in himself) would only have precipitated disaster.

In the $4° = 7°$ diagram we find represented the fall and the consequent rise of the dragon, which in the $3° = 8°$ Grade is represented coiled beneath Malkuth in the Kingdom of the Shells; but it only raises its head to the Sephiroth by right of the Crowns of the Kings of Edom.

These latter represent the Worlds of unbalanced force, before the Creation is established. They furthermore symbolize the places of the Sephiroth which are hollowed and before the light fills the cavities (The Light which comes down and fills the cavities is to be found allegorically set forth in the story of the usurpation of the younger brother in the story of Esau and Jacob). 'Before all things were the Waters, and the Darkness, and the Gates of the land of Night'. Note also the War of the Titans who rise and fight against Jupiter.

The Edomite Kings, therefore, are not altogether evil, but they are partly connected with Evil. They are the forces of restriction.

The result, therefore, on a higher plane, in the Tree, is that the Great Serpent rises to Daath, and if the Four Worlds be placed upon the Tree itself, it will be observed that the cutting off by the Serpent is between Yetzirah and Briah. Thus Evil cannot arise into the World of Briah, or indeed transcend the limits of Yetzirah. But if we seek for the correspondence of Evil in the Worlds of Briah and Atziluth, it will be found to consist in a lesser form of Good—a limiting, restricting and binding force without which you cannot have form on the higher planes. It is only in the Worlds of Yetzirah and Assiah that the analogue of this principle becomes absolutely Evil.

This idea was expressed by the Gnostics when they said that the Achamoth[2] attempted to comprehend the Pleroma, and could not understand it, and from the grief of her were formed the demons and the evil spirits.

If therefore we seek to institute an analogy between the Microcosm it will be seen that Nepheseh refers to Malkuth and Assiah: Ruach will refer to Yetzirah, which is the World of formation, therefore the formative principle operating in Ruach gives form to all ideas, and is that which weighs, balances and works in things. Ruach can also have an evil side.

Neschamah = the higher aspirations of the Soul, which aspire to the ideal. There can be no positively evil side to Neschamah:— there will only be a higher or lower aspiration.

If the Ruach overpowers the Neschamah; if the Neschamah seeks the lower good, both will be ruined. The following of a false idea cannot be said to be exactly evil, but is a lower Good than it should be.

[2] The Gnostics called this Achamoth, but probably this was a corruption of Chokmutha. (Original Note.)

Neschamah will answer to the World of Briah: — so also will Chiah, which is allotted to Chokmah; but you cannot touch the Yechidah part of you with your Ruach,—you must use the consciousness of the Neschamah. This Yechidah will, together with Chiah, be the 'Higher Genius', though this again will not be the *highest* self. For in and behind Kether will reside a part of the being, which it is impossible to understand, and which one can only aim at: this is the *highest* Soul, and answering to the highest part of Yechidah, cannot be touched by Neschamah. There must be a mode of transferring the synthesis of the consciousness making up the Man,—to this upper Sephirah. The Fall, which cut away the higher from the lower Sephiroth in Daath, was also our descent into this life, as it were, from that Upper and Higher Soul. Therefore our object is to get into contact with that again, which is only to be done through the Neschamah, which is the Divine Mother of the Soul,—our Aima.

When the Candidate enters the Vault and kneels down at the second point, he does so at the centre of the Altar above the symbolic form of the Adept, who is the synthesis of the sides of the Vault, whence he has come forth and occupies a central position between the Kether and the World of the Shades,—being there protected by the rising glory of the Golden Cross and the Rose. Then this Prayer is said: 'Unto Thee Sole Wise, Sole Mighty and Sole Eternal One, be Praise and Glory for Ever'. Now it must be the Macroprosopus, the Amen, who is addressed here, —the Lord of Kether who has permitted this aspirant who now kneeleth before Him to penetrate thus far into the Sanctuary of His Mysteries (which is in the centre of the Universe). Not unto us, but unto His Name be the Glory. (which is the name JHVH with the addition of the letter Shin) 'Let the influence of Thy Divine Ones descend upon his head,' (These Divine Ones are Angelic forces, and the higher Self is in the nature of the Angelic Forces, as the Highest Self is in that of the Divine One) 'and teach him the value of Self sacrifice, so that he shrink not in the hour of trial, but that thus his name may be written on high' (that is that the divine NAME formulated in him may be brought up, as it were, to the heights) 'and may stand in the presences of the Holy One' (which genius will be a mighty

Angelic power and in form far different from the petty person-
ages we are here) 'in that hour when the Son of Man is worked
before the Lord of Spirits and his name in the Presence of the
Ancient of Days'.

This will be the synthetical form of the Son of Man, the BEN
ADAM, who is the synthesis of the Ruach of the Universe: in
other words, the allusion is to the Great God of the World of
Yetzirah or the Microprosopus, the Son of the first Adam when
he is invoked before the Lord of Spirits, which can but be in
Kether; and his name in the presence of the Ancient of Days. 'He
who is ancient before the Gods, ancient before time, ancient
before the formation of the Worlds, He the ETERNAL AMEN—
or even He who is before AMEN and whom the plumes of
Amen's head-dress only touch'.

Now the foregoing partly represents the mode in which the
initiate becomes the Adept:—the Ruach directed in accordance
with the promptings of the Neschamah keeps the Nephesch
from being the ground of the Evil forces, and the Neschamah
brings it, the Ruach, into contact with the Chiah i.e. the genius
which stands in the presence of the Holy One = the Yechidah =
the Divine Self, which stands, as it were, before the Synthetical
God of all things. That is the only real way to become the
Greatest Adept, and is directly dependent on your life and your
actions in life.

And upon the lid of the Pastos this process is symbolically
resumed: there we see the suffering Man, pitiful and just, before whose justice and purity the heads of the dragon fall back,
but on the upper half there is depicted a tremendous and a
flaming God, the fully initiated Man,—the Adept who has
attained his Supreme Initiation.

It will be noticed that in the $4° = 7°$ Diagram the heads of the
Dragon have seized the Sephiroth but, as before remarked, on
the lid of the Pastos they are falling back from the figure on the
Cross: they are dispossessed only by the sacrifice of the lower
Self.

Recall to your mind that passage in one of the Eddas 'I hung
on the Tree three days and three nights, wounded with a spear,
myself a sacrifice offered to my (highest) Self,—Odin unto Odin'.

It will furthermore be noticed that this way of looking at the matter at once makes a reconciliation between the account in the Gospel of the Christ as a calm, peaceful and pitiful Man, and the representation in the Apocalypse of a tremendous and flaming God. A glance at the top half of the Pastos shows the descent as a flaming sword which casts out the evil,—the whole surrounding being white with brilliance. 'And He had in His right hand Seven Stars ... and the Seven Stars represent the (Arch) Angels of the Seven Churches', or abodes in Assiah, at His feet...

The Life of Nations is like the Life of men;—they are born, become intellectual, direct that intellect to black ends,—and, perish. But every now and then at the end of certain periods, there are greater crises in the World's history than at other periods, and at such times it becomes necessary that Sons of God should be incarnated to lead on the new era of the Universe. I do not affirm that Christ was necessarily a man who obtained Adeptship in that incarnation, but rather one who had obtained Adeptship and come down to be incarnated again to lead up the new era. It was, however, necessary in the crucifixion of so great a Soul,—so that the form might actually suffer,—that everything except the Nephesch should be withdrawn which would be the reason of the Cry of *the Nephesch*, 'My God, My God, Why hast thou forsaken me?' For the Nephesch which was temporarily abandoned in this case was the cloak of that incarnation. In other words, the only mortal part about the Man, or the God, and then only after incurring that physical death, as it were, could the other divine parts suddenly come down and make it the resurrected or glorified body, which, according to the description, had after the Resurrection, the apparent solidity of the ordinary body, and the faculties of the Spirit body. Because if you can once get the great force of the Highest to send its ray clean down through the Neschamah into the mind, and thence, into your physical body, the Nephesch would be so transformed as to render you almost like a God walking on this Earth.

The Ruach, then, has to undergo a certain check and suffering in order to attain its Apotheosis—which is the work of our Adept.

In the fully Initiated Adept the Nephesch is so withdrawn into the Ruach that even the lowest parts of these two principles cease to become allied to the body and are drawn into the first six Sephiroth. This is again brought out in the Obligation, where you say, 'I pledge myself to hereby give myself to the Great Work, which is so to exalt my lower nature that I may at length become more than human and thus gradually raise and unite myself to my higher and divine genius'. If it is a very great thing to unite yourself to the genius, how much more so must it be to unite yourself to the God that is behind it!

Looking at the Pastos, it will be seen that it represents a kind of triple cube, the whole of which is placed between light and darkness. The lid is half light and half darkness, the upper end is the symbol of light, and the lower, the symbol of darkness,— while the sides have the colours placed between the Light and the Darkness. At the head is placed a Golden Greek Cross, representing the Spirit and the Elements, and a Rose of 7 times 7 petals, and there are four rays which go out from it. But at the foot,—that which the feet rest on as if they were exalted by it,— is the Cross exalted on a pedestal of Three Steps, viz. the Obligation Cross. This latter is also to an extent represented on the top in the crucified figure, and symbolises the voluntary sacrifice of the lower Will, which is incidental to allying the intellect with the higher aspirations and to the establishment of your consciousness therein:— thus if the ordinary consciousness were centred in the Ruach you could touch the Neschamah, while if it was in the latter you could touch the Genius.

Now this transference of consciousness from Ruach to Neschamah is one object of the ceremonial of the $5° = 6°$ Ritual:— it is a thing which will be more readily understood when the Grade of Adept Adeptus Minor is reached. It is especially intended to effect the change of the consciousness into the Neschamah and there are three places where is can take place. The first is when the Aspirant is on the Cross, because he is so exactly fulfilling the Symbol of the abnegation of the lower Self and the union with the Higher Self:— and also there is the invocation of the Angel H.V.A.

The second place is when he touches the Rose on the representative of C.R. in the Vault, when he has taken on himself the symbols of suffering and self sacrifice, and says that his victory is in the Cross of the Rose.

The third place is when he enters the Vault in the Third point and kneels down and the Chief Adept says 'I am the Reconciler with the Ineffable: I am the dweller of the Invisible: let the White Brilliance of the divine Spirit descend.'

In these three cases a possible exchange of the consciousness from the Ruach into the Neschamah is initiated, so that whether he understands it, or not, the Aspirant actually approaches his own Genius.

(There are some cases where the Genius may have attained a height and fallen: — that is when, having touched the Ruach in one incarnation, it has been so wrought upon by the sufferings of the lower part that it has for the moment consented to slacken the tension of their union.

Now if the Genius part, instead of identifying itself with the God part, identifies itself too much with the Neschamah, a fall of the Genius takes place: which is not altogether evil, but may entail a certain evil effect.)

The most complete point of the actual contact is in the third point, where the Chief Adept says: — 'I am the Resurrection and the Life! He that believeth in me, though he were dead, yet shall he live, and whosoever liveth and believeth on me shall never die': i.e. if you can live at will in the Neschamah and touch the Genius, you will have made a great step towards the divine Elixir, for you will be worthy to sit with the Gods, and that which you drink of is the real Elixir, the Elixir of the Spirit of Life.

Then the Second Adept says: — 'Behold the Image of the Justified One, crucified on the Cross of the Infernal Rivers of death', and the Third Adept shows deific antithesis,—the exaltation into the Divine. Then the Chief Adept says again: — 'I am the First and the Last'—the Aleph and the Tau and the Yod and Hé final of the sacred Name,—'I am He that liveth but was dead, and behold I am alive for evermore, Amen', that is using the name of the Egyptian Deity AMON, or Amen, who represents the Ideal God force,—'and I hold the Keys of Death and of Hell'

(Because if you stand on Malkuth and keep your touch with the Gods, you hold the Keys of that which is below)—

But the lower self all this time has an existence, for it certainly is not quite eliminated:— it is cast forth from the Nephesch, yet preserving a link with it, it goes down into the Qlipoth, and in this connection, it is well to observe that what may be really Evil on this Earth plane, may be even as a God among the Demons.

The words 'He descended into Hell', have such a significance.

This Third point then represents the attainment of the Divine:— and the Second Adept proceeds to say:— 'He that hath an ear let him hear what the Spirit says unto the Assemblies' (i.e. in Malkuth) and if the Voice of the Divine is found in Malkuth it must find its echo in the realms beneath.

Then follows the exaltation into Neschamah of the Consciousness of the Chief Adept, whose Voice seems as if he were symbolically standing with his head in Atziluth, whence it reverberates through the Worlds, sinking down below Malkuth unto the dominion of the Shells and he says:— 'For I know that my Redeemer liveth' (the Redeemer is he that brings again) 'and that he shall stand at the latter day upon the Earth. I am the Way, the Truth and the Life. No Man cometh unto the Father but by me etc.' This whole passage of the Chief Adept is formed of a collection of utterances, which are, as it were, the speeches of the Great Gods, which he can only hear when he is still further exalted into Kether. 'I am the Way, the Truth and the Life', is the reflected Triad. No Man cometh unto the Father, but by me. Then the Neschamah speaks; down to 'I have entered into the Invisible'. Then it is as if the Consciousness went into the Genius, which says 'I am the Sun in his rising, I have passed through the hour of Cloud and Night'.

Then follows:— 'I am Amon the concealed one, the opener of the Day,'—like the Great God in Atziluth—'I am Osiris Onnofris, the Crucified One,' who is perfected in the balance and risen above all considerations that come from Maya, or illusion, and who only seeks the eternal life from above, and then, as if in a supreme moment 'I am the Lord of Life, triumphant over death, there is no part of me that is not of the Gods'. (That is the

voice of Kether.) This again is followed by a synthetical cul-
mination, as if all the divine ones united in the utterance: 'I am
the Preparer of the Pathway, the Rescuer unto the Light! Out
of the Darkness let the Light arise!'

Then the Aspirant is prompted to say—'Before, I was blind,
but now I see,'—representing again the blindness to the Neschamah Consciousness and the passage into this.

Whereupon the Chief Adept says:— 'I am the Reconciler
with the Ineffable! I am the dweller of the Invisible: let the
White Brilliance of the Divine Spirit descend'.

The Aspirant is now told to rise an Adeptus Minor of the
Rose of Ruby and the Cross of Gold, in the sign of Osiris slain,—
and then 'We receive thee as an Adeptus Minor in that sign of
Rectitude and Self Sacrifice.'

The affirmation of the three parts is then proceeded with.—
The Chief Adept says:

'Be thy Mind opened unto the Higher,' *Second*: 'Be thy heart
the centre of *Light*', and *Third*: 'Be thy body the Temple of the
Rosy Cross'.

The Pass Word is then announced, which is formed from the
Mystic Number of the Grade, 21,—this Pass Word, however is
the divine Name of Kether:— and it is used as the Pass Word
of this Grade of Tiphereth in order to affirm the connection between the two.

Then the Chief Adept says that the Key Word is I.N.R.I. The
three Adepts themselves represent Chesed, Geburah and Tiphereth. The Creator, the Destroyer and the Sacrificed One, ISIS,
APOPHIS and OSIRIS=the name IAO. The Symbol of Osiris
slain is the Cross; v is the sign of the mourning of Isis: the sign
of Typhon and Apophis: x the sign of Osiris risen: =LVX,
the Light of the Cross, or that which symbolises the way into
the Divine through Sacrifice. So that the symbolism in its
entirety represents the exaltation of the Initiate into the Adept.

PART FIVE

Esoteric Psychology

being
Flying Roll No. XX
Flying Roll No. XXI

For the sake of those readers of this book who are not familiar with the Qabalistic system used in the Western Esoteric Tradition I think it best that I should give a brief outline of that system as an introduction to the Flying Rolls which follow.

The Qabalah is essentially a system of classification. The various factors that make up both the universe (the macrocosm) and the soul of man (the microcosm) are classified in accordance with ten numbers, the Sephiroth of the Tree of Life, and twenty-two letters, the Paths of the Tree of Life.[1]

The manifested universe is further divided into Four Worlds, each containing a Tree of Life of its own. The Four Worlds are classified as follows:

Atziluth, Archetypal—Pure Deity
Briah, Creative—Archangelic
Yetzirah, Formative—Angelic
Assiah, Action—Man, Matter, Shells, Demons.

In each of these Four Worlds are the ten Sephiroth of that World, and each Sephirah in turn is divided into a Tree of Life made up of ten Sephiroth. This makes four hundred Sephiroth in all—the number of the letter Tau, last letter of the Hebrew alphabet, the completion of all things.

When the Tree of Life is applied to the nature of Man it is divided into three, Nephesch, Ruach, and Neschamah—roughly equivalent to the Body, Soul and Spirit of St. Paul.

Nephesch is equated with Malkuth and Yesod, the two lowest Sephiroth of the Tree of Life, and is usually translated as 'Animal Soul'. It is the vehicle by which the mind is brought into contact with matter and, broadly speaking, it corresponds with the 'etheric' and 'lower astral' bodies of Theosophical terminology.

Ruach, the second principle, is usually translated as Mind or

[1] These thirty-two factors were usually represented in diagrammatic form. This diagram—the Tree of Life—may be found in such easily available works as Dion Fortune's *Mystical Qabalah*, W. Gray's *Ladder of Lights*, and R. G. Torrens' *Golden Dawn—Its Inner Teachings*. (Editorial Note.)

Intellect. It is made up of the five Sephiroth (Chesed, Geburah, Tiphereth, Netzach and Hod) that lie above Yesod. Ruach is a set of five intermeshing intellectual principles, 'divided for love's sake, on the chance of union', concentrated upon their central core, the Sun of Tiphareth, the human consciousness and will, of which the other four Sephiroth are, after a certain fashion, extensions.

The Neschamah is subdivided into three; the Jechidah, or Divine Spark, the Chiah, or Will, and the Neschamah proper.

The Jechidah is the Divine Spark, 'that in me which is more than me myself', the deepest layer of consciousness. It is at the same time that which all men have in common and that which differentiates one man from another. On the Tree of Life it corresponds with the topmost Sephirah, Kether, the Crown.

The Chiah, or essential will, is the creative impulse of the Jechidah, through which the latter obtains its self-realisation. On the Tree of Life it equates with Chokmah, Wisdom.

The Neschamah itself corresponds with the Great Mother Binah, or Understanding, the third Sephirah of the Tree. It is the Jechidah's own understanding of itself.

It must be realised that Jechidah, Chiah, and Neschamah form a trinity—it is impossible to conceive of one of them without the other two.

Flying Roll No. XX

The following diagram will of course be immediately recognised by all of you: —

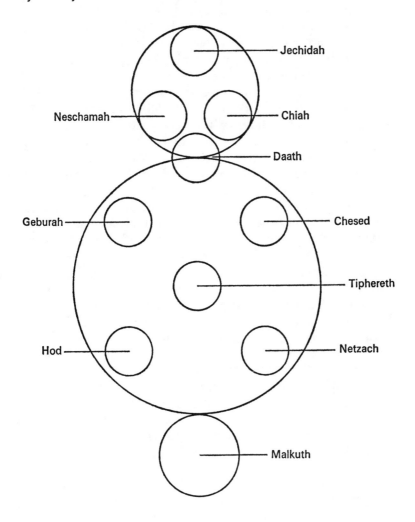

Now supposing a physical man to be here represented, Kether is the Crown and is above the head. The junction of Chokmah and Binah in Daath is in the head itself. Then Chesed and Geburah will correspond to the arms and shoulders, Tiphereth and Yesod to the trunk and body, Netzach and Hod to the hips and legs, and Malkuth to the feet alone.

Now I will put to you the question, where was the mystic body of our Founder, Christian Rosenkreutz discovered? In Tiphereth. And what is Tiphereth? The centre. That is to say it is in the centre of the middle Sphere and when that middle Sphere is projected what does it represent? The Polar Axis. Representing then the Polar Axis it will be in a sense invisible from the outside. Therefore the outermost form of the whole projection will be spherical. Now that would imply that Tiphereth corresponds to the heart and Tiphereth represents the place where the Chief Adept is found and it is the Polar Axis, and the influence which is surrounding this physical body of the man is a Sphere like that of the Universe. This Sphere then surrounds the body. Thus it will be the Assiah Plane of the Man, the Malkuth containing the reflection of the other Ten Sephiroth. Now this Sphere is what we of the Rosicrucian Order, call the magical mirror of the Universe, or the Sphere of sensation of the Microcosm. It is the Aura of the man. Now you will understand that as the Chief Adept is placed in Tiphereth you may expect to find the most vital portion of the body about the heart. The heart will therefore represent the King of the physical body. All this is, of course, much better explained in the lecture on the Microcosm which you will get later on.

This sphere, answering to the Sphere of the Macrocosm, you will naturally expect that it will have the forces of the Macrocosm reflected in it. Towards which part of the Zodiac then would you expect the man in the centre to face? He will face towards that point in his Sphere of sensation which represents the ascending degree in his horoscope and that ascending degree will therefore be the point which is opposite. His object is the development of the Daath principle which is in the head. This principle is, you will observe, the link between Ruach and Neschamah.

Now thus is the Consciousness attributed. In Chiah is the beginning of the Self of Man. The real Self is in Jechidah, and its presentment in Chiah. Thus Jechidah is called the Divine Consciousness 'Conscire' means 'to know with' and 'to be in touch with' and only your Kether can do this as regards the Divine and your Kether is then the Divine Consciousness. In Ruach is the human Consciousness and the human Will. In Jechidah is the Divine Will; so that the human Will is like the King of the material body. The automatic Consciousness, as it is called, is in Yesod, and has to do with the lower passions and desires. Being automatic, that is moving of itself, it can hardly be said to be Will. Now this is the danger which threatens the man who yields to the temptations of the lower desires. The Human Will which should be seated in Tiphereth, in the heart, is attracted to contemplation of, and union with, the automatic Consciousness so that the human Consciousness abdicates its throne and becomes automatic. You will find in the life history of men that vice brings about a species of automatic condition which compels them always to move in the same grooves, and it is a known fact that it recurs at regular intervals like a disease, and it is indeed a disease.

This automatic Consciousness in its right place refers to Yesod which is the part which attracts the material atoms, and here it is in its proper place. When, however, it usurps the place of the Human Consciousness then it rules instead of being subject to the Human Consciousness, and this destroys the balance of the Sephiroth.

Now in Daath is the Throne of the Spiritual Consciousness and Daath being the result of Chokmah and Binah it is the presentment of the seven following Sephiroth, that is to say that in the head are the seven planets of which the eyes will answer to the two luminaries—the right to the Sun and the left to the Moon.

You will now at once see that spiritual consciousness does not partake of the physical body but is the light which radiates. The way in which thought proceeds is by radiation, that is to say, its rays are thrown vibrating through this sphere of Astral Light. This will explain to you a very fruitful source of mistaken Clairvoyance. The many errors arise therefrom: It is really a selfish-ness of the thought plane. The Consciousness is content, as it were, to receive the reflections which are in its sphere and which have necessarily been modified by the person himself. Let us take an example of individual modification and we will choose that of the planet Mars. Fire will be red. That is to say, that in all cases of a fiery nature the judgment will be fairly accurate. But the fault will be manifest when you come to a watery nature. It will then be represented by violet instead of by blue as it should be, and he will always want to bring the nature of the Fire into the watery natures. Here then is a fruitful source of error in Clairvoyance, especially arising in natures which are not selfish in the ordinary sense, but which have that more subtle selfish-ness which arises from too much study of oneself. This is why, in our system of Occultism we are contrary or converse to that taught by the Theosophical Society. The Theosophists appar-ently advise the student to commence with the study of the Universe; and while I quite agree that he may arrive at his end by that means, there is the danger of that spiritual or thought-selfishness, and this is the reason why we study the Microcosm before the Macrocosm.

This continual dwelling on one's own nature with the idea of reforming and making oneself better is apt to give you too con-tracted a view, and you are threatened with the selfishness which you have yourself engendered. This is also the danger of too great asceticism, because it is apt to bring about the feeling that you are better than another person. These are the dangers. If you can escape these dangers you will arrive at the goal. There-fore to the student who is studying Clairvoyance, it is particu-larly advisable that he should rather repress that form of it which tends in his own direction, for fear of encouraging that spiritual selfishness which is so subtle as to escape his attention until it is too late. If he continues along this path his errors will increase, and he will arrive at a period of depression. From this will arise a series of miserable feeling which might have been checked in the beginning.

You see now that the sin of the Automatic Consciousness is what is commonly called vice. The sin of the Human Consciousness is that of the intellectual man.

The sin of the Spiritual Consciousness is the error of a somewhat psychic nature; you cannot have sin of the Divine Consciousness because you cannot have any error in Kether. Here again, you see, we have the representation of the four Planes in Man, or YHVH.

Flying Roll No. XXI
Know Thyself
Address to the Zelator Adepti Minores
of the Order R.R. et A.C. By
Vestigia Nulla Retrorsum 6° = 5°

Perfect knowledge of Self is required in order to attain Knowledge of Divinity, for when you can know the God of yourself it will be possible to obtain a dim vision of the God of All, for *the God of the Macrocosm only reflects Himself to Man through the God of Man's Microcosm.*

Therefore, before you would invoke the Shining Ones be certain that you have called upon the Lord of Yourself, that is to say, that the *You* in Daath (the seat of the Spiritual Consciousness) have allied yourself to the *You* in Tiphereth (the seat of the Human Consciousness) and to the *You* in Kether (the seat of the Divine Consciousness), and from thence the Kether sending rays downwards; from it to the Daath, from Daath to Tiphereth and from thence to Yesod, which is the seat of the Automatic Consciousness.

This combination must have taken place with the consent of the Lower Will (in Tiphereth) as being the Human Will.

If you have succeeded in accomplishing this you are commencing the real Initiation, (therefore, should an Adeptus Minor strive to begin the practice of such an operation).

It is said elsewhere that *The Beginning of Initiation is the Search for the Shining Light.* For if the Man through Pure Knowledge and Aspiration has been able to place himself with his head resting immediately under Kether the Crown, he has come into contact with his First Light.

But his Knowledge must be true, and his aspirations pure. How else is he able to wear his Crown, upon which poureth the Influx from Jechidah?

It is this development of the Man that must have been intended by the Apostle Paul when he said: — 'Till we all come... to the Knowledge of the Son of God, unto a Perfect Man, unto the *measure of the stature*, of the fulness of Christ.' That is, that Man must grow sufficiently in his Spiritual growth, that he may

151

attain to that stature where his head will come into contact with his Kether—that is, unto the Knowledge of his Higher Self.

Regarding this, I will also quote another passage from the New Testament in which Christ says:— 'Whosoever shall confess me before men him shall the Son of Man also confess before the Angels of God':— signifying that he who shall raise himself by linking his Human to his Divine Self, being consequently in touch with the Kether of his Assiah, he will be able to rise still further to the Plane of the Angels, that is to say, that through the Kether of his Assiah he can be admitted to his plane of Yetzirah, his Angelic Self; for he has accepted the Christ within him, his power of Ascent. 'But he that denieth me before men shall be denied before the Angels of God,' meaning that he who denies the *me*, the power of the letter Shin, the letter of the Holy Spirit that makes of Jehovah the Name Jeheshua, hath denied that Spirit, that Higher Self, which is his one link with the Truth of Life, and so hath refused the Christ that *can be* within him, the only part which would enable him to rise to his Divine Self, whence he could receive the descent of the Divine Spirit, which ever comes to him who seeketh for it.

Kether is the Crown, then, which is placed on the head of the complete Initiate; and a great King must he indeed be who is fitted to bear such brilliance, and well must he have worked towards the developing and perfecting of his Kingdom to have made it worthy of that Divine Crown.

Therefore must he whose aim is to become the Initiate, work well at the development of the Forces of the Being; seeking to purify and to exalt them.

He, the man, standing in his Sephiroth, can well be compared to a King in his Kingdom which if he wishes to govern well, he must first learn to know and understand, for only after having a complete knowledge of the constitution, character and inhabitants of his realm, will it be possible for a just Ruler to bring about such reforms as he may deem necessary;—hence the great assistance given to us in the teachings of our Order which insist on a careful study of the Kingdoms of the Macrocosm and the Microcosm side by side with our Spiritual Development, one study helping the other; in fact the two are almost inseparable.

Now the Kingdom of the Microcosm, the man, with which this lecture is chiefly occupied, has distinctly its character, its constitution, its inhabitants etc.—The King is placed in his sphere, that is the boundary, the frontier of his realm.

The constitution consists of his Sephiroth, upon which the principal scheme of the Kingdom is modelled.

Its character would be the general aim and tendency of the Kingdom. (This would depend on the inclination of the pole of its sphere as regards the Macrocosm.)

The King's abode is in Tiphereth where is placed his throne, the seat of the Human Will, whence he wields the reins of government either as a great ruler inspired by his masters above, the Spiritual and Divine Consciousness, or as the Ruler debased (inspired or, more accurately speaking, obsessed) by the voluntary abdication of his rule, through being led astray by the temptation of the Automatic Consciousness to descend therein and make Yesod his chief abode instead of Tiphereth, thereby permitting the usurpation of the Higher by the Lower.

This fall, according to the nature of the man, (besides leading to other evils) may bring him to the Phallic School of Symbolism or to the grossest sensuality, for these two things are merely the expression of the same error in different natures.

His people are the many Forces of the Sephiroth of Ruach, working in Malkuth through Nephesch (Nephesch=Malkuth) The Priesthood, or rather the Prophets and Magicians, alone ascending as far as their Daath, they dwelling on the Threshold of their Divine Consciousness.

The Nobles will be with the King himself, about his throne in Tiphereth; as well as all the petty rulers, and professions and trades governed by the Sun.

In Chesed are the various occupations under Jupiter.

In Geburah, Netzach and Hod are all those under Mars, Venus and Mercury.

Yesod, as the seat of the Automatic Consciousness, can hardly be said to be an inhabitant, a conscious being; rather might it be represented by the machinery, works and tools of the nation.

Of course each Sephira will have its own Ten Sephiroth within it, which would give its various types—professions, trades, etc.—for example—Chesed;—in its Kether might be the Priest (this naturally supposes the Priest to be true and upright; the Prophet as the inspired Priest, which we mentioned before, is placed in the Daath of the man.)

A Philanthropist would be in its Chesed; in its Tiphereth—a judge; and probably an artisan working under Jupiter in its Yesod.

Now he who is a just ruler will try to know well these people, his subjects; neither giving undue attention or preference to either one class or another, nor permitting strife in any one of them,—therefore must one of the works of a student for Adeptship be *to learn to bring perfect order into the Six Sephiroth of his Ruach,* then will the Qlipoth[2] who may be called the Wild Beasts of the Nation, be forced to retire, they only having been permitted to remain through Disorder.

He will then be able to banish them to their own plane, the land beyond Malkuth; as they, working in their own habitation, therefore in their own element, they will be as the lecture on the Microcosm says 'equilibrated therein and the Evil Persona (their synthesis) will become as a strong yet trained animal, whereupon the man rideth, this bringing added material strength unto the man', which is a thing to be desired, if it be completely governed by the Higher.

One school of Occultism insists on the Neophyte retiring from the world, on his leading a thoroughly ascetic life, and in every way trying to exist without thought or desire for anything of that which is Human.

Now to some of us this may appear to be the only method for the attainment of that self-development which we express in the Tiphereth clause of the Adeptus Minor Obligation, when we pledge ourselves to become *more than human.*

We know that all the works of Nature are gradual in their growth, therefore must a man also be gradual in *his* growth, and before attaining to that *more than human,* that is to say, Yetziratic, Briatic and Aziluthic planes he must certainly be the *Perfect Man in Assiah.*

It must be our object then, to become that Perfect Man, in

[2] The evil and averse Sephiroth. (Editorial Note.)

order to attain ultimately to that Angel, that Archangel, and that Divinity, which are in Yetzirah, in Briah, and in Atziluth.

And the Zelator Adeptus Minor, is not actually given any special manner of life to follow; rather is he advised to determine for himself what shall be his relations with his family business, society, etc., seeing that we human beings are so varied in our character as in our surroundings so that the discipline which will be beneficial for one may often be evil for another.

One thing, however, is greatly insisted upon, and that is that we should *not* retire from the world, for we can succeed in perfecting ourselves in what is required of us without isolation.

In certain cases, it might be advisable for the execution of certain experiments connected with more advanced studies to avoid contact with others for a short time; but this would only be permissible in special cases.

One of the reasons why we are told not to isolate ourselves is that isolation tends to make a man egotistical—it will become a habit to him to study and to pay too much attention to his own Microcosm, whereby he will neglect other Microcosms which together with his form part of the Macrocosm; and this Egotism of the Spirit, (though not so *gross* a sin as is that of the Animal or the Human Consciousness) will yet be a far greater snare to him, as being more subtle and therefore less easy to be perceived and checked.

For the chief danger of spiritual egotism lies in the self-righteous spirit so easily developed, which while gradually absorbing the true Occult Aspiration flatters its victim with the idea that he is rapidly attaining his proposed Goal.

It will be best, then, for us to live amongst our fellows, and in our contact with them are we advised to avoid preaching and proselytising; which often leads also to a condition of self-righteousness in the Preacher, and is generally useless to the listener.

Rather would we influence them by our example, and by keeping our thoughts as well as our actions pure.

Our Order teaches that one of our aims should be the Regeneration of the Race of the Planet.

We who are but beginners, and but on the Threshold of the

Second Order, can do but little yet in this Great Work, but we are daily approaching this end, if we are fitting ourselves to become the Perfect Man, for *he*, the Perfect Man, the Adept, whose Human Will is at one with his Divine Will, therefore always in contact with his Genius, or Angelic Self, can attract yet Higher Forces. These Forces sending down Divine Rays till they radiate through him, he, the Adept, is able to give out this Force to the human beings who are *ready* to receive it, and thus is he helping in their regeneration; an Angel or a God not being so fitted for the contact with ordinary mortals, as is the Adept who, though exalted is still a man, and of Assiah.

Most of you will recall that passage in Bulwer Lytton's *Zanoni*, (that romance which contains so many valuable hints on Occult study and which is a good lesson to us on the dangers of untrained Occultism) when he says, speaking of Zanoni, that 'those with whom he principally associated, the gay, the dissipated, the thoughtless, the Sinners and publicans of the more polished world—all appeared rapidly, insensibly to themselves to awaken to purer thoughts and more regulated lives.'

We who are but Neophytes in the Great Initiation, can only *at very rare moments* be so in touch with our Higher Self, that our head is immediately under our Kether. For those few moments we are standing in the position in which the Adept *ever stands*—yet must we on no account imagine that during those few seconds we have equal power with the Adept, for unaccustomed as we are to the Divine Vision, it almost blinds us and it can therefore only be partially transmitted to our Spiritual and Human Selves; yet is this partial vision greatly to be desired, for it is a *Force* unto us, and it also gives us a glimpse of what we may one day attain.

Let us try then to ascend unto our Higher Self, and to stand with our head under the Crown, before deciding on any great and important action in our life, *and especially, and this most especially,* when we are judging another, or trying to modify the life of another, for that is indeed a grave responsibility;— for we imperfect mortals are ever ready to lean towards the Pillar of Mercy or the Pillar of Severity, and even if we do remain standing in the Middle Pillar, the Pillar of Mildness; how few of us raise our heads to our Kether—only with his head touching his Crown, his Kether, can a man have perfect Knowledge of the things of his Assiah.

He who leans much towards the Pillar of Mercy, will think him the Perfect Judge, cruel when that Judge deems it necessary to *extend his arm on the side of Severity*.

He who leans to the Pillar of Severity will also have corrupted vision, for judging from thence, the action of the Perfect Judge will appear to him *feeble*, when that Judge may have found it well to *extend his arms on the side of Mercy*.

He who stands straight in the Middle Pillar will not be so prejudiced as his brothers who lean towards Severity or Mercy, but *unless he is linked with his Kether*, he does not take in the whole scheme of his Sephiroth;—is therefore incomplete, and his judgment imperfect. Let us be careful, then, in judging another, we see how easily we may be deceived, and let us insist and force ourselves to aspire to, and be convinced that we are indeed with our Higher Self, before pronouncing such a judgment, seeing how much mischief may be worked through the action of Unbalanced Mercy or Severity, or of the insufficient judgment of the Middle Pillar without the Crown;—as the Hiereus in the $0° = 0°$ Ceremony hath said:— 'Unbalanced Severity is cruelty and oppression; Unbalanced Mercy is but weakness and would permit Evil to exist unchecked, thus making itself an accomplice of the Evil'.

Referring again to the Six Sephiroth of the Ruach, and to the necessity of keeping them balanced; it will occur to most of us (who almost without exception are given to some profession or occupation) that we shall be delayed in Spiritual Development by tending, in our daily duties, to throw out more rays from the Spiritual Consciousness to some portions of our Sephiroth at the expense of the others, and thereby becoming unbalanced.

Though far more difficult to live than the life in which we can dispose of our time, more or less, at will, this need not be a delay in our development; these daily duties may indeed be an increased strength to us. But in such a case, must we aim always at the Purest and the Best of that occupation, whatever it may be, and attempt to develop in it those qualities that we may be weak or deficient in, such as courage, resolution, patience, concentration, etc., which can be learned in the performance of any work, however petty.

So that if we are really doing our best, we are bringing increase of strength to the Highest part of the Sephirah in which we may happen to be working;—and to increase the Power of the Kether of *anyone* of our Sephiroth can but be an added strength to the *Self* of the Whole; for the Kether of each of our Sephiroth is the reflection of that of our Microcosm, which again is a reflection of its Higher Prototypes, and being Kether (or rather its reflection) in its action, however great its strength, it will not become disorderly and attempt to over-ride another Sephirah, but will be reflected again into the Kether of the man, thereby becoming an increased force to him, for seeing that it is a presentment of the Divine no Kether can be unbalanced.

For we see that even the Kether of the Qlipoth can hardly be said to be unbalanced, being composed of Two Forces, ever contending certainly, for it is that quality of contention that makes them partake of the Qlipoth; yet are they balanced, for were they not of equal strength, how could they ever be at war with one another? Sooner or later *one* would have to surrender.

Therefore is it evident,—that many are the means to Knowledge, and many are the paths by which we may reach the Goal of the Initiate—wherefore—I would say to each of you;—absurd and ill-judged is it to rule that all shall crowd into one path, because that happens to be the one chosen by one member. There is too much tendency to wish all to follow the Ideal of one,—we are apt to forget that the Ideal of each will lead to the same Truth. We can help each other better, then, by helping each to rise according to his own ideas, rather than, as we often unwisely do, in advising him to rise to what is best in ourselves only.

That error of wishing to make another as ourselves is another and a very hurtful form of most subtle egotism. All we can do is to help him to *elevate himself* and to study to 'Know Himself', in order that by working at that Knowledge, he may cross the Threshold of the Portal, which leads to the Knowledge of the Divine.

Ex Deo Nascimur!
In Yeheshuah Morimur!
Per Spiritum Sanctum Reviviscimus!

PART SIX

Hermetic Love and the Higher Magic

being
Flying Roll No. XIII
Flying Roll No. XXVII

Flying Roll No. XIII
Secrecy and Hermetic Love,
By S.S.D.D.

We have all no doubt heard of the terrible physical tests applied in Egyptian Initiations and are aware that violence amounting to torture was used in the Ancient Mysteries before the Neophyte was considered fit to take the first steps in his Ascent of the Mountain of God.

Though the *methods* of *our* Order are different the Spirit is the same, and unless we have learned indifference to physical suffering, and have become conscious of a *Strong Will*, a will which fears *nothing* fate can do to us, we can never receive a *real Initiation*.

These ceremonies in the lower grades of Our Order are principally active in disciplining our minds; they lead us to analyse and understand ourselves. They deal with the Four states of Matter, the Four Elements of the Ancients which with their synthesis answer to the five Senses. Our Senses are the paths through which our Consciousness approaches the central power which for want of a more accurate word I will call the Will.

It is the object of *our* lives as initiates to bring this Will to such a state of perfection, strength, and wisdom, that instead of being the plaything of fate and finding our calculations entirely upset by trivial material circumstances, we build within ourselves a fortress of strength to which we can retire in time of need.

The natural Man is a chaotic mass of contradictory forces. In the higher grades of the First Order, (by presenting a perfectly balanced series of symbols to the senses) we endeavour to impress upon the imagination of the initiates, the forms under which they can obtain perfection and work in harmony with the world force.

In the o° = o° Ceremony the principles most insisted on are Secrecy and Brotherly Love. Apart entirely from the practical necessity for secrecy in our Order, it is the fact that Silence is in itself a tremendous aid in the search for Occult powers. In dark-

163

ness and stillness the Archetypal forms are conceived and the forces of nature germinated. If we study the effects of calm concentration we shall find that in silence, thoughts which are above human consciousness clothe themselves with symbolism and present things to our imagination, which cannot be told in words.

The more thought and concentration of purpose that precedes an action, the more effective and effectual it will be. Again in *talking* on subjects such as these, there is always a terrible danger of personal influence or obsession coming into action. The Eagle does not learn to fly from the domestic fowl 'nor does the Lion use his strength like the horse', and *although knowledge* is to be gained from every available source the *Opinion* of others should receive the very smallest attention from the true student of Life.

Free yourselves from your environments. Believe nothing without weighing and considering it for yourselves; what is true for one of us, may be utterly false for another. The God who will judge you at the day of reckoning is the God who is within you now; the man or woman who would lead you this way or that, will not be there then to take the responsibility off your shoulders.

'The old beauty is no longer beautiful; the new truth is no longer true,' is the eternal cry of a developing and really vitalised life. Our civilisation has passed through the First Empire of pagan sensualism; and the Second Empire of mistaken sacrifice, of giving up our own consciousness, our own power of judging, our own independence, our own courage. And the Third Empire is awaiting those of us who can see—that not only in Olympus, not only nailed to the Cross,—but in *ourselves is God*. For such of us, the bridge between flesh and spirit is built; for such among us hold the Keys of life and death.

In this connection I may mention that the $0°=0°$ of the Grade of Neophyte has a deep significance as a symbol; a o means nothing to the world—to the initiate in the form of a circle it means *all*, and the aspiration of the Neophyte should be 'In myself I am nothing, in Thee I am all; Oh bring me to that self, which is in Thee'.

Having so far considered some of the thoughts that the practice of silence may bring you let us proceed to the subject of brotherly love.

We must of course take the word, as we take all higher teaching, as a symbol, and translate it for ourselves into a higher plane.—Let me begin by saying that any love for a person as an individual is by no means a Hermetic virtue; it simply means that the personalities are harmonious; we are born under certain influences, and with certain attractions and repulsions, and, just like the notes in the musical scale some of us agree, some disagree. We cannot overcome these likes and dislikes; even if we could, it would not be advisable to do so. If in Nature, a plant were to persist in growing in soil unsuited to it, neither the plant nor the soil would be benefited. The plant would dwindle, and probably die, the soil would be impoverished to no good end.

Therefore brotherly love does not imply seeking, or remaining in the society of those to whom we have an involuntary natural repulsion. But it does mean this, that we should learn to look at people's actions from *their* point of view, that we should sympathise with and make allowances for their temptations. I would then define Hermetic or Brotherly Love as the capacity of understanding another's motives and sympathising with his weaknesses, and remember—that it is generally the unhappy who sin.

A crime, a falsehood, a meanness often springs from a vague terror of our fellows. We distrust *them* and ourselves.

It is the down-trodden and the weak whom we have to fear; and it is by offering them sympathy and doing what we can to give them courage, that we can overcome evil.

But in practising Hermetic Love, above all things conquer that terrible sting of love—jealousy. The jealousy of the benefactor, the jealousy of the lover, or the friend, are alike hateful and degrading passions. Jealousy is deeply rooted in human nature nourished by custom, even elevated to a virtue under the pretence of fidelity.

To see human nature at its very worst you have only to listen to the ravings and threats of a person who considers his monopoly of some other person's affection is infringed. This kind of

165

maniacal passion is the outcome of the egotism à deux, which has been so fostered by romance.

But it is natural to wish to help and be necessary to those we love, and when we find others just as necessary or helpful, to feel bitterly that our 'occupation' is gone; but these regrets will be impossible to us when we can live in the world realising from day to day more fully that the highest and best principle within us is the Divine Light which surrounds us, and which, in a more or less manifested condition, is also in others. The vehicle may be disagreeable to us, the personality of another may be anti-pathetic, but latent light is there all the same, and it is that which makes us all brothers. Each individual must arrive at the consciousness of Light in his own way; and all we can do for each other is to point out that the straight and narrow path is within each of us. No man flies too high with his own wings; but if we try to force another to attempt more than his strength warrants, his inevitable fall will lie at our door.

This is our duty towards our neighbours; our duty towards God, is our duty towards ourselves; for God is identical with our highest genius and is manifested in a strong, wise, will freed from the rule of blind instinct.

He is the Voice of Silence,
The Preparer of the Pathway,
The Rescuer unto the Light.

Flying Roll No. XXVII
The Principia of Theurgia or the Higher Magic
By L.O.

The obscurity reigning in the public writings of those who have treated of Occult subjects has had the effect of veiling to a very large extent, any clear conceptions, which might have otherwise been apparent, respecting the methods of the sacred Science, and it has occurred to me that it might be of service to such of our members who are entering the Second Order if I put down some ideas which it is well to have in mind upon approaching these studies.

To the merely intellectual eye, much of the more spiritual instruction hereafter given out will, perhaps, appear mere wild fantasy and be difficult to comprehend, and much more so to put into practice, unless, indeed, the real significance of the symbolism and teaching of the Outer Order has been to some degree assimilated.

The system before you is now only to be appreciated by a refinement of faculty, to be engendered through the recognition of certain principia which may be said to underlie all Occult operations, and the practices consequent thereupon.

These principia all logically proceed from one postulate,—viz. the Unity of all things in the Divine Being,—a conception which beautifully harmonises with the most venerable instincts of the Soul: 'In Him we, live, move and have our being!'

This divine basis of the Universe is omni-present,—endowing total Nature with consciousness in varying modes: no particle can be said to contain more or less of the Divinity than any other, but the modes of expression differ according to the type. Essential Divinity was called by Plato 'the same' and manifested Nature 'the other': Divinity is archetypal—Nature is anarchic. As it is said 'Between the Light and the Darkness the colours vibrate'.

'The colours' are due to the mingled proportions of the Elements which engender variety and form. The World of Forma-

167

tion is Yetzirah—the region compounded by the Six Sephiroth of Microprosopus.

Yetzirah is the Astral Light, which is especially the medium wherein operate the Ethers of the Elements under the presidency of the Planets: I use the expression *Ether of the Elements* in order to convey the significance of the Hermetic conception of the 'Elements'. The Elements of the ancients (called respectively Fire, Water, Air and Earth) are not at all the physical Elements but the subtle Ethers underlying these,—*the presence of which is necessary before the gross Elements can be manifested.* Hence the Altar symbolism.

Everything formed by Nature in the Yetziratic and Assiatic Worlds is ensphered and thereby individualised: such intangible and magnetic circuli are forces evolving form, form being static force. Each individual or entity,—whether a stone, a planet or a man, energises according to its nature, i.e. gives expression to the archetype of its sphere, and this is the work of evolution. All entities are vested in the Anima Mundi, directly or indirectly according to vehiculum. In the higher kingdoms increased complexity obtains, culminating in the human being, as it is said 'Oh Man thou subtle production!'

The Unity of the Divine One—'circumscribing the Heavens with convex form'—which is considered to underlie all manifestation is a necessary conception to the doctrines of Macrocosm and Microcosm,—the Greater and Lesser World: that which is a *part*, of necessity partakes of the nature of the Whole, and thus every entity is a Microcosm or Little World—reflecting the Greater World or Macrocosm after a certain formula. Reflection involves reversal and thus it is said 'Kether is Malkuth after another manner'.

For Occult purposes the crown of manifested life is considered to be the production of spiritually perfect Man. Spiritual perfection is the work of evolution, as physical perfection is that of evolution.

Once the projection into Malkuth is affected (for the second Adam must first descend and be born of her) the re-ascent commences:— with the 'recession of the torrent' comes the interior unfoldment, while instincts of association, co-operation and community enlarges the interest of beings,—spreads consciousness over a wider area,—and strikes a death-blow at the egotistic life.

Every thought evolved takes form: elementals coalesce with such forms and thus impart thereto, as it were, life of their own. The inherent force of any thought is proportionate to the intensity of the volition which generated it.

Most people are more or less at the mercy of their own creations having thereby gained a definite temperament, or character. Every man is thus the sum total of his creation plus X,—the forever unknown quantity; but as the creations of life increase so the power of X may be said to diminish and for this reason it was said 'Enlarge not thy destiny!'

At the dissolution the Soul enters the region of its own Yetzirah, and unless during life it has learned to be positive to its own astral nature, the unimpeded fantasy of excarnate life would involve a fruition of good or evil to which its creator would be subject. Such post-mortem experience is therefore considered illusionary, and hence the work of the Occultist is to render himself positive to his own astral nature by living as much as possible on the creative plane,—his Briatic World,—for, be it remembered, the Creator is also the Destroyer, and thus the true dignity of the Soul is maintained when in alliance with its own divine summit,—a condition involving a more or less complete detachment.

It is not necessary to study Occultism in order to become good,—but rather to become wise. The means which you are taught to employ are calculated to equilibrate the spiritual nature and implement spiritual growth.

The effect of spiritual growth is to extend the Consciousness in the direction of divine and superhuman things and correspondingly restrict the 'Automatic Consciousness' of animal Appetites and desires.

The methods handed down by the Golden Dawn tradition are those of the divine Theurgy.

Theurgia is the science of communion with planetary Spirits, the powers composing the Hierarchies of Being and 'Gods of Light'.

Two conditions are necessary for practice. The first is absolute purity and devotion to Truth. The second, the thoroughly trained knowledge of correspondences, the correspondences, that is to say, between the forces of the greater World, or Macrocosm, with those of the lesser World, or Microcosm, and the respective interaction of these.

The normal method of Occult development is a gradual retreat within—first to the Yetziratic World, and, then beyond it. The World of Formation which the student is now called upon to traverse, is the Yetzirah of Assiah,—hence the Elemental and Planetary forces are especially those with which he is brought into contact.

Man as the most completely evolved Microcosm of the Macrocosm synthesises in his own constitution the forces of the greater World of which he is a part; every entity is thus related to him, —and he to them. The World is, as it were, a vast animal, and its parts respond, being moved by mutual sympathies : sympathies obtain through approximation to type, antipathies when the types are imperfect.

Theurgia is operated through the harmonious combination of the forces of sound, Colour, Number and Form,—the whole attention being powerfully concentrated upon the plane of the force the *signature* of which is expressed.

The numbers from 1 to 10 constitute a complete progression : these are primal powers and the roots alike of force and form. Occult practice derived from the decimal numeration rests upon a basis of mathematical accuracy,—mathematics being an exact science. The number 3 is the first manifesting power, the number 10 is a return to Unity, or the commencement of a fresh series. For this reason the forms of manifestation are septenary and these are the roots of colours and of sounds.

The Theurgist commands mundane natures by virtue of his own divinity, but until apotheosis be achieved it is necessary in certain higher operations to stimulate the Consciousness by identification with the divinity.

The rule is 'Appeal to the Divine and Superhuman presences, and conjuration of those which are inferior'. The right to command is extended by subsequent progress.

When in mundane affairs you wish to gain information about a distant country, you do so either from those who have been there, or by yourself proceeding thither,—so with Theurgic operations,—you can either invoke the simulacrum of your subject, or travel by projection.

The intimate connection between forms and elemental forces has to be learnt and appreciated. 'Think of a place and thou art there already' says the old Hermetic axiom, and it might have added 'whether you realise it or not';—the Adept does!

The endeavour to picture to yourself persons and things seen is an invocation of the simulacra and presently, with practice, much plastic power of formation will be developed and the tinge of personality overcome. Of any place or being to which such thought direction is made the true conformation thereof serves as the ideal and archetype upon which the formative power builds and to which it tends to conform naturally, unless impeded by preconceptions in the sphere of the mind.

In ceremonial, let the drawing of a circle which, as you are told, is the key to all the rest, be the formulation of a true magical vortex,—raising about the sphere of the mind an absolute barrier to all extraneous impression,—thus enabling perfect spontaneity: as you are told the Mystic Circumambulation symbolises the dawning of Light.

It will be seen upon consideration that every thought which is creative and positive (as distinct from a passive and mediumistic reflex) must contain, as it were, within itself the complement and completion thereof,—i.e. Intuition. In just the same way as when along parallel wires an electric current is passed down one only, simultaneously inducing a reverse current up the other,—so the fruition of thought, which is perfect intuition, complements the centrifugal action of intellectual energy. The external mode of mental activity has engendered oblivion of the fact, and so men fail to realise their own possibilities: but that Invocation involves response is the testimony of psychic sensibility.

Thoughts which are expressed in some way, whether by speech or symbol, are by so much the more powerful than those unexpressed. Expression is the consecration of Will. 'The Paternal Mind sowed symbols in the Soul',—and regenerate fantasy shall reveal them.

Forces are entities; all entities are expressible by formula or signature. The Sigilla of Occult forces are employed because whatever has but a casual similitude to these forces directly participates therein.

Will is the grand agent of all Occult Work; its rule is all potent over the nervous system. By Will the fleeting vision is fixed upon the treacherous waves of the Astral Light, but, as it is said, you cannot pursue the Path of the Arrow until you understand the forces of the Bow.

The use of bright colours engenders the recognition of subsisting variety and stimulates that perception of the mind which energises through imagination, or the operation of images.

A picture which to the cultured eye beautifully portrays a given subject, nevertheless appears to the savage a confused patchwork of streaks,—so the extended perceptions of a citizen of the Universe are not grasped by those whose thoughts dwell within the sphere of the personal life.

It is selfishness which impedes the radiation of Thought, and attaches to body. This is scientifically true and irrespective of sentiment: the selfishness which reaches beyond the necessities of the body is pure vulgarity.

The road to the Summum Bonum lies therefore through Self-Sacrifice,—the sacrifice of the Lower to the Higher, for behind that Higher Self lies the concealed Form of the Ancient of Days, the synthetical Being of Divine Humanity.

These things are grasped by the Soul: the song of the Soul is alone heard in the Adytum of the God-nourished silence.

The force of association, or community, even in wordly affairs is very great, but far more so when the ties which link together take their rise in the profoundest recesses of Being.

Having entered the Second Order, you come within the radius of a psychic spiritual force, which, generated centuries ago, has acquired a momentum of its own, and silently exerts a protective influence. The isolated student lacks this advantage. The history and existence of this secret organisation is a monument to the energy put forth by our Golden Dawn Ancestors, 'Those who are of a most excellent genius, cultivated the divine science, while yet upon Earth.'

The legacy which they have bequeathed is perhaps something more than the actual knowledge preserved, great though this be, for, consciously or unconsciously, the forces they have put forward devolve upon us, and the very shades of the mighty dead stimulate to further exertion.

PART SEVEN

Alchemy

being
Flying Roll No. VII

Prefatory Note

The following material is of extremely early date, being originally given as a lecture by Wynn Westcott in 1890, well before the foundation of the Second Order. Although Westcott made some interesting points, notably his correlation of the chemical elements with the Qabalistic Tree of Life, he displayed no knowledge of the practice of alchemy as distinct from its theory.

Nevertheless, at the period in question a number of Golden Dawn initiates, among them the Rev. W. A. Ayton, were engaged in practical alchemical research. A few years later, after the foundation of the Second Order, a document known as Z2 was circulated and a section of this purported to apply the formulae of the Golden Dawn Neophyte ritual to alchemical operations. It is interesting to note that Aleister Crowley denounced both this section of Z2 and that dealing with ceremonial divination as complete rubbish; it is difficult to know on what grounds Crowley based his opinion as his diaries fail to disclose any attempt by him to put these sections into practice.

After the death of Ayton and his co-workers no initiate of the Order seems to have betrayed any interest in alchemy until the 'thirties, when Israel Regardie published his *Philosophers Stone*—a fairly orthodoxly Jungian interpretation of alchemical writings. A little later the members of a schismatic Temple, Hermanubis, began experimenting with alchemy on the lines of Z2. An alchemical ritual of this type is reproduced in my *Ritual Magic in England*. In recent years a certain *Frater Albertus*, who runs an organisation called the Paracelsus Research Society in Salt Lake City, has been engaged in reviving the alchemical tradition in practical form. *Frater Albertus*, who from his published writings on the Qabalah seems to be within the Golden Dawn tradition, attaches particular importance to the works of Basil Valentine. The former's *Handbook of Alchemy* has led many occultists into a complete retraction of the Jungian interpretation to which they formerly adhered.

Flying Roll No. VII
Alchemy
By S.A.

Chemistry, the modern science of which investigates the constitution of material substances, is the lineal descendent of Mediaeval and Ancient Chemy. The syllable AL is the Arabic indefinite article, like the Hebrew He, meaning 'The' chemistry —the Higher Chemistry, treating of the essential nature of the Elements, metals and minerals; while modern chemistry rejoices rather in being a science of utilitarian and commercial uses.

The earliest use of the word Alchemy is believed to be found in the works of Julius Firmicus Maternus, the Astronomer, who lived in the time of the Emperor Constantine. Firmicus wrote that 'he should be well skilled in Alchemy, who is born when the Moon is in the House of Saturn'. So he was an Astrologer as well; what house does he mean? the Day house (Aquarius), or the Night house (Capricorn) of Saturn? Or does he, like some modern Astrologers, allot one of these, Aquarius, to Uranus?

The Imperial Library of Paris is said to possess the oldest Alchemic Volume known; it is by Zosimus of Panopolis, written in Greek about 400 A.D. and entitled the *Divine Art of Making Gold and Silver*. The next oldest tract upon Alchemy known to exist is by Aeneas Gazius, written in Greek about 480 A.D.

The Mediaeval authors often call Alchemy 'Hermetic Art', implying an origin from Hermes Trismegistos of Egypt, the prehistoric demi-god, or inspired teacher, to whom we owe the Emerald Tablet. It it stated by one old Greek writer that the Hermetic secrets were buried in the tomb of Hermes and were preserved until the time of Alexander the Great who caused his Tomb to be opened, to search for these secrets, and that he found the documents, but that his wise men could not understand them. Many portions of human wisdom have from time to time died out of Human understanding.

After the Fall of the Intellectual freedom of Alexandria, scientific attainments were almost entirely restricted to the

Arabs, who made great progress in science—; yet some monks in Christian monasteries also studied these matter in retirement and some have become famous as alchemists and magicians; and further some of these rose to eminence *also* in the Church, becoming Vicars, Abbots, and even Bishops. Those who succeeded most, wrote least, and hence are almost, if not quite, unknown to us.

An infinity of books have been written upon Alchemy, and they are of all sorts,—good, bad and indifferent; learned and superficial; wise and foolish—some are by good men, some by great men, others are by fools, some are by knaves. This is because Alchemy has existed as a Science upon several planes; and there have been true and successful students of Alchemy on each plane; and there have been fraudulent professors and knavish authors concerned with the Alchemy of the lower planes.

Some modern students have written upon Alchemy wisely, and some unwisely; but the modern error has notably been in going to extremes of opinion. Some modern authors have insisted that all Alchemy was folly; some that all Alchemy was Chemistry; and a third party, dominant at present, have convinced themselves that all Alchemy was Religion.

I am firmly convinced that each class of teacher is partly wrong—let me take the middle path.

The science of Alchemy has existed, has been studied and taught upon Four planes.

Upon *Assiah*, there has been the Ancient occult Chemistry, the Chemistry of the Adept; who added to facility and knowledge of materials, the magical skill and Will Power of the ability to act on the 'Soul of things'—their astral counterparts. Here transmutation is a physical fact, and possibility.—This was both practised and pretended, and real Treatises were written.

Upon *Yetzirah*, is psychic alchemy, the power of creation of living forms.—This was practised, but rarely preached.

Upon *Briah* is Mental Alchemy;—the creations of Art and Genius, the ensouled music, picture and statue;—this was practised and not preached until modern times.

Upon the *Highest Plane*, the Spiritual, the practice was almost unknown except to a few entirely hidden Magi; but it was written about by some good and true philosophers, who couched their views on man's origin and destiny, his descent from God, and his possible re-ascent to God, in the language of the Material Plane to avoid persecution and destruction, at the hands of the priests of established churches.

By the pretence of chemistry, they saved themselves from penalties for heterodoxy : by the absence of Chemical apparatus, they saved themselves from extortion and torture as Alchemists.

As to Material Alchemy, the first mentioned, but few professors confessed to success and most of them lost their lives thereby. No man's life would be safe, or even tolerable—even today, who succeeded in transmutation, and confessed to it. I am entirely convinced that Transmutation of the lower metals to Gold and Silver is possible and that it has been often done; but not by Chemistry only, but by correlating with physical processes, the Will-action, and the power over the 'Soul of Nature', and the 'Soul of things', which the purity of life, and the training of the Adept can alone supply.

The true Alchemist would be the last to publish his success to the world—and if he did, he would probably thereby lose his power. His elixirs and powders that succeeded but yesterday, would be powerless today,—for Isis does not sanction any tampering with the Virgin purity of Her shrine. Personal aggrandisement, as an end, or as a result, would wreck any success in practical magical working; and the last student to succeed, would be he who cast a look behind upon the lusts of the flesh, pride of Life, and the ambition of the Devil.

Let no man study Alchemy to enrich himself. Let no man study Occultism to secure the gratification of passion; it is the unpardonable Sin. Hence we may say that even Material Alchemy is a high and gracious art, for success proves purity, Adeptship and spiritual power; the Chemist alone, may be successful in his limited sphere, whatever his character, and however soiled be his ego—intellect alone sufficeth him.

Pardon this digression, but alchemy has a moral and spiritual aspect, although it seems to me that my dear friend Anna

Kingsford erred, when she saw Religion and morals in every Alchemic process. The Alchemist professed the knowledge and encouraged the pupil to search for three things above all:

The Red Elixir to transform Base metals to Gold;

The White Elixir to transform Base Metals to Silver;

The Elixir Vitae to administer to Vegetable and animal; to intensify the life, to prolong life, and to expand the life.

Health and length of Life are much to be desired, for art is long, I believe the first and second Elixirs were not sought so much for their own powers, as because they were steps leading to the Elixir Vitae—the art of prolonging life and opportunities of the Adept, that he might lose less time in his progress to a spiritually exalted goal—less than he would lose by living more and shorter lives—with passive intervals.

Surely there is an advantage in living years after 'Adeptship in the Inner' is gained: — rather than early death followed by long periods of rest and then childhood. To the true student who learns to teach other men now, individuals and, perhaps, in higher lives—to guide nations; surely continuity is an advantage!

Spiritual progress, which hastens to be done with man and Earth is not (say the Easterns) the highest form of Buddhahood or Enlightenment. The Buddha of compassion, who renounces spiritual joys, to assist the grovellers upon earth, or near it,— is a higher type.

I believe then in the three chiefs of the Rosy Cross whose earthly years of work count by hundreds; they are allegoric and symbolic possibly in name and number of years, but they express a truth, that progress in adeptship links some great Souls to earth workers: and that such a goal for usefulness, is a worthy aim and aspiration for every one who enters here, and views the symbolic form of the Master C.R.

If I am asked why the Alchemic Books are so full of the Transmutation to Silver, and to Gold, I answer that these steps being necessary precedents to the art of the Elixir Vitae, have naturally had more attention and experiment, and more professors than the third superior step, which is almost altogether shrouded from the profane.

I must supplement these remarks by saying that I believe that many of the Alchemic treatises were really treatises written in the light of the Chemistry of the Age, and record real attempts at chemical processes in search of the secret of transmutation into Gold, by people who were really the chemists of the day, who did want real Gold, and who had no spiritual intuitions, and who did nothing but fail in Transmutation.

To return to physical chemistry and Alchemy on the plane of Assiah.—Note—the curious, and not denied, statement that certain Gold frames have been known to be struck by lightning and discoloured by the Flash, and that this discoloration has shown traces of Sulphur.—What of this incident? Either the Sulphur was in the Gold, as ancient Alchemy taught 'a Sulphur was'; or the Sulphur was in the Lightning, which modern Science says is Electricity and contains no Sulphur. But added Sulphur is not found in other matters which contain none, when they are lightning struck.

The Hermetic doctrine is that all Matter is but one in its essence, and is the lowest fall of the spirit, the most passive aspect of the Lux.

Spirit	—	Matter
Active	—	Passive
Motor	—	Moved

From the one Eus, came two contraries, thence three principles, and four elements;—on all planes of matter, the one base is Hyle—of the Greek philosophers. Then arose from the Homogeneous—variation. The Heterogeneous arose by development. Under Sephirotic impulse on the plane of Assiah, differentiation spread, and forms and combinations were produced during ages of time. During the ages of gradual concretion, and setting together of atoms, the elementary substance of modern chemistry, the Metals and the Matalloids, the halogens and the earths, became definite types and permanent of constitution. They became fixed in their molecular structure, and are now in the Kali Yuga, so far in time from their origin; practically Elements in the Modern sense of structure indissoluble to all known material processes. I assert that to the Adept they are still convertible and analysable, but even apart from Adeptship, some so called Elements will be even yet disintegrated by modern science alone. But while science prides itself on its progress, it is fatuous enough to demand implicit belief in its attitude of authority day by day. Modern Science howls down today the man who will tomorrow succeed in demonstrating its error. Science is but little less a Bigot than has Religion ever been.

The Metals then, and our present Elements must have been formed, defined, and set in their present type by the work of ages. By the slow processes of Nature, by heat, by light, by electricity, by condensation, by pressure, have the metals grown in the veins of stone. Sudden, and violent agencies no doubt also produced an effect, *perhaps* some metals, have been only produced by the convulsions, and not by the gradual processes of Nature.

Who knows but that the Gold found native and pure, as few metals are found, was produced by the Lightning and the Earthquake. Intense pressure and intense heat, would be likely to make a new combination from existing ones. Gold is intense in its weight—its specific gravity: intense pressure and high fusion point, would be likely to produce such a body, pure, homogeneous, heavy.

The Alchemist taught that the well known Metals, now called Elements, were not so—were not simple substances. The 'Elements' of the Alchemicist were states; states and processes. They taught that each metal, say lead, consisted of a Metallic Root, and certain other matter—sulphurs. The nature and quantity of their sulphurs, determined the Metal.—By taking a low metal,—coarse, common, easily altered metal, by purging it from these sulphurs, stage by stage, they taught that each metal might be produced in turn, until the last transmutation produced Gold. I believe the theory is true, I believe the practice is possible, by working in the astral, contemporaneously with action on the physical basis. But if Gold could be so made, Cui Bono? What good would that be? No sooner is Gold thus made, as it were from nought—than its value ceases—it is the rarity of Gold that makes it of commercial value—that makes it buy bread and luxuries. If it be produced at will, it will be of no more value than any other dust.

As to the Alchemist, who, as adept, does succeed in making transmutation, he will be so constituted that riches have no temptation for him and pride no attraction. He will know too, that wealth will be but ill spent, when gained, if squandered upon those who will not help themselves: he will know that individual progress, national progress, and world progress depend not on doles which pauperise, but on the will and effort of individual, nation, and world.

The temptation to wish one could but transmute a little, just to help some one friend, or neighbour, just to provide oneself with some thing earnestly desired—for one's good—is I believe a folly, and would be an evil if attained.

How few of us have not wished this tribute to our efforts?

How few men of the world do not wish it? What proportion of men who are wealthy, spend daily on themselves what is best for them and no more, and give the remainder to the friend, the neighbour, the deserving? Do you say—oh, I am an initiate, I should do differently? My friend—with greater opportunities, comes a great responsibility. I will not judge such, nor you, but in my heart, I thank God I have not the power of transmutation now. God knows,—and I know—how easy it is to fall.

But I constantly digress into the Spiritual, although what I really came to say, is a word on the material and physical aspect. I still defer these remarks, however, to quote two passages, one in prose narrating the sequence of the process of Alchemic work: and the other a poem written in English, translated from an old French prose account of Alchemic work, in allegoric language and myth. The first quotation is Astrological, and Astrology is inextricably mixed up with Alchemy. The second is beautiful in its poetry, and will well repay contemplation.

The first quotation reads:—

The Great Work must be begun when the Sun is in the
Night house of Saturn: the Blackness appears in
forty days when Sun is in the Day house of Saturn:

the Blackness deepens into the Night house of Jupiter
on reaching Aries a separation occurs. The Whiteness
of Luna develops when the Sun is in the house Cancer of Luna
The Sun begins his special form of change in Leo his
own house.
Redness is produced in the day house of the
Red metal of Copper, Venus, this is Libra, next Scorpio
follows, and the Work reaches completion in Saggitarius
the day house of Jupiter.

This is a good example of Allegoric description, which has
no doubt a physical basis,—and clearly refers to the Soul of
things, matters, seasons and processes on the astral plane of
evolution.
The second quotation reads : —

I

Within the golden portal
Of the garden of the wise,
Watching by the seven sprayed fountain,
The Hesperian Dragon lies.
Like the ever burning Branches
In the dream of holy seer;
Like the types of Asia's churches
Those glorious jets appear.
Three times the magic waters
Must the Winged Dragon drain
Then his scales shall burst asunder
And his Heart be rent in twain.
Forth shall flow an emanation
Forth shall spring a shape divine,
And if Sol and Cynthia and thee
Shall the charmed Key be thine.

II

In the solemn groves of Wisdom
Where black pines their shadows fling
Near the haunted cell of Hermes,
Three lovely flowrets spring:

The Violet damask tinted
In scent all flowers above:
The milk white vestal Lily
And the purple flower of Love.
Red Sol a sign shall give thee
Where the Sapphire Violets gleam,
Watered by the rills that wander
From the viewless golden stream:
One Violet shalt thou gather—
But ah—beware, beware!—
The Lily and the Amaranth
Demand thy chiefest care.

III

With in the lake of crystal,
Roseate as Sol's first ray
With eyes of diamond lustre,
A thousand fishes play
A net within that water
A net with web of gold
If cast where air bills glitter
One shining fish shall hold.

IV

Amid the oldest mountains
Whose tops are next the Sun,
The everlasting rivers
Through glowing channels run,
Those channels are of gold
And thence the countless treasures
Of the kings of earth are rolled.
But far—far must he wander
O'er realms and seas unknown
Who seeks the Ancient Mountains
Where shines the Wondrous Stone.[1]

---

[1] Le Dictionaire Mytho—Hermetique, states 'The Fountain found within the Garden', is the 'Mercury of the Wise', which comes from divers sources because it is the 'Principle' of the seven metals, and is formed by the influence of the seven planets, although the Sun alone is properly speaking the Father, and Luna, the Mother. The

You have already been taught two symbolic schemes for allotting the metals to the Sephiroth—each is capable of defence —for pointing out certain alliances and the alchemical relations of these Metals. I add here a scheme, of my own, for allotting to the Decad ten non-metallic lighter elements recognised by modern chemistry.

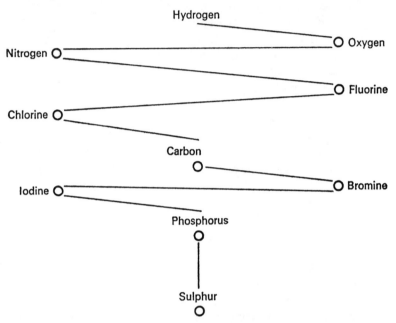

Binah=Nitrogen, always a Gas—very passive—neither supports life nor combustion.

Fluorine=a Gas—very active, almost intangible.

Chlorine=a Gas—yellow in colour like gold, acrid, caustic.

Dragon who three times drinks, is the putrefaction which overcomes the matter, and is so called from its black colour, and this Dragon loses his scales, or skin, when the Grey colour succeeds the Black. You will only succeed if Sol and Luna aid thee; by means of the regimen of Fire you must bleach the Grey colour to the Whiteness of the Moon (and then obtain the redness of Sol as the last stage). By the 'Fishes', is meant bubbles in the heated crucible. 'Lake' often means vase, retort, flask, alembic'. (Original Note.)

Bromine = heavier, baser, red liquid.

Iodine = a red copper and hermaphraditical Brass.

Carbon is Tiphereth, is the most notable non-metal—it combines with others, forming alliances with other elements of immense number—all vegetable and animal substances are compounds formed on Carbon as a Basis.

Phosphorous and Sulphur, represent Yesod and Malkuth, both solids, and complete the scale.

The analogies are very curious, and can be greatly extended. It *may* be possible also to rank the true metals along with the Sephiroth in the Chemical Order of their actual purity and as they the more nearly approach pure Basic Hyle, or the 'one matter', in addition to the G.D. Forms. The Sephiroth are progressive Emanations, each less exalted than the former, and they pass down plane after plane, and may be looked upon each as more material than the last. And in Assiah there may be scales alike of Metals, Metalloids, and other substances, in similar ratios. If such were the case, the Alchemical theory of successive steps of purification would in natural course transmute each metal into the one above. The Lead into Copper, the Copper into Silver, the Silver into Gold, the Gold into the Elixir Vitae, the gold of Vegetable and Animal life.

Alchemy taught that all metals consisted of the Mercury of the Philosophers and of a Sulphur, which *fixed* it—made it solid.

The Merc. Phil. was not the Quicksilver of commerce, not the Hydrogen of the modern Chemist—the one fluid metal.

Our Mercury they called Hydrardgyram,—Water of silver—fluid, silver-coloured. They thought it to be Silver in a state of 'low temperature fusion'—They also called it 'Proteus' = of diverse forms. The Alchemists found Gold to be extremely heavy, so they experimented chiefly with those other metals which were most heavy;—lead, quicksilver and copper, believing they must be nearest to Gold in order of steps of change, or that each heavy metal needed fewer processes for conversion, or less purification.

They argued—for example—Lead nearly resembles Gold in weight, therefore Lead consists almost entirely of Mercury Philosophorum and Gold. If a body be found, which will so work on the Lead, as to burn out of it all that is not Mercury Philos, and then we fix that Mercury by a Sulphur, we should obtain Gold as the result.

Relative weights of equal bulks are *about*: —

Gold 19
Mercury 14
Lead 11
Silver 10
Copper 9
Iron and Tin 7
Antimony 6
Arsenic 5

Many of the '*Elements*' so called from 1750 to 1800 have been since broken up, by analysis; notably Potash and Soda, which were shown to be compounds in 1807—by Davey. The Alchemist recognised three principal ways of making Gold.

First, by Separation; for many minerals contain some Gold.

Second, by Maturation, by processes designed to subtilise, purify, and digest Mercury; which convert it into a heavier body, and at last into Gold itself.

They looked on Mercury as an Alloy of Gold and Something: by processes of Fire, and by adding suitable material for combustion; the impurity was to be burned off and pure Gold to remain.

Thirdly, by fusing with base metals, some of that peculiar compound, the Stone of the Philosophers, a perfect transmutation was to occur, the faeces would be burned off, and the Metallic Root appear as Gold.

For example of Alchemical argument, I have read 'if we take 19 ounces of Lead and fuse it with a proper Agent, and so dissipate 8 ounces we shall have 11 ounces remaining, and this can be nothing but pure Gold, because Gold and Lead are as 19 to 11. Otherwise if the process be gradation, and we reduce 19 to 14 first, the result will be Mercury, but then the process may be continued and the further reduction to 11 will equally be Gold, as without the middle step'.

From another point of view, they said 'the Stone of the Philosopher's is a most subtle, fixed and concentrated fiery body which when it is added to a molten metal does, as if by a magnetic virtue, unit itself to the Mercurial body of the metal, vitalises and cleans off, all that is impure, and so there remains a molten mass of pure Sol.'

But as aforesaid,—I believe it is useless for any one to waste time on purely chemical experiments. To perform Alchemical processes, requires a simultaneous operation on the Astral plane with that on the physical. Unless you are Adept enough to act by Will power, as well as by heat and moisture; by life force, as well as by electricity, there will be no adequate result.

So far as I know,—I do not speak by order—power of transmutation may arise, side by side with other magical attainments —Labor omnia vincit. It is not conferred by any Grade—it is occasionally rediscovered by the private student: it is never actually taught in so many words. It may dawn on any one of you,—or the magic event may occur when least expected!

PART EIGHT

Christian Occultism

being
Hitherto Unpublished Papers of the Cromlech
Temple

On the whole the Flying Rolls and other instructional material produced by the schismatic fraternities derived from the Golden Dawn after that organisation had broken up in internecine disputes (*circa* 1900) are of little interest. Notable exceptions to the general mediocrity are the papers of the Cromlech Temple, a side order to *The Rosicrucian Order of the A.O.*—the name adopted after 1900 by those Temples loyal to MacGregor Mathers.

The membership of the Cromlech Temple consisted largely of dedicated Anglican clergymen, who seem to have found the Temple's brand of Christian Occultism much to their liking, and a Dean of Chester (who was also an initiate of the Stella Matutina) was a prominent member. In spite of the Temple's pretensions to Anglo-Catholic orthodoxy it is clear from the papers which follow that its Christianity was essentially Gnostic; the truth of the doctrine of reincarnation, for example, was taken for granted, in spite of its condemnation by a Council of the Church as early as the fifth century.

A certain confusion seems to have arisen between the Cromlech Temple and the Golden Dawn itself. Thus, in her article on the Golden Dawn published in Number 40 of *Man, Myth and Magic*, that distinguished Yeats scholar Kathleen Raine has written:

> Magic was indeed only one aspect of the work of the Golden Dawn.... Lectures and papers were circulated expounding the Catholic doctrines of the Apostolic Succession, the seven Sacraments, the Assumption and the Immaculate Conception of the Blessed Virgin, or teaching the three grades of prayer. None of these papers is included in Israel Regardie's four volume publication of the rituals; which gives in this respect, a one-sided impression.

All this is quite incorrect. The papers referred to, all of which are included in the following section of this book, were those of the Cromlech Temple, not those of the Golden Dawn—and, while a majority of Cromlech Temple initiates were also initiates of one or other of the fraternities derived from the Golden Dawn, the Cromlech Temple was a completely independent organisation. Details of its origin and development may be found in my *Ritual Magic in England* (Neville Spearman 1970).

Paper I
Received 18.4.24

To all my beloved companions of the Temple of the Cromlech, Greeting. We have watched you all with a great love throughout this time of pain and trouble and striving, and we commend your patience, hard indeed to attain when all are looking forward to the new life of service and advance.

Recall then all our teachings; that death must precede birth, old things must be broken up before the new things can be manifested. And so in yourselves must the same process take place, the breaking up of old ideals that the new ideals may be born and grow, the breaking up of the will, wherein is the self—that self, which though set to do the will of God, seeks to do it in the way of the lower self rather than in the way of the higher self, and long must it be ere the children of the earth can see that such efforts can only come to naught. Yet it is by the very failure of those efforts that they rise to the higher life. Not willingly doth the Supreme (Blessed be He) afflict His children, for in very love are all these failures set as stepping stones to Himself, and the only way to the final goal of Union with Him.

When this is realised, the heart is purging from the cloying of earth, and turned to a cup wherein to receive the wine of His Love. And in that prepared and spiritualised heart of man, all that comes, all that chances, may be as the varied substances put into the Crucible, out of which is to come the Pure Gold.

Ye have seen in our earlier teaching the World as a crucible —in which the Alchemic processes were proceeding in regular order. So now ye can look into the world of yourselves and see the same processes going on in the heart of each of you, pain and suffering, disappointment and mistakes all working to this ultimate end, and all good, when ye can see it with your spiritual eyes.

And now the Gold begins to be manifest, that which will in time turn all that is base to Gold. Yet think not that it will be apparent at once. The Fire must still work to bring all to

197

perfection. Yet not now the fire of sorrow and suffering, but the fire of love, and joy, and laughter known to those who are the Sons of God.

This year, that great symbol called the Fire of the World—the Sun, but called by us in truer phrase—the Sun of Righteousness, will arise with greater force than ever before since the coming of the Master. Therefore shall this year be known as 'The Year of the Risen Sun' to mark it out from all the rest. And ye Companions of the Sun will if ye set your minds and hearts to perceive it, receive the beams and the tenfold blessings they bring. Let not material thoughts like cloud-veils dim your sight. Look up and rise on the wings of Faith to that clearer air above the miasma of earthly things, and so shall ye be blessed indeed.

And for those who have passed on to a higher stage of work, never forget that they are still with you all, loving and working, and better able now that all material hindrances have been removed, to help and comfort you than ever before.

Well have ye all done, bravely have ye wrought and striven, and all your struggles and trials are known to us in ways that will be more clear to you when ye have learnt more of our teachings. 'If one member suffer, all the members suffer with it'. This is a scientific truth, explainable by our science, and gradually will ye learn it, and marvel at the love which binds us all together in bands that may not be broken. We bid you, as so often before, to rejoice and evermore to rejoice. For the great Master of all Masters is with us now in very word and truth, more closely than before, as we are growing able to receive His Light and Love.

Shemesh

Paper II
Easter Day 12.4.25

To all my dear Children and Companions of the Cromlech Temple—Greeting—and loving congratulations to you all—who each one, in his or her separate way, has striven to follow the command of the Master, and to rule and dominate that lower self which is the only curtain that veils Him from our sight.

In the Year of the Risen Sun now past, all were enabled to see more or less clearly those errors and imperfections, likes and dislikes, all that belongs to the narrow selfhood, and seeing more clearly in that Risen Sun, have desired to alter and change that which was barring the way and stopping the progress to the Higher Life. Hence, when the desire was born in the heart by the action of the intuition, has the clearing and purging process been begun in each. With some it has brought sorrow and bitter tears, with other bodily illness, with others a breaking up of outside circumstances, but with all there has been somewhat of the death that begins new life.

Look back, then, each one of you, to anything in the past year that has been akin to crucifixion, no matter how small, and rejoice that you have, even to a small extent, been following the Master and walking in His footsteps. For the divine law will work in each one of you, and after your crucifixion shall be a joyful resurrection, the greater the struggle and pain, the greater will be your joy and your own resurrection. Search your own hearts then, for the Holy Spirit will speak in each one of you without fail and without error. Having then, O my companions, been each one broken up and tested as ye were able to bear it, we come to a time of fresh life-effort, and the year shall be called 'The Year of New Beginnings', for the seed of a new life has been sown in each of you. See to it that it grow and bear fruit, for the Holy Spirit of God needs your co-operation, your desire, your imagination, your will. And remember, you who are attracted more to knowledge and the cultivation of brain power, that if ye see not in this also a development of character, a spiritual growth, it is empty and worthless. The desire to know more than your neighbours, to be more advanced, as it is said, is an evil thing, and will inevitably stop you, and finally, if yielded to, will draw you down, and you will come under the domination of an evil lower self whose power it will be difficult to escape from.

You are no teachers of each other, ye are fellow-students, fellow workmen, each for the good of all, each to be encouraged in his task, however humble, for all are working with the great Master Craftsman Himself.

We here do specially commend that little faithful Group in the City of Cromlech who have loyally worked in the best way to fulfil our behests, for all have been seeking unity with each other, and have been trying to overcome those fine and invisible, yet strong, barriers which the lower personality of each makes between souls who are very much at one on astral and spiritual planes. Verily brethren, this is the true advance, to try to look through the eyes of another, to feel with, for this is your first step in learning to Love. And when ye begin to love ye have joy—they cannot be separated.

So we send all our loving blessings, and may this Year of New Beginnings hold for you the best of all new things; the beginnings of Love and Joy in the heart of each one of you.

ShMSh.

Some teachings as to Post Mortem Conditions
For the First Five only

Some of you enquire mentally concerning the motives of the ancient Egyptians in mummifying the dead. The question could not then be answered—neither can it now be fully answered. But ye may know and bear in mind that a certain link usually remains between the freed spirit after death and its earthly surroundings. In the vast majority of cases the Spirit is not objectively conscious of this connection. Yet it feels a certain uneasiness at any sudden alteration of its former tenement.

The practical lesson of this highly occult teaching is that the survivors valuing the comfort of their departed friends should not suddenly nor hastily change the surroundings in which they lived, nor the things which they took pride in. For thereby unwittingly they may cause great discomfort, and pain to the spirit which is slowly, as it were, losing its hold on the things of the earth and is by no means parted suddenly from them when the breath leaves the body. Remember there are four Elemental Kingdoms and what we call physical death refers not to the Kingdoms of Air and Fire.

For those spirits now going through what is sometimes termed the cycle of Incarnations—the periods between two Incarnations are by far the most real and important parts of their existence —are in fact their true life. Those who teach that the Ego after an incarnation sleeps in Devachan, entertained by unreal illusions, or suffers in Avitchi—or wanders in Kama Loka—are in error, seeing only part of the truth—still more so are they who teach that the Soul's final and eternal destiny is fixed at the moment of death—for which there is no warrant in any revelation. For the truth is that in what ye earth dwellers term physical death the Ego returns to its full normal life, wherein indeed there is sleep, and dream, and suffering, and joy, yet these things are but part of its fullness.

To understand somewhat of the relation of an incarnation to the fuller and larger life—imagine a young lad who once or twice a week goes to a gymnasium or a drill hall. While there, the exercises he is engaged on take up the whole of his thought and energy, he is concentrated on horizontal bars, ladders and the like, and forgets everything else. Yet when he changes his gymnastic dress and leaves the gymnasium he resumes his real life, probably so much stronger and healthier for the keen exercise—yet, it may be, with a strain or bruise which will smart for days.

As it is the microcosm of the world, so it is in the macrocosm of the larger life. In the gymnasium there are but the pupils who are in the arena, and the instructors and such parents and guardians as may accompany them, but outside, in the more real life, are countless hosts of others, very many whose childish training is long over, and who are now training children themselves. Thus, in the discarnate life, the Ego meets multitudes of other spirits—some unknown to and unconnected with him, others who to him are in the position of parents and friends or guardians—with these he walks hand in hand, in loving converse, for the stress and striving of incarnation do not exist there and rebellion against wisdom and authority is unknown.

Yet note that these things in themselves are not evil—they form part of the gymnastic apparatus which ye call earthly life —and are hurtful only when an exercise is improperly done. Consider how the weight of a dumb-bell is a good thing—yet if the pupil lets it fall on himself its weight becomes a source of pain and trouble. As we have said, those going through the cycle of Incarnation are as small children—and their friends and guardians are close beside them.

These are not children themselves. As parents, friends and guardians on earth often accompany children to a gymnasium, assisting, advising, and watching over them—albeit it may be that the children lose sight of everything save the arena and its apparatus—so do these spiritual Guardians stand near those they watch over during Incarnation, albeit the strong development and vitalisation of material symbols in the Aura prevents the Ego from recognising (save fitfully and by vision or intuition) his beloved friend and guide of the larger life.

It is true that death is a very gradual process and that the separation of the consciousness from the material body is not accomplished all at once. But here then must we distinguish. The consciousness of pain and of discomfort is in the living body the resistance automatically established to that which infringes its law of existence. Now conservation of the form is the law of existence—whatever, then, tends to destroy the form is contrary to its law, and the automatic action of brain and nerve set up by Prana is termed pain.

But with physical death the law is reversed—dissolution of the form becomes law, and Prana is withdrawn, hence, though there is no doubt for some time a consciousness of the Physical Body—that consciousness desires its dissolution as much as in earth life it desires its conservation. The decay of the body is to the consciousness exactly as the sensation of its growing strength and vigour is to the youth or maiden—and the cause is the same viz. the fulfilment of law—sudden and abnormal development of strength is often painful and has been known to cause madness—because the law is slow development. So is cremation often painful in the West, because the law is slow decomposition. In the East it is different, for the law is much more rapid decomposition and much less consciousness of the body and its changes. In Egypt the case of mummification was different and arising out of the special circumstances of a nation of Adepts. Yet much pain was caused to the Astral thereby—voluntarily undergone for specific objects.

Burial at sea does not usually fulfil the law of the condition of death—yet in some cases it may. Perhaps of all forms burial in a cave—exposed to the air but protected by a stone from birds and beasts of prey—is in the most exact conformity with the laws of the condition—and thus was the Master buried, yet in death, as in life, the most perfect conditions are rarely attainable—expense and sanitary laws—the health and well being of survivors, and numberless other conditions prevent this.

A strong desire for one form of burial is mostly born of the mistaken view of post mortem consciousness, and of the non-recognition of the reversal of the law of the condition. If thou canst realise this reversal to thyself as did the Saints and Adepts who—as it were—practised death—thou wilt see more clearly what thou really desirest. Only beware of one marked danger. Those who practice this, very commonly get a delusive intuition of the time and manner of their own death—very few are allowed to know this—and those must be of an advance far higher than thine.... Beware that, though believe it not! For there be those who believing such delusive intuitions have brought about their deaths before the purpose of God had decreed them.

This is a species of astral suicide and very painful are the results thereof. Practice not much, then, this formula; only, when thou thinkest of death and burial—realise that thou wilt then desire gradual decomposition—as thou now desirest regaining of health and strength and that the decomposition—in the grave, the air, or the water, will not appear loathsome as it does when contrary to law—but lovely because in conformity thereto.

The Consciousness after death depends on the state of the Astral body here. In some cases it is weak and weary from its earthly pilgrimage here and requires a long sleep—in other cases it has periods of probation to undergo—or of purgation —but there are cases where the Astral enters at once on a career of help to those on earth—and to those also on its own astral plane.

Those of the grade of our beloved Frater ShMSh and myself are associated with many helpers on the astral—some of whom worked with us in life—and after death with scarcely a break continued to work on the astral plane—their relation to us being only slightly changed.

The Devotion of the Quipus[1]
Second Grade

It is well to recite this (at least the Key sentences) standing with the Arms extended in the form of a Cross. But to avoid fatigue—which is not desirable—stand with the back to a shelf

[1] The Quipus was a cord of seven strands which the initiates of the Cromlech Temple wore around their right arms. (Editorial Note.)

of convenient height—or put two stout pegs in the wall to support the arms—or put two loops of rope at a convenient height—or any other support that is convenient.

Do this occasionally only—the position itself—being that of the Master in the act of Expiation for the whole Order which he founded, is a most powerful symbol against evil or opposing forces.

Brethren for a long time now ye have worn the Sacred Quipus of our Holy Order, yet the deep and profound teaching and symbolism therefore have been hidden from you. It is time now that ye should learn some of the more elementary lessons thereof, that the Quipus may become to you a veritable guide, symbol and synthesis of truth and not a mere incomprehensible fetish.

Seven are its strands, and they are of different colours selected (but not as ye might suppose arbitrarily) from the spectrum, whereunto the rays of Our Lord the Sun are decomposed on passing through the triangular prism which is the symbol of the Fratrix through whom the pure white light must reach Frater Shemesh who passeth it on in the form of Love to the Outer Companions and thence to all the world.

Many are the scales of colour and almost infinite is colour symbology. That which is used in the lower grades of our Order, and which has been partially revealed to you, is that which is known as the Sacramental Scale, of which the mysteries will now be somewhat further shown.

Take the Quipus and lay it on the table before you. The central thread directed towards you. Next to it on the left hand the red, then the yellow, and then the blue, on the other side the orange, green and purple.

Now according to the Sacramental Scale the colours on the left hand represent the Supernal, those on the right the terrestrial. 'There are three that bear witness in Heaven, the Word and the Holy Ghost and these Three are One. And there are Three that bear record on Earth, the Spirit and the Water and the Blood, and these three agree in One'. And note that the One here is the White thread wherein all are included. The same was also the symbolism of the seven branched candlestick, as will be more fully shown later on.

But consider now the Blue Strand, the Ray of Power, the Father, Blue is also the colour of Water, but here of the 'Waters which be above the Firmament' viz. to our gross material senses, the Blue Sky. Its position at the outside of the group shows that here, by this gate, the Neophyte enters to the sanctuary at his first initiation, i.e. the purification by water. Hence in all Rituals is this purification by water the initial step, and thus in the rites of the Christian Church, wherein the form of the ancient mysteries is preserved, the first initiation is represented by Baptism.

In every form of the true mysteries it was taught that at the first initiation the Great Name of God entered into and united with the life of the Neophyte, forming a talisman invisible to every eye save that of the Adept, which saved him in the hour of need, helped, taught and comforted him through his life. Further teachings and other initiations taught him how to increase the power of this Name, how to recover it if lost, how to unite his own soul with it, and this last by lending his own soul to the constant adoration of the Great Name, till the Soul became absorbed therein. The utterance of the Soul expressing this is some form of the ejaculation 'Hallowed be thy Name', and in using it the Neophyte must regard the Name as the object of Supreme Worship in the innermost shrine of his heart, by the true hallowing of which, in constant adoration he shall attain unto his genius and become more than human.

Such then is the teaching of the Blue Thread. Learn to connect the following ideas:

Spirit of the Blue Ray
Spirit of Power.
  The Father
The Water above the Firmament.
  The Blue Sky.
The Purification by Water
  The First Initiation.
  Baptism in the Christian Scheme.
The Great Name of God thereby entering into the Neophyte.

His talisman unseen.

The Path to union with his genius.

The Hallowing and Adoration of the Great Name.

The Petition of Ejaculation—

'Hallowed be Thy Name'.

Consider next the Red Ray of the Quipus, the Ray of Love, the Son.

Red is the colour of earth, of Adamah, but here it is not the dull red of material separateness and of sin, but the triumphal red of heaven, the Royal Robe of the Monarch of the Kingdom of Love which is the Kingdom of Heaven.

When our Lord the Sun is transfigured in glory at his rising or setting and maketh to himself a royal robe from the Aura of the Earth the hue of it is red, the red of Love, with the scintillating orange and amber of the Wisdom of the Spirit. Thus when the Kingdom of Heaven is established in the heart of a man, the earthly red clay of Adamah is transmuted to the infinite Ocean of Divine Love, the lustrous red of Heaven, by virtue of the Mystery of the Atonement. The red then typifieth the Atonement, the establishment of the Kingdom of Love in the Heart of Mortal Man. How then shall this Kingdom be established? No man can of himself attain thereto. The Masters and guides, unseen yet verily present, acting under the Master of Masters must draw him. And these act upon the ordinary man through the ministrations of the Higher Adepts who work by the magical powers conferred on them. Hence the Supreme Initiation is the note which marks the establishment of the Kingdom. In the Christian Church this Supreme Initiation is signified by the ordination of the Priesthood, symbolically passing down the magic gifts received from the mighty Master of Masters, and hence is Holy Orders the Analogue of the Red Ray in the Christian scheme.

The command of the Master 'Go ye, and teach all nations' bids them exercise the Kingly function in bringing the world to acknowledge His rule, thence is Red the Ray at once of Love and of Kingly power. Hence also the Neophyte ejaculates Thy Kingdom Come'. Learn then to connect the following ideas.

Spirit of the Red Ray.

Spirit of Love.

  The Sun.

The Fire, the prismatic Red,

  The Grand Initiation.

Holy Orders in the Christian Church.

The establishment of the Kingdom of Love.

The ejaculation 'Thy Kingdom Come'.

Now look to the yellow thread of the Quipus. The Ray of Wisdom, the Holy Spirit. Yellow is the colour of Air, between Earth and the Firmament of Heaven vibrateth the Air, and the more inward and subtle mood thereof, the Ether, which conveyeth unto men the pulsations of Light, the pulsations of sound, whereby the messengers of the power of the Father are transmitted to the Divine Spark incarnate in man, to that composite Being which uniteth the prismatic red Ray of Heavenly Love with the dull red clay of Adamah, until, both being fused together and heated to a loving glow in the Power of the Atonement, they respond like a perfect instrument to the vibrations of the Amber Light from the Central Spiritual Sun, the Light of Wisdom guiding the Divine Love whose uniting rosy and golden rays herald the rising of Adonai, of Mithra the Lord of Wide Pastures in the radiant hues of the morning, which the ancient mysteries symbolised among much else of the profoundest mysteries of earth under the form of a Rose, and a gleam of whose marvellous teaching one of your own poets hath set forth in the line—'God made himself an awful Rose of Dawn'. Awful indeed, and when you know all the meanings of the Rose and the Dawn, and can go forth and learn without mistake or error the Lesson of the Morning, then shall you appreciate the full force of that line, and of the teaching of the Mystery of the Ages.

The Air or the Ether then, bringeth to man the message of the will of the Father, perfectly performed in the Blue, hindered and intercepted and limited in the Adamah, not through the aid, as transmitters, of the the Great Initiates, or in the Christian Church through the magic power of the priesthood. Not to all, but to a few is this magic power given, but to all under that, the Yellow Ray, the Air Spirits bring the mystery of the Father's Will.

Hence it is properly significant of the Second Initiation, which is universal in the Ancient Mysteries and is but the completion and crown of the first. In the Christian Church this is signified by Confirmation which completes and crowns the work of Holy Baptism.

Consider now, how each man within himself hath all these, for as in the macrocosm so it is in the microcosm. The Blue Ray belongeth to the intellect which is of power and is the Godlike directing force of the material man. The Red Ray belongeth to the affections which inspire and move the exercise of Power and the Yellow Ray proceeding from both, as the Holy Spirit proceedeth from the Father and the Son, and vibrating between them belongeth unto the Will animated by Love, to emulate the angels who in Heaven do the will of the Father. Hence then comes the ejaculation 'Thy will be done on Earth as it is in Heaven'. It will be seen how these three prismatic rays bring us into contact with the Heavenly Trinity—Pure and Transient out of the White Ray they emerge and into the White Ray they retire again.

Rightly do we rank them, as we consider the threads in the familiar order, Father, Son and Spirit. Yet rightly too do we lay them in order. Blue, Yellow, Red, for the Yellow the Spirit, ever vibrateth between the Power and the Love, carrying and executing the will, yet the Divine Love can only consummate the Atonement. Learn then, to connect the following ideas: —

Spirit of the Yellow Ray.
The Holy Spirit the Paraclete.
The Tongues of Fire at Pentecost wherein the Gold of the Spirit bore the Red of Love.
The Amber Light of Dawn.
The Completion of the First Initiation
Confirmation in the Christian Church. The will of God thereby done.
The Great Transmuting Medium.

Hence the Vehicle of the Atonement.

The Ejaculation—'Thy Will be done on Earth as it is in Heaven'.

Passing now over the White Thread as the synthesis of the central point and consummation of the Devotion shall be dealt with last consider next the Orange Thread.

In the Veil this Orange colour signifies Intellectual Wisdom, being compounded of their Divine functions. Wisdom judges austerely and righteously, Love embraces, being blind to offences. Love guided by Wisdom sees as God sees, and judging lovingly forgives. It must be that offences come. While the lower aspects of the Orange Ray present the snare of the Human intellect, the higher aspects show the pardon of God. But on the part of the person pardoned certain acts are necessary. First a token of regret for the injury wrought. Second an acknowledgement of the full extent of the injury, thirdly a willingness to repair it. On such terms is the forgiveness of God offered to us, and on such terms should we pardon our brother men, not with love only, but with wisdom and love. Hence the Orange or Flame colour was the robe of the priests in the ancient mysteries when declaring the acception of the purified candidate, his pardon in fact. Hence on the Day of Pentecost the commission was given to the Apostles by the cloven tongues in allusion to the Creative Word, and flame colour in allusion to the commission to pardon, the commission of the Spirit of Wisdom and Love, or of Loving Wisdom. Hence the ejaculation 'Forgive us our trespasses as we forgive them that trespass against us'. And on account of the condition in which this pardon is granted the Christian Church has united this power and this ejaculation with Penance, in which word are summed up the three acts above noted as necessary to make the pardon effectual. Mistake not Brethren and let no one mislead you here, the Christian Church follows the teachings of the ancient mysteries, and though the Priest has a certain magical power, it is in respect of Penance very slight, and he who claims more is acting contrary to the teaching of his Church. The Pardon comes from the Father through the Son, the Master of Masters. The condition to make it effectual must be produced by the penitent in himself, and consists of the above noted three-fold Penance. The function of the Priests is but to direct the penitent how to produce such condition of penance in himself, and, being sure that it is produced, to comfort him with the assurance that the Master pardons him. There are Protestant sects whose ministers take upon themselves to make enquiry into the hearts of their members and to pronounce Absolutions such as the wildest exaggeration of Priestly Authority has hardly attained to, but of these we do not speak, they are of man's invention, and shall fail accordingly.

Learn then to connect the following ideas:
Spirit of the Orange Ray.
    Orange cords of the Veil.
The tongues of Fire of Pentecost, Yellow and Red.
The Wisdom guided by Love.
    Seeing as God Sees.
    All pardoning and all wise.
Pardon on condition of penance.
Threefold penance in the Christian Church.
The ejaculation: 'Forgive us our trespasses as we forgive them that trespass against us'.

Consider next the Green Thread formed by the union of the Blue of Power with the Yellow which is the Wisdom of the Spirit, the Yellow which is the symbol of Air or Ether vibrating between Earth and Heaven and carrying the messages of the Father to man on Earth. Messages thus carried are teachings, and thence in the Mystery of the Veil you were told that Green was the colour of Doctrine and of Testimony, for it beareth witness. The message being brought to man is a witness of the Power that sends it, and hence again is the green robe of vegetation wherein the Earth is clad in spring, a witness of the life-giving power proceeding from the Blue sky and borne upon the Golden Light.

In this life of the Earth generation, maturity, decay, and renovation proceed without effort, without separateness, without sin. This is the great teaching of the perfect innocence of the processes of Nature, the standing condemnation of the false and morbid asceticism invented by man, which professing to lead to superior goodness more often actually results in sorcery and Black Magic. In all great Occult Schools of the World hath provision been made for this great and most essential teaching. And hence in those races which have most clearly followed the occult symbology of colour, Green is to this day the colour of marriage. In the Christian Church marriage is expressly stated to be for a remedy against sin, and is elevated to the dignity of a sacrament, as being a figure of the Mystic Union between Christ and His Church. To the Green Thread then and to the Sacrament of Marriage most fitly belongs the ejaculation 'Lead us not into Temptation'.

Tried we must be, when we are fit, yet we would not rush to meet the testing unprepared and unfit. The time will come to all of us when we shall be called to pass to the ascetic life, yet it is only the highest and purest of mortals who are called to this test. Of the College from whom these teachings emanate not all have yet been called upon to face it, many have rashly demanded to do so before the time, and almost without exception have fallen and failed and grievously delayed their progress. Pray then that ye be not exposed to trial until fit to bear it. Seek no trial rashly trusting in your own strength, lean on the Masters and be ready to face all trials when called on by them. The Christian Church which has mainly the correct symbology of colours still rightly uses green at all seasons where abstract teaching rather than commemoration is ordained. Learn then to connect the following ideas: —

The Green Thread.
The Spirit of Doctrine and Testimony.
The Message of the Father borne by the Spirit of the Air.
The Fertility of the Earth.
Sinless generation.
The Christian Sacrament of Matrimony.
The Ejaculation 'Lead us not into temptation'.
The Green colour used in the Christian Church.

Look now at the Purple Thread. In the curtains that hang behind our Altar, as in the curtains of the Tabernacle in the wilderness, this is the great mediatorial colour which unites the Red of Earthly Love with the Blue of the Power of the Father, typical, therefore, of the incarnation and of that Death of the Son which was the gate of a new life to all mortals who follow His footsteps. This Death, and new Life also, was taught to the Initiates in the Mysteries of the Old World and is now opened to the knowledge (but not the comprehension) of all.

Because it is the colour of the Incarnation and of all the suffering and the Death belonging thereto, Purple is appropriately used as the colour of mourning, of fasting, and humiliation in the Christian Church. This Church, watching and following all the life of her children from the cradle to the grave, blesses their last moments according to the holy custom of the Apostles in the Sacrament of Extreme Unction.

Here rightly do we ejaculate—'Deliver us from evil', or more properly 'from the Evil One'. Thus the parting soul is speeded and guided on its journey through the Valley of the Shadow of Death, till, in the language of the Alchemist, from the blood of the Black Dragon ariseth the Green Lion soon to be transmuted, by the Power of the King and of the Bride, to the Pure and Living Gold.

Learn then to connect the following ideas:

The Purple Thread.
The Mediatorial Colour.
The Purple Robe thrown in mockery over Christ.
The colour of Mourning and of Death.
The Christian Sacrament of Unction.
The Ejaculation 'Deliver us from the Evil One'.
Death the Gate of Life.

Observe now that as the first three colours brought us in contact with the Divine Three Persons, so do these last three show us their work on Earth, being called secondary colours, and note also that they are secondary in the blending of pigments and not in the blending of Rays, for if you superimpose the

Yellow Ray on the Blue it maketh not Green, showing that the Earthly nature, typified by the pigments of Earth, must be properly prepared and harmonised in order to obtain the operation of the Divine Spirits of the Holy Rays thereon.

All these colours lead up to and concentrate in the central White Thread, the Great Three in one of Purity Sublime. It is impossible here to enter into its complete symbolism, for it is the synthesis and key of all.

In the Christian Church it is typified by the Holy Eucharist and it naturally leads to the central Ejaculatory Prayer 'Give us this day our daily bread'. Bread here meaning everything necessary for bodily as well as Spiritual Health and Life.

Such, Brethren, are the Elementary Meanings of the Seven Strands of the Quipus, and of the Seven Sacraments of the Christian Church according to the Sacramental Scale. They have their relation also to the Seven Lower Sephiroth on the Qabalistic Tree of Life, and the Qabalistic Sign of the Cross, as it was in use among the Hebrews of Old, concludes the Prayer of the Master.

This symbolism of colour was in use among the Incas of Peru and in the Temples of Mexico, and by its aid, even now, if you obtain a correct representation of Temple or Shrine you may learn much of their mysteries.

Ye should then constantly, or as often as may be, place the Quipus before you and go over the Summary of the ideas as herein before expressed, placing a finger meanwhile on each thread, and finishing each meditation by repeating the Ejaculation aloud, speaking as it were in the breath, monotonously slowly and dwelling with distinct outbreathing upon the vowels.

When all the ideas have become so knit in the mind that any one naturally, and without effort, recalls the others, it is no longer necessary to use the Quipus always, a series of coloured beads on a string, touching each one as you repeat its appropriate ejaculation, is commonly used in the Order and serves well; some use a model of a Rose of Seven Petals, which may be made of silk or coloured paper.

Above all things in this exercise, as in everything occult, we must earnestly beseech you to cultivate the greatest possible exactness. Every word should be accurately learned, every symbol accurately drawn, every colour brilliant and pure. It is a favourite device of the Adversary to hinder the Student by suggesting that it is sufficient to get only the sense or the general idea, that is the Spirit that matters. Observe that this is the spirit which denyeth the Incarnation, for the material form encloseth the Divine Spirit and the Two (not the one alone) are One Christ.

In all occult matters, then Brethren, let all your learning be exact, allow not a single mistake. So will you progress and be conscious of your progress, not otherwise. We who address you have trod the path ye are now treading. We have seen our comrades fall and fail from the very faults of which we warn you. Under the Shadow of the Wings of I H V H rest ye ever.

Farewell.

Shemesh.

Second Grade

The Eagle

Lecture on the Introductory Knowledge of the Second Grade.

The element of this grade is Air.

The Kerubic Sign is the Eagle, and it is under the patronage of St. John the Beloved Disciple of the Master. In the Gospel of St. John, therefore, may be found much of the learning appropriate thereto.

The special number is that of the Hebrew letter Shin, or 21.[2] Seek ye then in the 21st Chapter of St. John's Gospel and ye shall learn how the Master shows Himself to His Disciples, and thereby also ye shall learn how the Master shows Himself to each man who has purified his heart to receive Him.

And here also ye shall learn to interpret many things in our ritual, otherwise dark and incomprehensible. A few of the secrets of this interpretation we will unfold. Others will be told you later and some may be divined by your intuition. Consider first to whom He was shown. 'There were together Simon Peter, and Thomas called Didymus, Nathaniel of Cana in Galilee and the sons of Zebedee and two other of his Disciples'.

Observe that there were seven, answering to the Seven Principles of Man, and the other Seven whereof ye have been taught. Observe also that of these seven, five only are named, the two others are hidden. As in our ritual there are Five Companions, Priests of the Order, with whom two Invisible, yet present, Masters make up the Seven.

Observe also that they are named from the lowest upwards, and that Simon Peter therefore represents Sthula Sharira, the lowest and most material, as is shown by his name meaning a Stone, or the Syriac Cephas, also meaning a stone, but of a different character. A stone being the emblem of all that is dead

[2] This is not the Qabalistic number of the letter Shin (which is 300), but that of the Tarot trump corresponding to the Path of Shin on the Qabalistic Tree of Life. (Editorial Note.)

and inanimate—yet in another sense it is the Stone of the Wise —the Rock whereon the Church of the Master is built, and it is further the Flint of the Mysterium Magnum of Paracelsus wherein lyeth fire, and hence it corresponds also with our Frater Shemesh, whose symbol denoteth fire and heat, and the red of whose stole shows the fire of Love, the first Key to the Mysteries. Meditate on these things, Brethren, and on these correspondences. Equally appropriate are the names of the other Disciples and the correspondences therewith, but of these we speak not now. Love is the first Key, therefore we express this at present.

Observe also, that all Seven were together, and learn from this that only when all the Seven Principles in each man are in thorough accord can the Master be manifested to him. Only when a group of occult students are working harmoniously together can that group advance, and hence until such an harmonious group is at least potentially formed the higher messages of the Master cannot be delivered. Now to such a group 'Simon Peter said I go fishing'. The material body, the Sthula Sharira, desired the Ichthus the Christ—whose meaning has been shown you in this grade. And not until such a desire is present in a such body is such a manifestation possible.

Again it is Love which suggests the search for the Ichthus. The Stone of the Wise thus operates the change whereby in fullness of time the Divine Light shall dawn.

But immediately the Word goes forth from the material Love, all the Principles unite to carry it out. 'They say unto Him we also go with Thee'. Hence in the initiation of this Second Grade it is Frater Shemesh who craves admission in the name of the rest.

Observe now further what they do. 'They went forth and entered into a Ship immediately'. This ship as ye have been taught is symbolic of the Golden Ark and means the same. In the same way did Noah enter into the Ark, in the same way was the infant Moses laid in the Ark, and both emerged to higher and nobler life. Thus too does the Life principle enter into the Womb and emerge to complete human life, and in the same great symbol lies hidden all the mystery of regeneration.

This Universe is but the first step. Note that Love in the

material body must take the iniative, then all uniting must enter into the Golden Ark which is the mystery of the Covenant of God with Man.

And thus the seed is shown, the process of Generation of a New Life commenced, but not as yet is the fruition. Forty days was Noah in the Ark amid the waste of waters. Moses passed a long period of seclusion and study before his mission was announced. The child in the Womb is matured into human form and life through a period of darkness and of silence. The seed lies dark and silent in the earth before its time of germination comes.

It was night when the Seven entered into the Ship 'and that night they caught nothing'. Notice now especially the manner in which this first manifestation of the Master is made and the time. It was 'when the morning was come' in the light of the Dawn, and when our Lord of the Sun was risen on the Earth— the Seven were still in the ship—that is the new life had not yet attained to separate incarnate existence—the new body was not yet born. And the Master 'stood on the shore'—He was perfectly incarnate—He had descended into matter. The body of the New Association in which hereafter He was to be manifested was yet in embryo—still in the Ship or in the womb—surrounded by the Waters—unborn. And they knew him not—yet He spoke to them.

Learn from this that before ye can know the Master He will speak to you as He speaks constantly to everyone. Sometimes by the Beth Kol, sometimes by the thought-flash, sometimes through the voice of a material human being. Watch therefore and be ready to listen for His voice though Himself ye may not know.

'So he said to them "Children have ye any meat?"' They were seeking material food—in parable also they were the perfect man—the seven principles in harmony seeking the Ichtus, the Christ—and they had not found what they sought.

The Voice of the Master now gives them directions how to seek. 'Cast the net on the right side of the ship'. Many are the meanings involved in this direction which will gradually be unfolded to you. Meantime note that the Ichthus, the Christ giveth no benefit to mortal men till enclosed, limited or brought within their sphere by their own actions and that the nature of this action must be dictated by the Master, those who profess to serve the Master by doing so in their own way cannot take the Ichthus to themselves. They toil all night and take nothing.

Observe too that the casters of the net would stand with their faces to the prow which was pointed to shore and facing the Master who stood on the shore—the right side of the ship would therefore be their right and the action of obedience in casting would be the second sign of this grade, which therefore also signified 'obedience'.

Thus far then, Brethren, ye see that before ye can recognise the Master three things are needed.

First, harmony of all the principles, whence ariseth the prompting of love to desire the Ichthus, the Christ, the Spiritual food.

Second, patience, whereby after Love has sown the seed, and the Seven Principles have retired into the darkness of night and the ark during the period of incubation, the seed is matured.

Third, obedience, whereby although ye may not yourselves recognise the Master yet ye believe and cheerfully perform the behest of the Voice ye hear.

Strive then to follow out this process accurately in yourselves, if ye would see and speak with the Master face to face. Note then, that he who recognises the Master is the Disciple whom the Master loved. That is according to common speech, in each individual man is his higher self. And to no other doth He declare it—except to Simon Peter. Not to the intellect, not to the emotions, but to the material corporal body on this Earth plane, to the pure Spiritual Love which is its correspondence on the higher plane. That disciple said 'It is the Lord'.

So to the initiate man, when the process of his regeneration is about to take place, the Higher Self will suddenly reveal to the lower material body that the voice from the shore, the material voice which has given good and wise counsel whose source was not perceived before, is the Voice of the Master.

Now observe the action of the body when this great intuitive knowledge is given, 'When Simon Peter heard that it was the

Lord he girt his fishers coat unto him'.

Therefore is it in this second Grade of the Companionship that ye, who have as a group recognised the Master by confessing the Faith of our Lord and Saviour Jesus Christ, do gird to you symbolically the Fishers Coat, thereby asserting that ye will follow St. Peter in asserting boldly before men without equivocation or reservation the faith of Christ.

He also cast himself into the sea—the waters of putrefaction —the lustral water of Regeneration—the holy water of Baptism, showing that the shtula sharira, the material flesh and blood, first emergeth from the ark which is the Womb of the new birth. Despise not then, Brethren, the body, for it shall see the Lord, when it is purified and all the principles shall worship Him, but the material body first.

The other disciples however came in a little ship. Whence ye are to learn that during this material life the supersensual principles of man, all, that is, which lie beyond the body or house of flesh are not yet born into outward objective life, but can lie, so to speak, in the womb. Yet as the child in the womb can be influenced, modified and developed so is it possible to work, change, transmute and purify in the mental, moral and spiritual nature.

For understand that Peter stood with the Lord on the shore, and the others were still coming towards land in their boat, in obedience to the Master's Voice. Hence ye may learn how to purify the inner man, the imagination, the thought, the desire, by appropriate ceremonies. And all the ceremonies of this grade are based on the true understanding of this great ceremony, when the Master Himself, the first Dictys, initiated the first supreme group.

Now whereas the Group had been in the Boat, now did the group come to land, or in other words, all the principles were able to function on the material plane and the incarnation became completely perfect.

So then when by Harmony, Patience and Obedience, ye recognise the Master, the Voice of the Higher Self by Divine Intuition reveals the Mystery to the material body, and the **material body thereupon emerging in the new Birth purifies** itself in the Lustral water of Creation.

Then by the following of the other principles into incarnation may the Christ within be made manifest and the true Adeptus brought forth. There are mysteries in connection with the distance of the ship from land (200 cubits) and the number of fishes (153) in the net which shall be unfolded in the further ceremonies and teachings of this grade, as also will the nature of the communications made after the disciples were on the shore, signifying the teaching given by the Master to him who has purified his heart sufficiently to receive them. These things however belong to further and higher teachings.

Having learnt, then, how the Master shows himself to each man and how each may expect to receive communications, it remaineth to show you the practical working thereof. And know that as there are hierarchies of angels charged with the office of ministering to humanity, and below these again many elemental spirits of mixed nature, partly good and partly evil, all of which may be controlled and put into subjection by man. So hereafter ye shall be taught their names and nature and how they may be summoned and made to appear so that ye shall be able to call those most fit for the work on which you are all engaged and compel their assistance. At present however ye must learn to use a simple and elementary formula, that ye may become accustomed to the commanding of the ministering Spirits and may learn their efficiency.

Let us suppose that the disciple hath discovered in his material body some thing which is unharmonious—some breach of the law, some imperfection he desires to cure. Thus shall he proceed. First let him carefully seek in the realm of thought or imagination for the seed of the evil. Perchance it may be over indulgence in meat or drink, or it may be uncontrollable violence or irritability of temper. Impurity of thought or deed, or carelessness, idleness or self-indulgence. Whatever it may be, let him raise his thoughts out of himself. Look down on himself as a stranger, and see himself persecuted by an evil spirit. Let him imagine the personality of this spirit, clothing it with all its filthy hatefulness in God's sight—and extenuating nothing. Let him contemplate the image so raised and reflect that he, the Divine

Man, made in the image of God, does in his thought world, whereof he is Sultan and Supreme, caress and hug to his bosom a filthy swine, by the influence of his own weakness and permits it to trouble and possess him.

He must give some time to the realisation of an outward form for the trouble he desires to purge from his body, for it is the vagueness and intangibility which gives these foul spirits their power over men. Like the cuttle fish they surround themselves with a dark cloud of their own secretion. But the Adept must force them to at least visibility to the clairvoyant, that they may be dealt with and repelled.

Now must the material body like Simon Peter seek the Master of Masters, casting himself into the sea, and thus must he do it.

First, choose a time when not assailed by temptation, when calm and resolute (otherwise the ceremony will bind up the evil thing in thine own aura where it will torment thee).

Second, retire to a place where thou canst be absolutely secure from interruption. If thou hast an occult room or oratory it is better, but any secluded place will serve. It imitates the isolation of the disciples entering the ship or Ark.

Third, cast from thy mind all thought of worldly anxiety or passion, all irritability, all love and hate or annoyance, and endeavour to harmonise all thy principles.

Fourth, realise that if the night seem long and the answer be delayed, thou wilt exercise patience till the dawn.

Fifth, resolve an absolute obedience to the Divine Will in all things.

Note: though this takes long to describe it is the work of a few moments only to properly pose the mind. If from a disturbed mental state the harmonious pose and calmness be hard to get, it is better to put off the operation for the time is inappropriate.

Sixth, stand in the centre of the room facing East, make the sign of the Cross from brow to breast and from left shoulder to right, with the right hand saying 'In the name of the Father and of the Son and of the Holy Spirit', clasp thy hands and say Amen.

Seventh, trace with the right hand in the Air before thee a Cross keeping the hand extended, call on the name of the Lord

Jesus. Pronouncing the Most Holy Name as it were whispered in the breath, and lingering on the syllables, bowing the head as you do so.

Eighth, keeping the hand extended turn to the South and do likewise.

Ninth, the same to the West.

Tenth, the same to the North.

Eleventh, bring the hand round again to the East so as to complete the circle.

Twelfth, standing in the midst of the circle so formed, picture to thyself that a great ring of Shining Ones is formed around thee, and so facing the East, clasp the hands, raise the eyes to a point slightly above the head and say 'Lord Jesus, now verily on this earth, who hast conquered all forces of matter, add thy force to mine that this evil thing may be expelled, and let the Guardian ring of Holy Angels protect me now and evermore'.

Thirteenth, close the eyes and breathe as deeply as possible three or four times in the fourfold rhythm, then, holding the breath, pronounce mentally the name of the Lord Jesus three times and raise mentally as clearly as thou canst the picture of the Guardian Circle of the Shining Ones under the Presidency of the Master of Masters, and of the hideous personification of that which thou desirest to expel shut without the circle and still striving to enter.

Fourteenth, close with the sign of the Cross as in the beginning.

Fifteenth, in turning away from the East be careful to turn to the right hand by the South, the path of the Sun.

Note—it is well thou shouldst know the operation of this ceremony though its full meaning can only be told later. In fact thou dost put forth and project from thyself a certain ray of power of which the nature is to attract from the Astral Light[3] a similar force and the concurrence of the two formeth a vortex attracting and compelling the Guardian Spirits of a high and pure nature.

[3] 'Astral' is used here in Eliphas Levi's sense of all planes above the physical, not the Theosophical sense. (Editorial Note.)

But seeing thou knowest not yet their nature and disposition and mightest ignorantly call on those prejudicial to thy work in hand, or actually evil in operation, so must thou as yet entrust this whole matter to the Master of Masters.

If the spirit thou desirest to cast out assail thee at any special place or time, there and then shalt thou face the East and tracing the Cross in the Air shall pronounce the Master's Name and recall the protective circle.

Know that the initial force is taken from thyself and marvel not though after the ceremony thou feel tired—thou has formed an Astral fence. Lie down then and rest if need be in calm reliance on Divine Protection.

Expect not that immediate and perfect success will crown thy efforts. The Astral forces of evil will beat against thy fence and may break it down, for they are strong and thou art weak as yet.

But learn perseverance and, so often as the evil thing finds admittance, as soon as may be repeat—recover the proper pose of mind and repeat the ceremony. Striving to put forth more force and to repair the broken fence. At each attempt thy powers will increase and the powers of evil be depleted.

But give heed that thou work not the ceremony for any but thyself at present, for thou art not yet strong enough and mightest do mischief to thyself and to that other also.

There be further ceremonies of great importance and power belonging to this grade. Such are the consecration of the Golden Ark, and the Mystic devotion of the Quipus. Also the investing of the newly initiated brethren with the insignia pertaining thereto.

Eagle M.S. and the Purpose and Goal of Development

The Ceremony given at the end of the Eagle M.S. is merely a carefully designed and elaborate formula for the same end as every Christian's daily acts of prayer and penance. The difference in degree if the former be performed with earnestness and Faith, is very great—the difference in character and intention, if the latter be genuine and not mere formal repetition—is nil.

Our experience is that when a Companion of Our Order having attained the Second Grade has once performed the Ceremony in the Eagle M.S. with power and effect—his daily prayers—his confessions—his penances—thereafter all bear the glow of reflection from that Ceremony and are immeasurably increased in faith and earnestness—in other words he becomes a more real and devout Christian.

To establish closer and more personal relations with the Lord Jesus, the Master of Masters, is, and ever must be, the ultimate object of all the teachings of Our Order. Many are admitted to the First Grade who know Him not—and follow Him not. If they diligently keep our rules and follow our teachings their prejudices must break down—their ignorance is dissolved—insensibly they are led to the Master's feet.

They who know Him by the teachings of their pastors and masters—and their parents—who have never doubted—but never realised Him, are brought to know Him. Every bit of teaching we give is derived from Him—the powers we teach our disciples to use are bestowed by Him according to His promise. Only the doubting, the hesitating, the timid, fail to realise how completely Our Order emanates from Him and leads to Him. Closer and personal relation with Him is indeed our object and there is no other. Let all disciples cast off doubt—tread boldly in the way we have trodden and we will lead them to Him even as Philip led Nathaniel.

Teachings on the Church
Apostolic Succession

There is most undoubtedly an Apostolic Succession by the laying on of hands in all Three Branches of the Holy Catholic Church—viz. the Roman, the Greek and the Anglican. The Exoteric doctrine and the historic evidence with regard to the Anglican Church is well set forth in a work by Arthur Haddan on the Apostolic Succession.

The Esoteric, and for the Adept really conclusive, evidence is furnished by sensitives and clairvoyants and by those who have the power to read and to see on the astral plane. Let any such who are under no delusion of prejudice compare the Holy Sacrament as consecrated in any of the three true Branches of the Master's Church with the parody of that Divine Rite as performed in Presbyterian or Protestant Meeting-Houses. Yet in the latter the intention is usually extremely reverent; the faith often fervent—the partakers sometimes of higher ethical character and greater devotion than in the true Church.

Were it possible for men by their own will and effort to invoke the Holy Spirit doubtless these would do it. And doubtless also many priests whose lives are evil, and who have no faith, could never of themselves invoke that Holy Spirit. Whence, then, can come that Power? Only from the Master Himself—according to His promise—and by His own appointed means.

The Assumption

The 14th of August is the eve of the Feast of the Assumption of Our Blessed Lady. Natural therefore is it that Her influence at that season emanating like the scent of the Mystical Rose should penetrate through the serried ranks of the Companions or Our Holy Order vowed to the Quest of the Ruby at the Heart of the Rose—and should come to thee who hast so lately been added to the ranks of those bound on that Holy Quest.

The Immaculate Conception

The Immaculate Conception of Our Blessed Lady thou hast

228

done well to ask about. The whole teachings as originally given to Our Order are contained in a very ancient M.S.S. known among us as the Book of the Negative Existence. More than 600 years ago this Book was for very sufficient reasons withdrawn from the knowledge of the lower Grades of the Order, and is now in its entirety only to be studied by Companions who have attained to a great advance. Yet as with others of our great teachings is it permissible that certain elementary portions may be given out in such form as may be readily comprehended when any student hath sufficiently advanced to ask concerning them.

Accordingly I ShMSh have now received from the Custodian of our Ancient Wisdom certain excerpts from this book—which in its entirety I have never seen—and have been commanded to adapt these to the mode of thought and the comprehension of the modern student.

It is in Our Order an opinion—yea and much more than an opinion, for it is held by our most advanced Brethren as an absolute certainty and confirmed by those workers who are beyond the Veil—that Our Blessed Lady was verily and indeed born without the taint of original sin and was so also conceived in the Womb of her Mother.

Yet we seek not to impose this great truth upon any—the Master is very tender to the ignorance, the prejudice, and the foolishness of His children and we would fain follow Him in His tenderness. As regards the Assumption of Our Blessed Lady— remember that she typifies and sets forth for us the Root of the Negative Powers. The force of the Negative and receptive, which is indeed the very germ of Faith, and has been known in all ages of the world, and is the necessity thereof before any manifestation of the Master could be—even in the soul of a man. Thus did the great Initiate of the elder world write 'Be still then and know that I am God'. In modern language the idea might be more accurately rendered 'Let thy whole being become Negative and thou wilt know Me'.

Hence before the Word could become flesh it was necessary that there should be a perfect manifestation or incarnation of the Negative and that this Negativity should be absolute—and hence the Immaculate Conception—the Virgin Birth of the Master. This, and the perpetual virginity of Our Blessed Lady are not theories or myths superstitions or corruptions, but the absolutely essential concomitants of His Divinity. But in passing out of Manifestation into the Spiritual Plane, the sequence is otherwise—for here the Positive—the Master—first enters—and when He hath prepared a plane there entereth also the Negative which shall be the entrance or first receptacle for them that follow Him.

For indeed entering to His Own Kingdom He needeth no Negative receptacle as He did when He descended to earth. But we who follow Him entering by His Grace a Kingdom He has won for us do need such Negativity. Hence when He called Our Blessed Lady to Himself it was first as it were, the more positive side of Her Negativity—namely Her pure and sinless soul, that ascended to the Throne of Grace, and thereafter her ever-Virgin Body, which saw not corruption, was taken up in order that in the presence of the All Supreme there might be the positive Mediator, the Master—and the Negative recipient the welcomer —who guideth souls to Him.

Hence much to blame are they who say that in the Cultus of Our Blessed Lady we detract from the honour due to the Master. For She was necessary to His Birth on earth but detracted not from His Glory. Great is the Mystery of these things.

Some Notes on the Church and Church Teachings

The Master left no room for opinion. When He founded His Church He impressed thereon a definite form—His immediate followers from His instructions filled up the details, and the Rulers of the Church in all ages so far as they have been faithful have been guided by Him—and thus His Church hath grown and is alive today. 'Other foundation can no man lay than that which is laid.' Thus every society—which hath rebelled against the Church and the Rulers thereof is cut off, even if built on the foundation of the Church it is but wood—hay—stubble—that is built thereon—and it is condemned, but observe only if necessary—the Society—the men and women composing the same are oftimes young souls learning elementary lessons—thou mayest freely do justice to all noble qualities each individual may have, but no more consort with them in their worship than thou wouldst go into an infant school to learn to read with children of eight years old.

The Three Great Branches of the Catholic Church contain among them all the truths taught by the Master. Their errors are in their schisms—in their separation and their opinion of each other—from any of them thou canst learn much.

A Presbyterian as such is in great error—yet in spite thereof he may have much that is pure and holy to teach yet always with danger—for because he is a Presbyterian he is below thyself and the causes that make him or keep him so are points of error and thou mayest perchance be unable to sift the false from the true. Why read such where lifetime would not suffice to read the writings of the Saints?

The Master of Masters hath so planned that all that is absolutely needed of His teachings are recorded literally by certain of His followers in what are known as the Four Gospels—but seeing that to human comprehension these can neither be grappled with nor understood—He has further revealed to certain special teachers appointed to guide His flock certain glosses and interpretations of His teachings whereby they may be brought down to the physical brains and translated into rules of physical conduct for certain sections of Mankind. But observe that these of their very nature are limited—only the Master's own words being universal. Therefore is closeness of touch with Him the solution of all difficulty.

Thus to take one instance—the great Initiate whom we term St. Paul was specially inspired and specially trained to speak forth the Master's teaching and expound it to his own time and the countries and races committed to him. To him was given to lay down rules for the new-born and growing Church which are still valid, and therefore has that Church by Divine guidance incorporated the Epistles of St. Paul into the infallible and divinely inspired Canon of the Scripture. Yet they who set the words of St. Paul which are infallibly true considered in their connection and circumstances on a par with the words of the Master, which are infallible without limitation for all time and for every place, do greatly err.

Consider now the Master's own words 'Other sheep I have which are not of this fold'—them also I must bring. 'Feed my sheep' 'We forbade him because he followeth not with us—forbid him not'. 'Feed my sheep'. Brother in these words of His the Master speaks to these (this message was sent to a priest, a member of a Temple).

Now look back and see how thou thyself hast drawn night unto Him. It was by one of the most perfect expressions of His Divine Spirit. The formularies of the Catholic Church. This was the step that lay before thee and thou didst mount thereon and find the Lord.

Highly privileged wert thou for there is no other road whereby so rapidly or so nearly approach to Him may be won. This step is a White Stone—but if thou shouldst make a fetich thereof as the Moslems do of the Caaba and say there is no other way —thou wouldst greatly err. For herein do men often confound what is useful discipline and of immense value to those who are at the stage to profit thereby with the absolute essential of the Master's teaching and the New Revelation.

These limitations are easy—therefore dear to the human hearts of human teachers—very easy it is to say 'My way is the only way—walk ye in it'. Very hard it is to see the way that lies before another and to aid him to walk in the path that the Master has traced before him—much easier to force him if it may be—to walk in thy path. Much easier—but not the Master's method. 'Forbid him not, because he walketh not with you'.

Now what said the Master is the highest duty? 'Be not afraid, only believe', over and over again reiterated, and what is belief or faith? 'The evidence of things not seen.' They, then, who put all their trust in what they can see and touch and handle and examine—the agnostics—the rationalists and the like, these are they who offend the Master, and any touch of faith that can be given to them is a service to Him. But they who strive to believe —who are straining their eyes into the darkness to obtain the evidence of things not seen—all these, though they see falsely and imperfectly, yet are they on the road to the knowledge of the Master. Hence have all the mystic and supernatural religions the germs of truth more or less developed and all are energising upward. All materialising, denying, doubting, religions (whereof are most of those which termed themselves 'Reformed') tending away from the Master.

Thou shouldst call nothing common or unclean. That man or woman who seeks a good or fancied good be it what it may— even if it be merely sensual lust (which to him or her appears the best thing) is, all unknown to him or herself, seeking Him, the Master—the soul is young, the ideal is low and primitive, nevertheless it is an ideal—by degrees will higher ideals be substituted for low ones—'Feed my lambs' the Master said, not drive them into your own favourite pastures.

Nothing is common or unclean—the sacrifice He asks of thee is the sacrifice of thy prejudices, thy limitations, in order that thou mayest feed His Sheep, above all His Lambs.

Well canst thou guide members of the Catholic Church in Catholic ways. This is easy and demands no sacrifice. Thou art asked to see His hand everywhere—to recognise that faiths thou callest heathen may have a knowledge of Him. That there are grains of Truth everywhere—that thou art called to be a shepherd.

PART NINE

Hermetic Wisdom and Mystical Prayer

Being
Further Cromlech Temple
Papers

Three Grades of Prayer

Know, Oh Companions, that there be Three Grades of Prayer, appropriate to the Neophyte, the Initiate, and the Adept. The nature of these I will unfold as far as may be. Seek in your own hearts for that which ye can pray with all your mind and soul and strength, and strive not to use a grade higher than that which ye can put forth your whole strength in, thinking thereby to please God the Vast and Mighty One—for ye shall not so please Him. But rather try to develop yourselves so that ye may attain to a higher Grade, and pray naturally the prayer thereof. Herein I take no account of the mass of mankind who have not yet learned to pray at all with concentrated force and intensity on every plane of being at once.

The neophyte prays for what he desireth—either for himself or others—and he prays with confidence, because he is a member of the Great Master, an integral part of that Divine Body wherein dwelleth the Divine Spirit—and he receiveth that which he prays for. The Initiate trusteth that the Lord of All knoweth his necessities before he asketh, and his chief prayer is 'Lord make me pure—make me Holy as Thou art, and bring me to Thy Eternal Glory'.

Yet the more advanced Initiate prayeth also the Neophyte's prayer therewith, for he knoweth the power thereof and he prayeth for Wisdom to use aright the power of prayer.

Yet notice that these prayers are self regarding—they are prayers of separateness—even at the highest, when for others. The Neophyte, moreover, cannot pray with his whole soul to be made pure and holy, for as yet he only partially desires it. He putteth force upon himself to pray this prayer, yet in his inmost soul he knoweth that it is his own prayer in the same sense that a prayer for the health or life of one near and dear to him is.

The chief prayer of the Adept is 'Lord let me be an instrument in thine hands for good or for evil as it pleaseth Thee, for all that Thou desirest is good—use me O Lord to fulfil Thy purposes, and teach me as part of Thyself, to yield myself at once to Thy Will.'

For ye know that the Master needeth not only all whom the

world calls good and holy—but those whom the world calls evil are a part of His body and move with His Will—the outer and uninitiated unconsciously—the Adept consciously and willingly. The Pharisees and Scribes despised Mary Magdalene—the woman who was a sinner, yet was she at that very time developing towards the highest Adeptship to which she afterwards attained, and why? 'Because she loved much.' She yielded herself willingly through her love to be a vessel—whether to honour or dishonour, in Her Master's hands.

Few can attain to this height but one lesson ye can learn of infinite importance in this Fire Tatwa. Any person so ye see, may for aught you know be on the path of Adeptship, and in love yielding himself to the Master's Will, though seeming evil to you—as Mary Magdalene seemed to the Pharisees—therefore condemn not and ye shall not be condemned.

Various Teaching on Church for Second Grade only

Some notes on the Sun Order and the Church.
The first foundation of our Order was long pre-Christian—but seeing that our highest Adepts always maintained (as did the Hebrew seers and Prophets—many of whom were also members of Our Order) an intercourse with the spirit world.

Our Order recognised only those faiths which had acted on a direct Divine Revelation. Such a revelation was, as all Christians admit, given to the Hebrews. It was also given to some before the Hebrews, as Enoch and Noah. Further it was given to the Egyptians, since Moses was learned in all their wisdom—which would not have been the case had their Revelation been false. And the same may be said of other faiths, whose revelation, though in them it degenerated and became corrupt, yet at first was pure.

In all these faiths there were members of our Order, and it was known to us and is recorded in our ancient Archives that in all of them was the prophecy of the coming of the Incarnate Word in Human Flesh.

To this, therefore, we ever looked forward, and when the Master came, Our Order all over the world knew and recognised Him, that is our Higher Adepts did so, and the knowledge was communicated to every Temple throughout the World—there then being some thousands.

The chief of the whole Order—whose title is never revealed to the lower grades—did homage and laid down his office at the feet of the Master—who became the actual Living Head. Thus every word of the Master became and remained for ever an infallible and unalterable part of our teachings.

When a society was formed to promulgate those teachings many of the most eminent and advanced of our Order assisted therein. By reason of our Organisation—its secrecy, its detachment from all material considerations and by the preservation of our ancient M.S.S. we believe that we have been able to preserve all the pure doctrines of the Catholic Church and to know

239

and reject those which have been introduced by corruption, or for material or political ends, most of which have already been discarded by the true Catholic Church in its Three Great Branches.

Our Order then—meaning thereby the governing and teaching body, is absolutely therein, as all its members are actually members of the Holy Catholic Church. Yet we do not refuse to teach Neophytes of any other faith. *Only they cannot advance to higher grades unless they be Christians and members of one of the Branches of the Catholic Church.*

When the Master came, the question was definitely raised by what title should He be referred to in our Rituals—and should the existing system of Initiation be changed. After careful consideration it was resolved to make no change. One strong reason being the desire to emphasise the fact that His coming was in fact revealed to all the great revealed Religions on Earth—as was shown in the Homage of the Three Holy Kings—Magi—or Wise Men.

To neglect, as some have neglected, all the history of the prophecies of His coming and to commence Christian doctrine with the Birth of Christ is to disregard the Master's own teaching and the place of that Supreme event in the World's history. To confine these prophecies, as some others have done, to the seers of the Hebrew Faith is to disregard the evidence of history and the Master's own teachings and both these errors give great occasion to those who impugn the justice of the Father in leaving the greater part of mankind in intentional darkness and ignorance.

It is certain that some of the immediate followers of the Master were parties to this decision. Indeed some think that the Master Himself was consulted—but of this there is no evidence. Yet are we fully persuaded that the course resolved on was the only one consistent with His teachings—and with the doctrines of His Incarnation; it was further said that when in time to come Neophytes should ask 'What mean ye by these ceremonies?' the explanation given would bring them to a clearer understanding of the Father's dealings with the world and the purpose of the coming of the Master.

240

Dost thou not know that there are many titles belonging to the pre-Christian systems in constant use in the Liturgies of the Church as applied to Christ—and still more to Our Blessed Lady, who is frequently invoked with the very titles of the Greek Aphrodite? The images and symbols used are also drawn, almost always, from some pre-Christian system—and in every case the occult reason is to connect the coming of the Master with the preparations made for His coming in all Nations of the World. He who came 'not to destroy but to fulfil'.

How canst thou greet the Master as the Sun of Righteousness and Our Lady as the Star of the Sea—if thou thinkest it is a transgression of Scripture? Know that the whole of our teachings as applied to that Branch of Our Order whereto thou belongest is founded first, on the very words and acts of Christ—the Master—second, on the Words of His Apostles—third, on the earliest Fathers of the Church—fourth, on the Decrees of General Councils as setting forth the voice of the Living Church—fifth, on the Decrees of certain other Councils setting forth the voice of the Church as applied to certain of Her Branches—sixth, on Catholic Tradition—and in the whole of our teachings there is nothing contrary thereto.

Now in the messages and replies to queries these principles are applied to particular cases—and herein is much instruction—for wheresoever thou, or any Companion of Our Order, seest or fanciest any divergence from the true teaching of the Master and His Church—then thou mayest be sure thou hast misunderstood either our teaching or the authorities whereon thou restest—and thy duty as a Companion of the Order is at once to set forth such fancied divergence—and thereby wouldst thou receive full explanation. And know, that for this purpose, are continually labouring a group of learned theologians, all Companions of the Order of the second and higher Grades—many of whom are priests devoted to the service of the Master and His Church—who gave their labours ungrudgingly with no thought of fee or reward to bring wandering souls and those in difficulty to a more perfect knowledge of Him.

And now when we say that in no iota do any teachings of ours differ from the teaching of Christ and His Church, we say it with a full conviction of the seriousness of the statement. But let all who profess the Catholic Faith beware lest they reject the commandment of God that they may keep their own tradition.

On Divine Names
Second Grade. General Circulation.

Supreme over all that is, is the Most Holy and Undivided Trinity in Unity known partially through Divine Revelation by some of the sons of men; known completely by none—nor indeed knowable, wholly unknown to some.

Known unto all men in part, at all events, is the Visible Universe of things. This being finite is knowable by finite man... the only bounds of his knowledge being his own intellectual capacity.

Besides the Supreme Eternal and Ineffable Three in One, and the Material Universe, there exist vast multitudes of beings invisible, imperceptible to the bodily senses, usually imperfectly known, and barely, if at all, comprehended, yet having a vast and most important effect on the Material Universe. Of these beings, from the human standpoint, some are good, some evil, some a mixture of both, some are higher and some lower, than mankind. We say 'from the standpoint of humanity' because all are created by the Supreme God, none can do aught save what is permitted by Him, therefore none can be in essence aught but good, yet, seeing that there are some of these beings whose effect upon humanity is to persuade men to act contrary to those laws which the Supreme God hath imposed on men, and thus bring about their own destruction, so unto men they are evil and must be shunned and resisted accordingly.

More of this mystery will be shown later. Now these beings are partially and imperfectly recognised in every religious system in the world. Thus in modern Christianity, Archangels, Angels and Devils are universally acknowledged. The more advanced Christians recognise also glorified Saints and know some of the names of Angels and of Demons. In the Bible are also the beings alluded to as the Four Beasts, the Four and Twenty Elders, Thrones, Dominions, Principalities and Powers, and the Hebrew Qabalah frequently recognised by quotation in the New Testament, adds considerably to the list, recognising the Domi-

243

nant Spirits of the Elements and the sub-human Kingdoms of the Qliphoth.

In the Brahministic and Buddhistic systems these beings—or rather such of them as are superhuman, are termed Devas, and their kingdom Devachan—where the souls of the first wait and rest—this is the same state as the waiting Church of the Christians, though, as it were, a different section of the plane. Of this more hereafter.

When men lose the knowledge of and belief in the Supreme God—they worship these beings—and, truly, it is no sin in those who worship the highest that they know. But to those who know the Infinite Supreme, to worship any of His creatures is a deadly sin—and for a Companion of the Sun Order to worship any such beings may entail expulsion from the Order and further penalties.

The Ancient Greeks had lost the knowledge of the Supreme Gods and worshipped mainly the Dominant Spirits of the Elements, of whose nature powers and attributes they knew much. They also worshipped the planetary Spirits.

The Phoenicians had in their later period lost, not only the knowledge of the Supreme God, but also that of the Angels or Devas; they had some imperfect knowledge of the Spirits of the Elements and Nature Spirits, but the real objects of their worship were the subhuman Qlippoth, and their cult was a species of Devil worship, this prevailed also among the Philistines of the coasts of Canaan.

The purest of all the nations of antiquity after the sacred tribe of the Jews were the Persians and the Ancient Egyptians and, more recently, the Incas of Peru and the (so-called) Druids of the North. All of these knew and worshipped the Supreme God. They also knew, and revered, and studied the nature and attributes of those beings whom He has created and through whom He works.

To study the nature and attributes of these beings is as lawful and as meritorious as to study any other of the works of God. Even as Astronomy, or Botany, or Chemistry are termed sciences, so is this truly termed the sacred science—for if we truly know the nature of Devas, or Angelic hosts, we know the link between man and God. Yet the study is fraught with grave dangers, for among these beings there are many who crave worship—who would set themselves up to be Gods and would deceive men. Against such, the Christian who truly believes in the Master of Masters who is Jesus Christ the Incarnate Word, the Co-Eternal Co-Equal Son of the All-Father—has a perfect protection.

Therefore this teaching is withheld till considerable progress be made—see O Companion that thou reveal nothing of this—for the temptation to the Worship of Created Things is strongly subtle to some minds.

You may compare this branch of the sacred science to the study of bacteriology. Not to the unexperienced medical student is this study with its enormous possibilities, its vast results, its danger in inexperienced hands committed—but to him who has learned care, who knows all the dangers and how they may be avoided, who works calmly, methodically, taking no needless risk but fearing no danger. The powers he wields and investigates may bless or ban mankind, for the bacteria, like the spiritual beings we now write of, are necessary to our existence—yet may destroy millions of men in an hour.

In Persia two opposing forces are recognised as incessantly contending—Ahura Mazda and Ahriman. In later times the knowledge of the Supreme God became dim in ancient Iran and the contending forces alone were recognised. The heretical Gnostics, especially those of Samaria, imported this idea into Europe—and it infected the Christian Church through the Manichaeans—thence reappearing at intervals among the Albigenses, Lollards, Hussites and Calvinists. Yet in origin the idea was the same as that expressed by a Master Initiate of old; 'There was War in Heaven Michael, and his Angels fighting the Devil and his angels'. Yet Ahura Mazda is not precisely Saint Michael, but rather the synthesis of the Four Archangels.

The name is retained in our rituals because there is no other name that precisely represents what is meant. But observe, O Companion of the Sun Order, that Ahura Mazda is a created being even as thou art, and is thy fellow servant. Worship then God only. Yet shalt thou ask the blessing and illumination of Ahura Mazda even as thou mightest of any wise and Holy man from this Earth.

Furthermore, note that Mithra representeth all the beneficial powers of Fire. He is the Chief and Ruler of the Spirits of Fire, who as regards humanity are good—Many are his names—yet that of Mithra best expresses his attributes. He it is, who, guided by the Holy Spirit, stirs the zeal and energy of the souls of men. Hence, when the Holy Spirit descended at Pentecost He came in the special symbol of Mithra—the Tongues of Flame— Mithra too, it is, who stirs the germinant heat of the Earth, bringing forth life and vegetation in the spring. Yet he too is a created being—lower indeed than Ahura Mazda. Worship then God only.

Yet the benediction of Mithra thou shalt ask for—for unto thee he is the means whereby thou shalt receive the Holy Spirit. Thus, O Companion, shalt thou read our Rituals. Change not the names there set down for they have a meaning thou canst not yet know.

The salutation of Iran with which the Ritual of Initiation commences, i.e.

The Inspiration of the Supreme!

The Illumination of Mazda!

The Benediction of Mithra!

is no essential part of the ceremony, but rather is a hymn or anthem in the Christian Ritual. Yet it containeth deep knowledge to be unfolded later. Therefore should it by no means be omitted.

If thou desirest, O Companion, ask any questions upon this teaching. Let no part be dark unto theé. Those who guide the Order deem it a privilege, and a service meet for the Lord of Hosts, to answer all questions relating to the teaching of the Order. Woe only to those who will not ask but yet condemn that which they understand not.

Four States of Ordinary Prayer
Permission only. Feb. 1924

Writers on Raja Yoga, which is the Eastern equivalent of the At-One-ment, or perfect Union with the Divine, after giving elaborate instructions as to means and exercises, conclude by saying that the alternative method of devotion for those who can practice it, is far simpler and easier. This is the method of prayer as taught by the great mystic writers of the West, and advocated in our Order. Prayer does not attain to this union— but it is essential for bringing the soul into the Mystic State wherein this Union may take place.

We must, therefore, in the first place, carefully distinguish between ordinary prayer, as it is called, and the Mystic State.

Now, if we take the world in which we live as a magnified image of the human personality, we shall find some very useful analogies. The solid globe may be figured as man's corporeal body, and the Atmosphere as the Aura. The living creatures of the earth, then correspond to man's conscious life. Those that are, so to say, bound to the earth, the animals, answer to his material consciousness.

The birds which live in the air are his immaterial thoughts, which pass to and fro in his Aura, perching on the Earth— therefore affecting his material body, but not limited or bound thereto. His prayers are therefore appropriately represented by birds. Now birds rise in the air by the efforts of their own wings—but they cannot rise beyond the air, or even to its extreme limits. This then is the analogue of what is termed 'Ordinary Prayer'.

It is made by man's own efforts. But here observe that, though a man's own effort is needed, his effort is not the force by which he rises—that is the force of Divine Grace which he is permitted to call into action by his own efforts. Even as an engine driver does not supply the force that drives the engine, neither can the engine move without his efforts, but when he pulls the lever the force of the steam is set in action. Now conceive— when the bird has risen as high at it can, a Divine hand takes

247

it and lifts it to higher levels. Hence forth the bird can do nothing, it can but lie perfectly passive and trusting in the hand that carries it upward. This is the mystic state, wherein at length Union is attained—but such Union is the free gift of God, and due to no effort of the man, nor even in any sense earned by him.

The consideration of this state we must defer for the present, and consider the ordinary prayer which fits the soul to receive the Supreme Grace. Resuming our analogy of the bird—we know that different birds have different powers of rising above the earth plane—from the heavy and clumsy birds who can only rise a short distance, and that for a very little time, to the eagle who soars almost out of sight and whose mighty wings seem tireless.

These differences, by the great mystical writers, have been grouped into four called 'The four states of Ordinary Prayer'. This is the classification of St. Theresa of Jesus—(whom, as being a Member of Our Order of very high grade, though writing for outsiders and for the uninitiated, we shall mostly follow).

These four states we shall name as follows: 1. Vocal prayer. 2. Meditation. 3. The prayer of affection. 4. The prayer of simple regard, or simplicity. These being the nearest English equivalent to the terms used by St. Theresa. The first two of these are well known and need very little comment.

Vocal prayer may be either the repetition of a set form of words—as prescribed by the Master in the 'Lord's Prayer' and countless others—or maybe an extemporary voicing of our own needs. The former being adapted for the collective prayer of a number—the latter for private and solitary devotion.

Vocal prayer has been called 'Spoken Meditation', and meditation has been called 'silent prayer'. Excellent models of both abound in books of devotion, and the Catholic Church of the Roman Obedience makes a special point of teaching meditation.

From the Occult point of view the repetition of a definite formula aloud may act as a mantra and produce certain effects in the body favourable to prayer—also the practice of meditation, by obliging the brain to remain fixed on certain definite trains of thought, may avail to steady the Aura. But these physical effects are not the primary intention. To be regarded definitely as states of prayer, the attention must be alive, the brain and the will must concur with the physical act, otherwise it becomes mechanical and automatic. The third and fourth states therefore should exist, even though unconsciously, in order that the first two may be effectual. We shall therefore proceed at once to examine these.

Recurring for the moment to the image of the bird, we may say that the first two forms of ordinary prayer may be compared to a wild bird flying low in short flight, say from branch to branch in affective prayer—but where the will and the intention go not with the act, it is like the common barndoor fowl, having wings indeed, but unable to do more than flap helplessly on the ground.

Assuming that the student has attained some success in the practice of meditation, he will understand that it involves reasoning. In these qualities St. Theresa was deficient. She says herself 'God never endowed me with the gift of making reflections with the understanding—or with that of using the imagination to any good purpose. My imagination is so sluggish that even if I would think of or picture to myself Our Lord's Humanity, I never could do it'.

As, then, we pass from the meditation to the Prayer of Affection we leave reason and imagination behind.

Now although we class numbers two and three as different states, it must not be thought that there is any fixed line between them. One melts into the other. Reason, memory, imagination gradually decrease—Love increases.

Consider a man who has a woman comrade. His reason presents to him the causes for their friendship. Similarity of ideas, of pursuits, of sports—her intellect, her constancy, her sweet disposition—a thousand reasons.

Memory calls up instances—imagination intensifies them. But if he falls in love with her, all these gradually fade into insignificance. He thinks of her continually, but it is always with the same object, with little or no variety. He is content to contemplate her mentally and seeks not the reason why. The reasons which swayed him before now only appear as justifications of himself, to himself, for an admitted state of mind, then grow fainter and fainter and vanish. It has been well said, that a man who can say he loves a woman does not begin to love her— so with simple souls having only a few ideas—only to be nearer to God is happiness to them, and the prayer of affection is consequently easier to them than to the more developed and intellectual.

St. Theresa reproved certain great preachers who had got so into the habit of expanding and expounding a subject that they acted in the same way during prayer. She says they continue preaching, but to themselves.

The true prayer of affection is that of Her of Magdala, of whom St. Francis de Sales says 'Behold her I beseech thee, Theotimus, she sighs not, he stirs not, she prays not ... and this Divine Love, jealous of the love sleep and repose of this well-beloved, chides Martha for wanting to awaken her'. (*Treatise on the Love of God.*)

Another example may be that of a mother watching over the cradle of her child. She thinks of that child lovingly for hours together, if interrupted she resumes the contemplation— and this without arguments she never reasons why she loves that child—the thought would be absurd.

We have said that intellectual natures find greater difficulty in reaching the prayer of affection than do simple ones. Loving natures are naturally attracted towards exercises wherein acts of love predominate over acts of understanding. Women, generally speaking, have more capacity for very simple forms of mental prayer than men. Men in celibate life, who have no experience of the human passion of love, find greater difficulty than others in reaching the third stage of ordinary prayer. Well said the Master 'If a man love not his mother whom he hath seen, how can he love God whom he hath not seen?'

For all those who are in this state and have taken the vows of celibacy, the very difficulty constitutes the exercise whereby the necessary strengthening of their souls is to be accomplished —and by hypothesis, their souls are strong enough to face and overcome the difficulty. But for others there is no doubt that the knowledge of human love is the best preparation for the knowledge of the Divine Love—as was said of her of Magdala '... for she loved much'. It is well therefore that they who would attain thus far should cultivate and intensify in themselves the power of loving.

The third state is produced sometimes with consolation—but very often with suffering, and with what St. Theresa terms aridity, when the soul is unable to meditate, and the inaction is extremely painful. This aridity will be more fully explained, and the means of combating it described later on. But in the meantime the student should realise that it is a universal experience, and should be very careful not to be discouraged.

Real prayer and meditation are for most people comparitively easy—but when we quit this degree it is no path of roses, as we may be inclined to anticipate—there are many crosses. Father de Caussade says truly 'There is nothing more sublime than contemplation as we find it in the books—there is nothing more beautiful or grander than the prayer of affection, or the prayer of simplicity—in theory, but in practice there is nothing more humiliating or more crucifying. Hence it is a worthy offering to the Lord of Light, a costly gift—like the Magdalen's vase—for which He will fully reward us'.

We are apt to say 'If God approved of my praying thus, He would give me proof of His approval by consolations. I am simply wasting my time'. To which St. Ignatius replies—'Oh poor in faith and weak in love wilt thou then depart from God, because to try thy love He seems for a moment to hide Himself?' If the student then expects periods of aridity, he will not be disturbed thereby, he will know they are inevitable and will pass. Moreover, that the more completely he reaches the prayer of simplicity, the more he can render himself passive, the less will these painful interludes be,—and further—if he be assailed by doubts and difficulties, as all the Saints have been at times on reaching this state, he must recognise that this is a sure sign that he has not fully arrived at the State of the prayer of affection. For its essence is that it transcends reason.

Reason is left behind, as I have already explained. But doubts spring from reason which must still be present. He must endeavour therefore to attain more completely to the state desired.

I have mentioned the difficulties experienced by different types of persons in attaining this state, and the analogy pointed out by the Master Himself of human love. All the experience recorded points to this as being a most valuable, and in many cases essential, stepping stone, especially for those who, one account of the activity of their minds and the development of the reasoning faculties, find their progress impeded by doubts, difficulties, and times of painful aridity. St. Mary of Magdala has left in on record that the practice of the body in perfect self-forgetting human love for another person, by some sort of reciprocal action trains the soul to the power of experiencing a perfect love for the Master, who said 'In as much as ye have done it unto one of the least of these, ye have done it unto me'.

Meaning thereby that He accepts even an intensity of devotion shown to a fellow human being sent by Him, as though it were shown to Himself—as she showed it—in His Incarnate Human Body. Take the example of a woman meditating on the man she loves—to all the rest of the world he may be mean, contemptible, eminently undesirable, but what cares she? To her he is her hero—she no more questions or reasons why she loves him or weighs his good points, his virtues, than she does those of her child.

Now if such a woman can experience this human love, and take it as an example, a model—she will reach the state of affective prayer (or the prayer of affection) quickly and readily—she will be able at once to dispose of all doubts and difficulties; times of aridity will have little terror, little pain for her—all will be simple and easy—she will pass into the third state, and rest secure in the infinite love of the Saviour, conscious always of His Divine Presence—and from thence glide easily into the fourth state of the prayer of simplicity or simple contemplation.

There be some who would affirm this state, by reason of its quiet and silence, is a state of inertia. As well say that the painter whose brush travels silently over his canvas is less actively employed than the blacksmith who deafens us with the clamour of his blows.

In passing upward through the four states of prayer to meditation we drop the external bodily action, that, namely, of repeating a certain formula of words—but we still retain reason, memory, imagination. In passing to the third stage we gradually part with these also, and in their place we develop the sentient or emotion of love. Passing to the fourth state—that of the prayer of simplicity—we drop also all active emotion, and remain in passive contemplation of God. But seeing that we ourselves do this—that it is we who place ourselves in the presence of God, it is not the mystic state as yet. This state gives great vitality to the will, but it is a vitality not at once perceived.

Imagine a meadow under the direct rays of the sun. All the hidden forces of nature do their work slowly, and in silence. As one great Adept has said—'all those millions of molecules of sap circulate like a crowd of workmen engaged in building a city. So with the prayer of simplicity—the soul is like a field exposed to the rays of the Central Spiritual Sun.' We shall see the Adept, after reaching the mystic state, recurs to vocal prayer, but in a wholly new manner, for he now knows the meaning and occult force of 'The Word', and can formulate for himself how from the Transforming Union, or Spiritual Marriage, the Thought of God is conceived, and how through the Prayer of Quiet and through Contemplation, as in the darkness of the womb, it is matured, till at length the Word is made flesh in vocal prayer, and thus the process is reversed: God coming down to Earth and manifesting Himself.

In conclusion of this first paper, I append some brief rules which may be of some help to the student.

Ia. Produce a retired place free from interruption as far as possible.

b. Calm and equilibrate the mind, banish all thoughts of worldly matters. Try to realise that 'Your Father knoweth what things ye have need of before ye ask Him.'

c. Kneel down and say the Lord's prayer very reverently, trying to realise the full force of every repetition. It is well to couple this with the ideas of the devotion of the Quipus.

d. Stand facing the East, and say the Ave Maria, striving to picture to yourself Our Blessed Lady before you, and a dim vision of the Saviour behind, whom you approach through Her.

IIa. Now sit in a comfortable and symmetric attitude, and let the vision gradually glide into a meditation, say on the first of the Joyful Mysteries—the Annunciation.

b. Picture to yourself the scene—Our Lady engaged in prayer —the gradual sensation of an Angelic presence—the thrill of colours in the air—the formation of the Angelic appearance— the Words of the Salutation—Our Lady's reply 'Be it unto me according to thy word'.

c. Consider the Faith, Humility and Obedience manifested by Her.

d. Apply these to yourself.

e. Resolve to imitate Her and to follow Her footsteps as far as humanly possible.

IIIa. Try to hold this vision and accentuate the impression of the form of the Master, and the Magdalene at His feet.

b. In thought centre yourself with Magdalene, Say mentally 'We love Him because He first loved us". Seem to hear Him say : '... For she loved much'.

c. Let all faculties of reason etc. gradually sink away. This will follow naturally in most cases if the feeling of love be gradually intensified. These faculties are not banished or violently expelled, but with regard to them the sensation is as of falling asleep, till only love is left—and this is love for the Creator, and all that He hath created. As a man who loves a woman will treasure all that comes from her, whether in itself desirable or beautiful, or the reverse, and will love a soiled glove or a torn fragment of lace that she has worn—so the soul in this state loves not only the image of the Master, but all that comes from Him with great intensity.

IVa. For some time it will be well for the beginner to pause there. For the preceding stage to be of benefit should be maintained for some time, say ten minutes to a quarter of an hour at least. (The great mystical writers advise longer, but their times were less restless than ours.) It will however be found naturally after some practice, that the active emotion of love is of itself giving way to a passive happiness of contemplation only. In human love this is exemplified by the joy the lover takes in merely being in the presence of the beloved, not speaking, not moving, content simply to exist, bathed in the atmosphere that is so dear. Finally, we reiterate here the advice given by all the great mystical writers—not to force the soul at this stage to uncongenial acts.

First, for those acts for which the soul has no inclination, never to force ourselves to produce them.

Secondly for those to which we have during prayer an inclination or facility—to yield to this inclination. Therefore if during the prayer of simplicity we have a strong inclination to offer a petition to God—let us do so, notwithstanding that we have resolved to banish all active thought.

Thirdly, as laid down by St. Francis de Sales and by Father Balthasar Alvares—outside the time of prayer to profit by all opportunities of arousing the will, and thus training it, as it were, for the prayer itself. And here, says St. Gertrude, in a private letter, quoting from St. Mary Magdalen, 'They who are permitted to enjoy human corporeal love have great advantage for they have something wherewith they may compare this Divine contemplation, and whereby they may excite the will thereto'. And this must and will suffice for the present.

They who shall well practice this Devotion shall at least be ready, if it shall please God, as I have no doubt it will do, to take them of His infinite grace into the Mystic State.

Hereto I ShMSh add a note of my own. In modern life an aeroplane is a more perfect example than a bird, for the man rises, not sails, not by his own effort but by the force generated by his engine, which is like the Grace of God, but his own effort is needed to pull the lever and the machine is given thus into his control. The two lower grades may be compared to flights through the lower atmosphere comparatively easy and safe among all the familiar sights and sounds of the earth. Then soaring higher, the man passes through the clouds, typical of the doubts, difficulties, troubles, aridity etc.

At the entrance of the third State—after which he reaches the calm and silence of the upper air, and soars as high as the atmosphere will support him. After this, whatever lever he pulls, whatever power he applies, he can go no higher unless God take him.

APPENDIX A
An Exegetical Note Upon the Flying Rolls

In all there were thirty-six Flying Rolls circulating among the Adepti Minores of the pre-1900 Golden Dawn.

Flying Roll I was partly concerned with administrative details (how to contact the headquarters of the Order etc.) and these would be of little interest to the present-day reader. The remainder of this Flying Roll is printed in Part I of this book.

Flying Roll II Included in Part I of this book.

Flying Roll III (On Procedure) Purely administrative, and therefore not included in this book.

Flying Roll IV (Spirit Vision) Included in Part II of this book.

Flying Roll V (Thoughts on Imagination) Included in Part I of this book. Originally issued on November 30th 1893.

Flying Roll VI (A Supplement to Flying Roll II) Included in Part I of this book.

Flying Roll VII (Alchemy) Forms Part VII of this book.

Flying Roll VIII (On Tracing a Pentagram by Geometry) I have not thought this purely mathematical piece of instruction worthy of reproduction. It was written by Dr. Pullen-Berry (Frater *Anima Pura Sit*).

Flying Roll IX (Right and Left) Included by Regardie, under the title *The Diagrams*, in *Golden Dawn*, Volume I, pages 161-2. This Flying Roll was originally issued on March 26th 1893.

Flying Roll X (Self-Sacrifice) Included in Part IV of this book.

Flying Roll XI (Clairvoyance) Included in Part II of this book, and originally issued March 30th 1893.

Flying Roll XII (Telesmatic Images) Published by Regardie, in somewhat disjointed form, as part of Volume IV of his *Golden Dawn*. The first paragraph of the Flying Roll is also the first paragraph of page 61, Volume IV, *Golden Dawn*. The remainder of the Flying Roll is to be found on pages 62-3 of the same book under the title *The Vibratory Mode of Pronouncing Divine Names*.

Flying Roll XIII (Secrecy and Hermetic Lore) Included in Part VI of this book.

Flying Roll XIV (Talismans and Flashing Tablets) Printed by Regardie on pages 51-6 of *Golden Dawn* Volume IV. Regardie's version is not quite complete and omits a supplementary note by *Sapere Aude* (Wynn Westcott). The note, which is to the word AL on Regardie's page 56, line 20, should read as follows: 'e.g. for Fire, put Shin first, then three Fiery Signs, then AL. So far for elementary ones. For Planetary ones you may add AL to the Planet's letter or to the Planet and its Houses—the letters of them; and the Planet and Triplicity, use the hexagram made six times. For Zodiacal ones add AL to the letters of the sign and use pentagram five times. When you use the three letters of three Signs of a triplicity for elemental working you should put as the initial letter that of the Sign principally invoked as most useful to you'.

This Flying Roll was originally issued on January 15th 1893.

Flying Roll XV (Man and God) Included in Part IV of this book.

Flying Roll XVI (History of the Rosicrucian Order) Included in Part III of this book; originally given as a lecture on August 17th 1893.

Flying Roll XVII (The Seven Sides of the Vault) Like the preceding Flying Roll this was originally given as a lecture by Westcott on August 17th 1893. It can be found on pages 280-6 of Volume II of Regardie's *Golden Dawn*.

Flying Roll XVIII (Progress in the Order) This Flying Roll was written in June 1893. There is a certain confusion as to its authorship. Some copies attribute it to Annie Horniman (*Fortiter et Recte*) others to Elaine Simpson (*Fidelis*), who later became the mistress of Aleister Crowley.

Flying Roll XIX (Aims and Means of Adeptship) Included in Part III of this book.

Flying Roll XX (Constitution of Man) Originally given as a lecture by Mathers on September 23rd 1893 and included in Part V of this book.

Flying Roll XXI (Know Thyself) Originally given as a lecture by Mathers' wife on September 24th 1893 and included in Part V of this book.

Flying Roll XXII (Free Will) I have been unable to trace a copy of this Flying Roll.

Flying Roll XXIII (Visions by V.N.R.) This account of visions experienced by Mathers' wife is printed on pages 43-6 of Volume IV of Regardie's *Golden Dawn*.

Flying Roll XXIV I have been unable to trace a copy. I am told that it dealt with Horary Figures in astrology.

Flying Roll XXV (Clairvoyance) This, written by J. W. Brodie-Innes, is included in Part II of this book.

Flying Roll XXVI (A supplement to XII) Included in Part II of this book.

Flying Roll XXVII (Theurgia) This Flying Roll, written by P. W. Bullock (*Levavi Oculos*) is included in Part VI of this book.

Flying Roll XXVIII (On Robes) I have been unable to trace a copy.

Flying Roll XXIX (On Lieutenants) I have been unable to trace a copy; I understand that it was purely concerned with administrative matters.

Flying Roll XXX (Clairvoyance and Hierophant Signs) Included in Part II of this book.

Flying Roll XXXI (Ethiopic Letters) I have been unable to trace a copy, but I am told that it dealt with the numerical value to be given to the letters of the Coptic alphabet for Qabalistic purposes. If so, the information can be obtained from Crowley's *777*.

Flying Roll XXXII (Theban Letters) Once again, I have been unable to trace a copy, but I am told that it dealt with the letters of the Enochian alphabet, sometimes (wrongly) referred to as the Theban alphabet. If so, it was probably identical with the table given by Regardie on Page 299 Volume IV, *Golden Dawn*.

Flying Roll XXXIII (Visions of Squares in the Enochian Tablets) Seven visions are described, of which four may be found in Part II of this book. The remaining three visions may be found on pages 318-22, volume IV, *Golden Dawn*. Regardie's first vision is also the first vision of the Flying Roll—it is by *Vigilate*. Regardie's second vision is the sixth vision of the Flying Roll (by *Shemeber*) and his third vision is the Flying

Roll's seventh (it is by *Resurgam*), Dr. Berridge.

Flying Roll XXXV (Notes on the Exordium of the Z Ritual) Printed on pages 150-1 of *Golden Dawn*, Volume III.

Flying Roll XXXVI (Skyring and Astral Projection) Printed on pages 29-42 of *Golden Dawn*, Volume IV, under the title *Of Skyring and Travelling in the Spirit Vision*. The earliest copy I have seen is dated October 1897.

APPENDIX B
Enochian Magic and the Enochian Language

This subject is one of great complexity and it is possible for me to give only a brief outline of the system in this short appendix.

While some occultists have claimed that Enochian Magic was known in fifteenth century Florence, and others have gone so far as to state that it originated in the mythical drowned continent of Atlantis, there is no hard evidence of its existence before the last quarter of the sixteenth century. In any case, whether or not the system is of any real antiquity, there is no doubt that in the form we have it available to us it is derived from the crystal-gazing activities of the Elizabethan occultists, John Dee and Edward Kelley. These two claimed to have received from 'Angels', seen in the magic crystal by Kelley, who acted as skryer, the following material:

(a) Nineteen invocations, known as Keys, or Calls, in an unknown language called Enochian, or Angelic.
(b) Translations of these same Calls.
(c) An Enochian alphabet of twenty-one letters.
(d) Over one hundred large squares, each divided into smaller squares (usually 2401 in number) containing letters.
(e) Instructions for using these squares.
(f) Much miscellaneous occult teaching.

As far as the Enochian language is concerned it suffices to repeat what was said by the early Chiefs of the Golden Dawn. by Aleister Crowley, and by Israel Regardie—that it is a real language, with definite traces of grammar and syntax, and not a mere gibberish.[1]

[1] For those who regard the statements of such occultists with a certain amount of scepticism it is worth stating that a professional philologist has recently done some work on Enochian and has confirmed their essential correctness. It should also be borne in mind that the language is sufficiently complete to enable translation from English into Enochian; Aleister Crowley did this with the invocations of the grimoire known as the *Lesser Key of Solomon*.

Most of the occult teaching received were extremely obscure; the following extract from a message received on May 23rd 1587 is typical:

I am the daughter of Fortitude, and ravished every hour, from my youth. For behold, I am Understanding, and Science dwelleth in me; the heavens oppress me, they covet and desire me with infinite appetite: few or none that are earthly have embraced me, for I am shadowed with the Circle of the Stone, and covered with the morning Clouds. My feet are swifter than the winds, and my hands are sweeter than the morning dew. My garments are from the beginning, and my dwelling place is in myself. The Lion knoweth not where I walk, neither do the beasts of the field understand me. I am deflowered and yet a virgin: I sanctify and am not sanctified. Happy is he that embraceth me: for in the night season I am sweet, and in the day full of pleasure. My company is a harmony of many Cymbals, and my lips sweeter than health itself. I am a harlot for such as ravish me, and a virgin with such as know me not—[2]

Of the squares received five are of much greater importance than the remainder. They are, firstly, the 'Great Eastern Quadrangle of Air', secondly, the 'Great Western Quadrangle of Water' thirdly, the 'Great Northern Quadrangle of Earth', fourthly, the 'Great Southern Quadrangle of Fire', and, lastly; the 'Tablet of Union', sometimes referred to as the 'Quadrangle of Spirit'. Each of the four Quadrangles of the Elements is divided into one hundred and fifty-six squares while the 'Tablet of Union' is divided into twenty squares from which, by methods too complex to be explained here, are derived certain Divine and Angelic names. Furthermore each Tablet is sub-divided into four other Tablets attributed to the Elements—so in the Northern Quadrangle are contained Tablets attributed to Earth of

[2] In fact I do not think this statement quite so obscure as it might appear to be at first sight. The 'speaker' is clearly Binah, Understanding, the third Sephirah of the Qabalistic Tree of Life, and the Science to which 'she' refers is the Gnosis, Knowledge, Daath, the invisible eleventh Sephirah. In Crowleyan terms the 'speaker' may be identified with Nuit, the Egyptian Star-Goddess, or perhaps with Nuit's reflection in Babalon, the Bride of the Beast.

Earth, Fire of Earth, Water of Earth and Air of Earth.

From each of the six hundred and forty-four lettered subsidiary squares of the five Tablets are derived the same number of truncated pyramids. On the apex of each pyramid is the letter of the square and each side of the pyramid is attributed to either an Element, or a Sign of the Zodiac, or a planet. In addition the cards of the Tarot pack and the symbols of geomancy are also attributed to the sides of the pyramids. Such pyramids are reproduced in Flying Roll XXXIII, and are to be found in Part II of this book. With each pyramid is associated a Sphynx, a composite form built up in accordance with the attributions of the four sides of the pyramid.

The Keys or Calls—the strange invocations received by Dee and Kelley—are designed to be used with various parts of the squares received. Thus the third, seventh, eighth and ninth Keys are used in connection with the Tablet of Air (Eastern Quadrangle); the third used in the invocation of Air itself and the other three Keys with, respectively, Water of Air, Earth of Air, and Fire of Air.

APPENDIX C
A *Stella Matutina* Flying Roll

After the split in the original Order the appearance of various schismatic Orders (see *Introduction*) there was a considerable amount of unintelligent tampering with the Flying Rolls. This was particularly noticeable in the fraternity known as the Stella Matutina.

The Stella Matutina also produced several supplementary Flying Rolls. I have examined several of these and I am of the opinion that they are of little value save for one on the Tarot trumps, written by Dr. Felkin's wife, Soror *Quaestor Lucis*, and one on the use of the Vault, written by Dr. Felkin himself. Both these late documents are included in Regardie's *Golden Dawn*.

The Chiefs of the Stella Matutina were responsible for rewriting many of the Flying Rolls. In my opinion their versions of this material are not only quite different from the originals but markedly inferior. As a specimen I reproduce herewith the Stella Matutina version of Flying Roll XXV—a very different piece of work to the original included in Part II of this book.

'Consider the relationship of Man as Microcosm to the Universe as Macrocosm. The former is a reflection in miniature of the latter, in the same way that in a field a dewdrop might present a tiny image of trees, fields, mountains etc.

'Thus everything is pictured in each man's Sphere of Sensation, or akashic envelope. If he is conscious of the picture as reflected he will be possessed of all knowledge. Initiation makes such knowledge possible and available.

'Seeing that the brain and sensorium are physical, it is necessary at first to use physical means to produce the sensitivity required to perceive images consciously.

'The readiest way is the use of symbols. These produce visions in the physical brain and make it more sensitive. A large number of well-known symbols have a definite relationship to certain portions of the Sphere of Sensation, the corresponding regions of the Cosmos, and the related regions of the physical brain.

'The experimenter must thoroughly know the attributions

and meanings of the symbol employed, as this knowledge produces an immediate concentration of thought, vital energy, nerve force, and actual physical blood in the part of the brain related to the chosen symbol.

'For example, if the Tejas Tattwa be taken, the knowledge that it belongs to fire will at once charge with nerve force and blood all the brain centres relating to fire. It will involuntarily recall the various Divine and Spirit Names learned beforehand; the vibration of these Names will increase the effect. The force will be further increased by gazing fixedly at the symbol and holding the appropriate magical implement, which is also a symbol of the same tract of the physical brain. Eventually every other brain cell is muted and inhibited, and the whole consciousness concentrated on the function of Fire. Thus the physical brain becomes sensitive, translucent, and able to perceive the Macrocosmic Fire as reflected in the Sphere of Sensation.

'The sensation is as if one had stepped out of a door into a new world. At first it seems as if everything one sees is just the product of one's own imagination. However, experience shows that 'the next country' has its own inviolable natural laws, just as the physical world has. One cannot make it and unmake it at will. The same actions produce the same results—one is a spectator, not a creator. The conviction dawns on the experimenter that he is perceiving a new and extended range of phenomena—the Astral.

'Taking every symbol whereof you know the meaning, the abstract idea associated with the symbol comes first (as Fire or Water in the abstract), then comes a pose of mind cognate or sympathetic thereto, a *desire* of that particular element—not keen but perceptible. Then, gradually, comes the feeling of the physical effect of that element. Attention is slowly withdrawn from all surrounding sights and sounds. A grey mist or steam surrounds everything and from this the form of the symbol is projected—this is due to the withdrawal of blood and nerve force from other centres of the brain and their consequent inhibition.

'The consciousness then seems to pass through the symbol to realms beyond it: probably visions and pictures from other planes come on to the hypersensitive brain centres. The sensation is as if looking at a series of moving pictures, and although there are beings with whom one can converse and animals one can dominate, there is no more solidity than in a cinema film. In time, however, the sensitivity of the brain increases, and one gains the power of actually going to the scenes of the visions and seeing them as three dimensional—indeed, one actually becomes capable of doing things in the vision and producing effects upon it. This is what is technically known as 'Travelling in the Spirit Vision' and whether it is more than an extension of the power of seeing the moving pictures on the Sphere of Sensation (the akashic envelope) is difficult to determine. The stages of 'Travelling in the Spirit Vision are as follows:—

(1) To become conscious of a figure walking amidst the scenery of an unfamiliar country.
(2) To realise that it is one's own figure.
(3) To look through the eyes of the figure.
(4) To feel with the figure's sensations.
(5) To gain the ability to consciously direct its operations, to control its inhibitions, and to get it to visit unfamiliar people and places.

'It is as though consciousness was extruded from one's own body and taken over a body either created for the purpose or invoked out of the astral sphere. It seems probably that as the Sphere of Sensation reflects everything on the physical plane it contains a reflection of the material body of the percipient. If this is so it would follow that the body could be made to travel within the Sphere of Sensation and visit all things reflected therein.

'The perception of the Astral Plane is peculiarly liable to delusion arising from defects in the sensorium or physical brain —an object seen through a faulty glass is distorted. As the brain can be rendered sensitive is any particular direction by symbol, so these errors can be corrected by symbol. The various qualities in each man's mature nature are symbolised by the planets, hence planetary symbols can be used to correct such errors.

'The visions experienced may be merely compounded from memory. In this case build up, in brilliant white light, in front of any image suspected of being compounded from memory, the Hebrew letter Tau, symbol of the Qabalistic Path of Saturn, the 'Great One of the Night of Time', whose sober influence causes memory pictures to disappear. Similarly the Hebrew letter Beth (for Mercury), formulated in the same way, dissipates the products of lying in intellectual illusion. The Hebrew letter Daleth (for Venus) is used for intellectual vanity; the Hebrew letter Gimel (for the Moon) is used for wavering mind; the Hebrew letter Resh (for the Sun) is used for delusions caused by intellectual haughtiness; the Hebrew letter Kaph (for Jupiter) is used against imagination, and the Hebrew letter Peh (for Mars) is used against revenge and hatred'.

APPENDIX D
The Fugitive Flying Rolls

In a postscript to his Preface to *The Magicians of the Golden Dawn* Ellic Howe describes the last-minute discovery of a cache of Golden Dawn documents that included the parchment Rolls of the Inner and Outer Orders and the official address book, all of which provided him with invaluable biographical information. Three years after the publication of his book Mr Howe introduced me to the custodian of these documents, who, in due course, permitted me to use further material from them for some of the Appendices in my own study, *The Golden Dawn: Twilight of the Magicians*. What neither Ellic Howe nor myself had realized, however, was that this second 'Private Collection' contained far more than we had at first seen or suspected, for its custodian had no idea that either of us would be interested in anything but the dry bones of the Order's history.

When he learned that my own interests extended to the rituals and teaching of the Golden Dawn, the custodian showed me some two dozen bound volumes of miscellaneous rituals, essays, and records of magical working, in the autographs of Ayton, Westcott, Florence Farr, and other members of the Inner Order. Among them was a fat octavo labelled 'Flying Rolls etc', which I borrowed—largely for the sake of the 'etc', a blanket covering revised (and unrecorded) rituals of the Neophyte and Zelator grades, records of the workings of the Sphere Group, and the Minute Book of the Ahathoor Temple in Paris. Out of curiosity I decided to compare the Flying Rolls with the printed texts in *Astral Projection, Magic and Alchemy*, and found that they included all the missing Rolls that Mr King had been unable to trace, together with variant texts of the early, and rather dull, Flying Rolls.

Some were in the hand of Westcott, others were transcriptions by Percy Bullock, but the majority had been diligently copied in 1898 by Frater Tenax Propositi. This was the motto of Colonel Sir Henry Edward Colvile, who became a member of Isis-Urania Temple in November 1896, on the same day as his wife, progressed rapidly and entered the Second Order on 5 December 1897 (Lady Colvile entered the Second Order seven months later than her husband). Sir Henry was a diligent student, not only copying the Flying Rolls but making notes on his work in Florence Farr's Sphere Group. His associates in that group—

Mrs Rand, Colonel Webber, Blackden, and Palmer-Thomas—later followed A. E. Waite at the time of the schism of 1903 (although Florence herself did not), and it seems probable that Sir Henry also supported Waite, although there are no records of his activities in the Order after 1901.

Whether or not Sir Henry Colvile followed Waite, his papers certainly did, and Waite catalogued them, bound them and preserved them for occult posterity. Now that after eighty years they have finally come to light, it seems fitting to me, if only for the sake of completeness, that the missing texts should be published. I have my own opinion as to their literary merit, but this I shall reserve to myself, presenting the texts as they were written and passing no judgement upon their intrinsic, magical worth—for I am no magician, and this is a question I must leave to others to decide.

Flying Roll No. XXII

Issued by N.O.M. 8 October 1893, being Essays by V. H. F. Quaestor Lucis on:
  (1) Free Will and the Theory of Separateness
  (2) River of Life
(No official G.D Authority)

While Oriental Theosophy postulates the unity of all Life in its basic source, it makes the attainment of conscious union between the lower of intellectual aspect of mind with the Soul or Higher Manas dependent on the effort of the former, or in other words of the striving of the personality.

Again in the Hermetic School, of which Dr Hartmann is an independent interpreter, the freedom of each person to decide whether to climb the Mount of Initiation or to remain on the lower plane of intellectual rational life is strongly insisted on.

The position of these schools would apparently be that Primordial Being differentiates itself into Units or atoms, each of which contains the potentialities of its original. Free Will being attributed to original Being, it follows that each unit or atom possesses Free Will in potentia. Finding himself in incarnate condition, living in the sense-mediated planes of self-consciousness, it may strive or decide not to strive to attain union with its Higher Principles, or to bring the illumination of these higher aspects of its being, into functioning conjointly with the rational intellectual plane of normal life.

This can only be effected, according to these schools, by the outer or personal degree of life reaching up and striving to come into contact with the inner principles.

This is apparently one of those veils which oriental and ancient systems considered to be necessary till the student dared himself to tear them asunder, but its retention in the sense of the teaching of transcendental philosophy ceases to be reasonable. It is in contradiction also with those portions of Theosophic teaching which condemn 'the illusion of personal existance' and the 'Heresy of Separateness'. It is also untenable in the face of Mr Maitland's theosophic teachings with the reference to the centrifugal current in man, which returns from the circumference of Being as centripetal, thus inferring that re-ascent is the sequential effect in continuity of descent, that evolution is self inherent in involution, that unfolding is implicit in involving.

To teach that conjunction with the higher principles of consciousness may be effected by the will of the lower personality, is to attribute a vitality to the personality which Theosophy itself contravenes in its teachings as to the illusion of personal existence, and to lose sight of the fact that man is not the former but the formed, that personality is but the external manifestation of the one self determinating power.

To teach that each atom or unit, differentiated from original Being possesses Free Will, is to imply that they are separated from Original Being and possess existence in themselves; or to fall into the 'heresy of separateness' and to forget the identity of the unit and the Universal of the self-reference which is implicit in experience and demonstrates the permanent relation, ever present, which links the unit with the fountain source. To imply that the lower aspects of mind have separated off from those which are left and dwell in the higher planes, till conjunction or reintegration has been effected by the lower, is to lose sight of the fact that, while aspects of consciousness may [be] distinguished, they cannot be separated without destroying the unity of Being.

To imply that instinctual rational man may develop his own Will power, that he may make his own condition of life, is to arrogate to the external personality the prerogative of disposing of that one self determinating power which manifests through him, of which he is the instrument or media, the expression the unfoldment.

The original plan of the Great Architect cannot be altered by the external manifestation thereof. The successive unfolding of the inner aspects of man's consciousness must be subject to the Law of the One Determiner, which alone knows itself from centre to circumference, a ground and a fulfilment.

The action of the one determinating Power on the plane of nature illustrates its mode or process. It shows results achieved by a continual, gradual, consecutive unfolding from within. The Sun builds up vegetable forms of life from the seed, beginning with the root, stem, bud, blossom, fruit. The uniformity of law manifesting in the correlated modes in different planes is a generally accepted axiom in occultism, so, by analogy, must our internal state be successively unfolded from within by the rays of our Spiritual Sun or Centre of Life. So also must the recognition of the permanent relation with our Ground of Being or Fountain Source return Man's will to its Central Source.

If for effort of the Personality we substitute the desire to have ever present recognition within us of the reception of all power from the central Source of Being, the desire to be able permanently to associate our lives, in thought, as an external manifestation of the One Determinating Power, and thus relate our actions to the original Source of Being, that will probably be more likely to contribute towards unfoldment from within.

Some Considerations on the Sepher Yetzirah

Transcendental Philosophy shows that the unit is permanently related with its Source or Fountain of Being. Experience, when analysed, is found to bear relation or self reference between the permanent element of Being, which is ever present, which wells up in thought and forms the ground of cogitation on the one hand with the actual 'I' on the other. Thought is a relation and the subject identity recedes ever behind the regarding mind. Hence events may be said to be in time and knowledge out of time. The phenomenal world is then related in experience by the Thinker to the subjective reality.

It is this 'relating' present in thought, the self reference implied in experience, which ever unites the Unit with its ground or source — its permanent element, and this would appear in the Path, on the Tree of Life by the ☽ or reflection which unites the Microprosopus with the Macroprosopus, its source: it would also appear to be symbolized by the River of Life 'Nahar' which unflows from the Supernal Eden or Spiritual Being or Microprosopus or Being manifested in Time.

But the permanent relation between the unit or 'I' and its subjective ground must probably have an occult natural aspect as well as the metaphysical one I have illustrated. In other words there must be a force behind thought of which what we cognise as thought is the manifestation and it must be that force which constitutes the real relation between the Unit and the Universal. That permanent relation, that Force manifested as thought I believe is the River of Life bearing within it and unfolding the four elements of Being; Spirit, Soul, Mind, Instinct.

That emanation of Life or Spirit, the Sephira, the Sepher Yetzirah says extends through all things. Through God's power and existence every element has its power and source from a higher Force and all things have their common origin from the Holy Spirit. So God is at once both the matter and the form of the Universe, yet He is not only the form, for nothing can or does exist out of Himself.

The suggestion arises whether we can form any concrete conception of that Emanating Force—the 'River of Life' which permanently relates the 'I' with its source, as well as the metaphysical relation described and which we cognise as thought. Will not the conception of the centrifugal force in which the centripetal is inherent and inseparable, assist us, carrying as it does that unfolding is implicit in involving, that evolution and development is the sequential effect in continuity of involution.

The circuit of electricity will help us further, issuing as positive until its reaches the negative pole, when it returns on itself to its source. In this indeed we have an illustration of a positive Universal Ground or Brain, as it is well known that electricity is not created *de novo* by the dynamo. It is generated or emanates from an under[lying?] source of which the Earth is but one reservoir or condenser. Edison's experiments, the similar research of Greenwich Observatory, show the magnetic storms of Earth which coincide with and are correlated with the Sun spots, thus showing the lives of our coal miners to depend on the state of the Sun. It is well known that magnetism is an effect of electricity. The passing of a current of electricity through a bar of iron converts it into a magnet. The presence of a current in one wire 'induces' a current in any wire near it.

The action of the Sun on the Earth above referred to is under the same law. The presence of electricity in our Earth, itself entails its polarity, its positive and negative poles—consequently its attracting and repelling force or its centrifugal and centripetal currents. The Aurora Borealis of our Earth and the Solar Corona or photosphere are probably similar effects with regard to these orbs. So what the magnetic field or radiation is to a magnet, which though not seen visually is illustrated by iron filings spread on a piece of paper and held over a magnet—What these spheres are to a magnet, the Earth and Sun, most probably our aura is to us. This aura Madame Blavatsky described as a magnetic aura, a psychic effluvium partaking both of the mind and of the body. It is Electro-vital and Electro-mental.

Have we not in these examples illustrations of the force pervading the Universe, coexisting in the unit and in the whole, inter relating all into one Unity, manifesting in each in accord with one universal and all-pervading law.

We have here, I think, the illustration of the one determining force, the River of Life, manifesting Unity and its media, and cognised by these units as thought.

In this connection a further reflection suggests itself for consideration with regard to the Sepher Yetzirah. While the four planes of Being may be viewed a distinguishable, they must be inseparable, as the unity of Being cannot be divided, and, as the Sepher Yetzirah itself says, the Elements of Being each have their source in a higher form and all from the Spirit which is both Form and Substance and in which are all things. In accord with the Law of Uniformity, these Elements must coexist in Unity, as well as in the Universal, in the microcosm as well as in the macrocosm. It is probable therefore that we may consider the Four Worlds as the planes through which the unit descends from its Fountain Source to its present circumferential state and by which descent it obtains a vehicle in each element or relation in each place.

Is not the Wheel of Life in the door of the Vault a key to this question? showing, as it does, all four elements coexisting in the Unit. But this cannot be considered as an integration of four living creatures, each separate and having to be integrated into Unity, in as much as the Unity of Being could never be divided up and separated without entailing annihilation and chaos. If these four Elements are viewed as Spirit, Soul, Mind, Instinct, it is evident that these do not co-exist in each unit. The problem suggested is or may possibly be to attain conscious functioning of each of the elements of Being in relation with its place or World.

These descending states in the ultimation of the Unit find their parallel in the process of thought. Every thought has an objective aspect, as well as its subjective aspect, and one may say, like the unit of being, thought emanates from original Being, is produced from the unmanifested in Atziluth, takes shape in Briah, form in Yetzirah and ultimates in Assiah, in which consideration we return to the two aspects of the River of Life, we referred to at the beginning of this paper, viz. the metaphysical and the occult.

What constitutes the difference between that part of the River of Life which takes shape in Briah, and incarnates as volition, and that which emanates through us as thought, remaining disincarnate, and what becomes of that River of Thought which takes disincarnate form and is ultimated through us?

We ourselves must have been produced from the unmanifest in Atziluth, taken soul and shape in Briah, mind and form in Yetzirah, a concrete shell and instinct in Assiah. Yet we remain permanently attached to our own source, by a River of Life or electricity, which conveys to us in reflection and intuition what we cognise as thought from our original source. Is this the continuation of the River of Life which produces us? Does that River still flow through us its self-deluminated vehicles, and manifest as thought? Then is not our personality an objective representation of the attributes present in that River of Life? Or a reflection in form of the type on the sense mediated plane of that which involved itself by determination and is now unfolding to our consciousness, as the centrifugal current returns on itself as centripetal?

The conception of the Duality of Will, good and evil, must have arisen presumably from the appearance of there being a conflict between the 'River of Life' flowing through man and the impediments or obstructions raised on the circumference by the atom cells or lives used in the construction of the outer shell or organism and which were drawn from the animal vegetable and mineral states. But these are only manifestations of the One Universal Life, equally with the Primum Mobile of Man, and the relation or reaction between these lives or states of consciousness and the consciousness of the Entity using them must in reality be a relation of harmony though in appearance there may be conflict, and it must not be forgotten that the Primum Mobile or Entity using these lives on its circumference is in reality the one River of Life, and let me now again suggest the question of what becomes of the Thought thus ultimated? and which we find to be manifested as the River of Life.

275

The relation between the cells or lives used by the Unit in the integration of its form or its body and the Primum Mobile which has integrated that body, has its parallel in the Greater Universe in the relation of the Unit or outer Manifestation to the Universal, then determination whose body they form. The ultimation of each unit is undoubtedly in accord with the archetypal plan, of which we are parts, manifested objectively, yet there is all appearance of revolt, of conflict between the unity, occupying the schools of Atheism, Materialism, Evolution and their Determination.

The conflict between these units of manifestation and their Determination is probably as real as that between the Wills and Lives, making up the shell or organism and its constructor or controller or Primum Mobile. It is [unclear: 'it with the Sun', but that makes no sense. RG] the same 'River of Life' acting in the next or more external plane, that of the shells or matter. Let it be remembered that it is the interaction between the 'Unit of Life' or Primum Mobile in Man and the other units and particularisation of the Universe that begets the manifold of experience, which is the function of the unit to relate and unify.

Flying Roll No. XXIV

Part of a Lecture on Horary Astrology delivered in 1892 to the Adepti in college assembled, by V. H. Frater Resurgam.

Verified Horary Figure by Nemo. *Question*—Will queried [i.e. the subject of a query] die of his present illness?

Hearing by letter that my maternal uncle, an octogenarian was seriously ill from pneumonia, I drew a figure for the moment of intuition to do so, which was while reading the communication. His illness had commenced about February 7th and he was now confined to bed.

The student can easily cast the figure for 11^h45^m a.m. February 26th 1887 London W. RA of M $22^h25\text{-}6^s$ and $332°21'24''$ in arc. ♓ 0.17 culminating ♈. ♋ 4°45 ascending; ☉ in ♓ $7°32'47''$, ☽ in ♈ $16°23'$, ☿ in ♓ $23°19'$, ♀ in ♓ $27°54'$, ♂ in ♓ $20°32$. ♃ in ♍ 5°48, retrograde, ♄ in ♋ $15°54'$ retrograde, ♅ in ♎ $11°46'$ retrograde, ♆ in ♑ $25°10'$. Declination ☉ $8°43'$ S. ☽ $2°47'19''$ N. ☿ $2°29'$ S. ♀ $1°56'$ S. ♂ $4°31'$ S. ♃ $12°9'$ S. ♄ $22°25'$ N. ♅ $3°59'$ S. ♆ $17°25'$ N. The Moon's North node was in ♌ 27.35 Pars Fortuna was in ♌ 13°32. The Moon's motion in longitude was $11°49'56''$ in the 24 hours.

As the querited was the fourth of my maternal uncles and aunts, my mother being the youngest of the family, I took the 10th House of the figure for herself and the 12th (or 3rd from the 10th) for her eldest brother or sister, the 2nd for the 2nd, the 4th for the 3rd and the 6th for the 4th, the querited, and correspondingly the 1st (or 8th from the 6th) for his 8th or House of Death. There ♂ ruled querited's 1st House and ☽ his 8th, the aspect being ☽ 25°.51. ♅ , separating from the quindecile (24°) and applying to his semisextile. The past aspects being good but very weak showed his past state of health, which had been very fair considering his age, but not robust—the applying aspect being good and stronger than his preceding, ♂ moreover being dignified by triplicity, term and decanate and also receiving Luna by House, sure recovery from illness was shown, but at the same time not absolute restoration to health. Had the significant been applying to a Δ or even a *, I should have predicted not only complete recovery from his acute attack, but also a continuance of a vigorious old age. Had the case been chronic I should have predicted a partial restoration of health at the time indicated, In this instance however, acute pneumonia being a self limited disease, I predicted a complete recovery from the pulmonary attack itself and an escape from death, but not restoration to vigorous health. Nevertheless the severity and danger of the illness was shown by *Cauda* in querited's 4th House, by ♄ lord of his 4th posited in close ☐ to ☽ ruler of his 8th posited in his 6th and slow in motion. As ☽ the applying significator, was in a movable sign and a succedent house, each degree signified a week; therefore as wanted 4°9′ of the complete semisextile, I judged that querited would be convalescent in 4 weeks and 1 day, or March 27th. On March 29th he walked out in his garden for the first time and fully recovered from the pneumonia. *Observations* (1) This shows the necessity of selecting the exact house corresponding to querited and not generalising. Had I taken his 12th house of the figure as signifying maternal uncles and aunts in general (being his 3rd from the 10th, and the 7th (or 8th from 12th) for querited's death, the aspects of the Lords thereof would have been ♀ 105° ♄ exactly, and applying to ☐, showing present fair health and danger to life in 8 weeks, which was not the case (Future 1.106).

(2) It made no difference to the selection of the 6th house of the figure as the querited's 1st, that two elder brothers (the 1st and 3rd of the family) were deceased. They has to be taken into consideration in the calculation of his appropriate house, just the same as if they had been living.   277

(3) Had I taken the 8th house of the figure as signifying querited's death, the aspect would have been ☌ 115.22 ♄, applying to 108°, signifying recovery in 7⅓ weeks which was also not the case (Future 1.107).

(4) The ☽ was in latitude 3°58′ S and ♂ in 0°50′ S, adding the sum of these to the degrees and minutes required to form the perfect semisextile, and converting the total amount so obtained into time, would have prolonged the time of the event by 4°48′ or nearly five weeks; yet recovery occurred only two days after the exact time predicted (Future 1.60).

(5) The ☽ was 13° distant from the cusp of the house in which he was posited, yet this made no difference whatever in the calculation of time (Future 1.60).

(6) The ☽ applied to par. decl. ♂ being 1°43′4″ distant; yet no danger to life occurred at the corresponding time (Future 1.109).

(7) As the question was concerning the querited only, Scorpio, the sign of his 1st hour described him, a corpulent, strong, able body, somewhat broad and square face, short necked, a squat well-trussed fellow (Lilly p. 63). But the ascendant of the figure does not describe myself, because though the querent, the question was not concerning myself (Future, 1.171).

(8) ♅ is strongly dignified in Scorpio; but the sign is not its diurnal home. Were it so, the aspect would have been ☽ 175°23′ ♅ separating from ☍, implying past danger to life and applying to the quadrasextile (150°) Signifying some illness in about 25⅓ weeks, neither of which significations were in accordance with facts (Future 1.29.30).

(9) As ♂ ruled both the querited's 1st and 6th Houses no judgement could be formed from the Lord of the 6th, otherwise it would have entered in the calculation, though in a question of the duration of life, I consider the 8th House *coeteri paribus*, the most important (Future 1.108).

(10) In this figure ♂ was in the 10th, subradius and applying to combustion, also ♄ Lord of the 7th, was in his detriment and retrograde both being therefore 'unfortunate.' Nevertheless I did not 'end in the discredit of the artist' but the reverse, neither was I unable to 'scarce give a solid judgement' (Future 1.109-1).

[Note by F. K. The significance of such notes as 'Future 1.108' is not known to me. Presumably as a result of textual corruptions, RA and ST as given are incompatible.]

Flying Roll No. XXVIII

On the value of Magic Implements and Insignia in methods of Divination. By D.D.C.F. and N.O.M.

As far as the Adeptus Minor is concerned, the successful practice of Divination, whether Astrology, Geomancy, or Tarot depends upon the training of intuition. The rules of Astrology, the dots of Geomancy and the law of the opening of the Key are the guides which lead the intuition and limit its function to definite aims and ends.

All processes of Divination require a concentration of mind and of the vital and astral forces of the operator upon the subject matter; this being so, it is of vital importance to success that the mind does not wander, the body be at rest and peace. No opposing forces intervene. That the personal and social attitude be cast aside. These things being so, it is of great value to furnish the physical with symbols of protection and power, and the astral form with the astral counterpart of their insignia and implements.

For by such means are the lower Elementals forced to abandon their attacks and they being absent, the opportunity is presented for the access of Superior Powers. For it is the Higher Self which receives prompting from Higher Powers at those times when the Lower Self is set aside, and when the interference of Elementary and Qlipothic forces is provided against.

Do not attempt Divination when angry, when anxious and worried, when ill, when fearful, for under all these circumstances the tendency to obsession is great.

As an Adeptus Minor, Divine when calm, peaceful, healthy and courageous. To supplement your power, use the means provided by your Adeptship: the white robe, emblem of Purity. The yellow sash of 5=6 rank. The Rose-Cross, that comprehensive symbol, so well able to afford mystic protection and which itself affirms the support of the knowledge and the virtues of the keys of Wisdom you have already attained. Hold, or have at hand, the magic sword of Mars and Geburah to hinder the attacks of opposing forces acting with hostile intent, and of errant forces crossing your path. It will also increase the power of your resolves. The Lotus Wand should be in frequent use, because it gives precision to your working and supplies a ready means of appeal to any special force, zodiacal or planetary, by hour or present position; or elementary by triplicity.

The four Elemental Implements should be all laid on the table before you for immediate use as required: the whole four must be present to preserve a certain Balance and Harmony in the sphere of your aura, and yet it is desirable to take up and hold with concentrated idea any one of them when trying to form an estimate of the strength of the corresponding force in any detail of your work: or you may hold one of them to secure physical or astral power and intensity of that character or again to preserve your own natural equilibrium. For example, in the act of judging an astrologic Figure. Suppose you find the ascendant in Aries and Mars is found in Virgo. To ascertain more accurately their effects in the case, take the Lotus Wand in the Right hand and use the left for the Elemental Implements. Hold by the scarlet band of ♈, consider, take up the Fire Wand, consider, then shift the grasp to ♍ and lay down the Fire Wand and take up the Pentacle for that earthy sign.

Again, suppose the end of the matter to be in ♋ and the ☉ in ♑. Take the Lotus Wand first by one sign band and then by the other, taking up with the left, the Cup and Pentacle in succession. Or if ♄ be in ♎ in ☐ to the ☽ hold the Wand by the emerald band and take the air dagger in the left hand, if you wish to consider what mischief the square of ♄ does to ☽. The same method will apply to a Geomantic Consideration, and the Lotus Wand is here especially suitable, for Geomantic Working is markedly Zodiacal rather than Planetary.

If a Divination *must* be done when you are in trouble, use the sword to give strength in working and fortitude: holding it in the right hand and wand or implement in the left hand. In a Tarot judgement the same mode of working conduces to accuracy of result. In Geomancy also you may hold the sword in the left hand, while making the dot with the right hand. The actual presence of your mystical motto, painted upon your magical weapon has its special use of 'identifying the Power of the weapon with your own force.'

You should *not* imprint your own motto upon a telesm or flashing tablet given by you to another member. But you *may* add it to such a design intended by you, for your own wearing or use. This caution does not apply to a Telesm drawn and energised by you for presentation to the Chiefs for purposes of examination or for tests of your ability: in such case you may preferably write your motto on the reverse side of the Talisman or Design.

[Note by F.K. Some copies of this document give it the title 'On Robes.']

Flying Roll No. XXIX

Notice to all Members of the Second Order. By G. H. Frater D.D.C.F. 7=4, Chief Adept.

On their attainment of the Grade of Theoricus Adeptus Minor I appoint the four following members of the Second Order, viz. V.H. Fra. Levavi Oculos, V.H. Soror Sapientia Sapienti dono data, V.H. Fra. Resurgam, V.H. Soror Fortiter et Recte, to assist the G.H. Frater Non Omnis Moriar, Chief Adept in Charge in Britannia Magna cum Hibernia et Coloniis suis, in ruling and management of the Second Order, as his immediate Lieutenants and under his immediate orders. And upon these Four, as a badge of their office I have conferred the symbols of HORUS, ISIS, AROUERIS and NEPHTHYS as a distinctive mark of the authority of each, a higher ranking superior to all other members of the Second Order until further notice; and to show to which particular one of them appeal is to be made by other members in case of difficulty.

And the decisions of these Four are to be subject to the approval and ratification of the G.H. Fra. Non Omnis Moriar.

To the V.H. Fra. L.O. I have given the symbol of HORUS showing that appeal is to be made in all grave matters coming under the dominion of Horus . . . such as Disagreement. All things pertaining to wrath, misunderstanding and irritation between members. Enforcement of the authority of the Chief of the Order. All frankly suggested plans requiring energy in their carrying out. Also the administration of advice to inferior members of the Second Order on all matters requiring decisive action.

To V.H. Soror S.S.D.D. I have given the symbol of HICE, ISIS showing that unto her appeal is to be made in all grave matters coming under the dominion of Isis . . . such as the maintenance of peace and harmony between members. Instruction in doubtful application of occult correspondences. Decision in cases of vacillation and doubting of mind of inferior members, and decisions in matters affecting the harmony existing between different methods of occult working.

To V.H. Fra. Resurgam I have given the symbol of AROUERIS, showing that unto him appeal is to be made in all grave matters coming under the Dominion of Aroueris . . . such as all cases of doubt and difficulty in the application of rules for divination. Matters requiring subtlety and tact, and all decisions regarding the formulation of ideas.

To V.H. Soror F et R I have given the symbol of NEPHTHYS showing that unto her appeal is to be made in all grave matters coming under the dominion of Nephthys . . . such as all cases of difficulty in the application of given rules to material correspondences. Difficulties in the ordering of studies of inferior members. All questions regarding difficulty in the selection of Forces to work, under or with, for a fixed end. All cases of doubt or difficulty requiring a right application of rules already given.

These four members aforesaid to be coequal in authority under the super-intendence of the 'Chief Adept in Charge' and in all matters of difficulty their decisions being submitted to him for ratification. And if (which is not frequently probable) a case shall fall under more than one of their heads, it is to be submitted equally to the judgement of those two or more Theorici Adepti aforesaid under whose office it is classed. And I trust that members of inferior rank will not abuse the faculty of appeal herein accorded, by constantly harassing the members aforesaid concerning trivial and unimportant subjects.

(signed) Deo Duce, Comite Ferro 7=4

[Note by F.K. 'Resurgam' was, as stated, earlier, Dr Berridge; 'Sapientia . . .' was Florence Farr; 'Levavi Oculos' was P. Bullock; and 'Fortiter et Recte' was Annie Horniman.]

Flying Roll No. XXXI

Correspondence between the Enochian and Ethiopic Alphabets, by V.N.R. and V.H. Ad.Maj.

In the Book of the Concourse of the Forces it is stated that the letters of the Enochian Alphabet are of the nature of sigils and can therefore be better employed for magical purposes than our ordinary Roman characters, and we find proof of their force and correctness as to correspondence in the skrying of the squares of the Enochian Tablets. One or more of these letters being placed on the particular square employed in a vision, instead of the Roman letter will aid the skrying power by compelling the force of concentration on to the one square in question and on no other.

For however great may be the power of Clairvoyance, the student will find himself obtaining erroneous results should he not carry his correspondences to the last detail. Therefore it is wise to use the particular sigil of the square, as well as the general one of the Tablet, and naturally as well the ruling Names (Deity, Angelic and otherwise) with the correct pronunciation and *vibration* thereof, the colours &c &c.

The descent of the Book of the 'Concourse of the Forces' from the Egyptian Wisdom is undoubted, for we find that the very key note of the scheme of these tablets is the esoteric meaning of the Great Egyptian Symbols of the Pyramid and the Sphinx. The probability is then that this Tablet language has its origin in the Egyptian and its close resemblance to the Ethiopic (which is generally supposed to be derived from Egyptian) is very marked as the Table on page 000 will show.

Certainly, certain of these letters have a resemblance only when inverted or transposed, but this is not surprising when we consider the nature of hiero-glyphics, which can be read from right to left or vice versa and downward or in groups, and that a letter may also be turned in several directions.

The Ethiopic is composed (according to Gesenius' Heb[rew] Gram[mar]) of 26 letters all consonantal (as are most Semitic languages) the vowels being expressed by little curves or dashes seven in number, for instance ʊ , ʊ (here the curve or dash is at the right side and further it is half way up. In the second case the curve is at the top.)

In the Tablets, when written in the Roman character the vowels are sometimes omitted. It is for this reason that we have been told to pronouce certain vowels after certain consonants. e.g. If B in an Angel name precedes another consonant, as in SOBHA thou mayest pronounce it SOBAYHAH (Book of the Angelic Calls).

[There follows a table of Ethiopic and Enochian characters for comparative purposes, with a guide to pronunciation, and a table of the Ethiopic alphabet giving all the diacritical marks. R.G.]

Flying Roll No. XXXII

Theban Letters. Issued by N.O.M.

In the Flying Roll which explains the Yetziratic formation of an image of Adonai ha-Aretz it will be noted that the name is written upon the girdle in Theban characters. Many members having asked for this alphabet, I now issue this roll to furnish the required knowledge.

[Here follows a table of Theban letters, as found in Barrett's *The Magus*, on the plate facing p. 64 of Book II]

These letters are recorded by Peter of Abano, also called Petrus di Appone who derived from Honorius the Theban. This Honorius is said by many to have been a Pope. There have been four Popes named Honorius, but neither [*sic*] of them was called 'Theban'. Peter of Abano flourished circa A.D. 1300. This Alphabet is found in Cornelius Agrippa's *Works* and in Barrett's *Magus*.

[Note by F.K. The so-called Theban letters were also printed, along with other 'magical alphabets', as an appendix to Mathers' edition of *The Key of Solomon*.]

Flying Roll No. III

1. If you are leaving home, or will be away, or if there be any reason why these messages should not be sent to you—you must inform the member *from* whom you receive messages.

2. Messages are to be returned to N.O.M. whenever they cannot be sent to the proper member; and a note is to be added, stating the reason why this is necessary.

3. A time for keeping each message will be written upon each:- any member who causes unnecessary delay will incur the risk of being omitted from the next circulation.

4. Each member must sign the form and add data of receipt and

sending on, under a similar penalty on failure to do this duty which is required for the common good.

N.O.M.

5. Do not keep anywhere, the address of the office, written out, or only written in Hebrew.

Flying Roll No. VIII

A Geometrical Way to Draw a Pentagram

Let AB be any line of the length required for the distance between the points of Earth and Fire. Bisect AB in O and from O draw OH

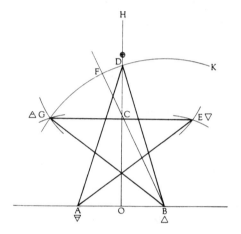

perpendicular to AB. Cut off OC to equal AB.

Join B with C and produce the line BC to F making FC to equal OA. From centre B, with radius BF, draw the circle FDK, cutting OH at D. D is then the 'Spirit' angle of the Pentagram. With the centres B and D draw circles with a radius equal to AB, and they cut each other at E which will be the Water angle. In a similar way [i.e. by drawing a circle of radius AB from centre A] find G the Air angle. Join A, B, D, E, and G in the usual way.

R. A. Gilbert

285

APPENDIX E

Among Westcott's papers is a manuscript 'Catalogue of Flying Rolls' which lists not only the dates of issue but also the prices charged to members for copying. It is of further interest in that it gives the original titles of those Flying Rolls whose content was later changed.

Flying Rolls, Catalogue

		Issued on	
1	Warnings	Nov. 7, [18] 92	2/6
2	Purity and Will	Nov. 24	2/6
3	Instructions	Nov. 24	2/6
4	Spirit Vision, S.S.D.D. and F. [Later re-numbered 6. The authors were Florence Farr and Annie Horniman.]	Nov. 28	2/6
5	Imagination by Resurgam [i.e. Dr Berridge]	Dec. 11	4/-
6	SRMD Note on 2 [i.e. Mathers' Note. Later re-numbered 4.]		4/-
7	Material Alchymy	Dec. 27	6/8 (7/-)*
8	[Enoch Suggestions: erased] Geometric Pentagram [Altered to '95' when the content was altered.]	Feb. 25, [18] 93	1/-
9	Right and Left	Mar. 27	1/6
10	Self Sacrifice	Apr. 8	6/-
11	Clairvoyance	Apr. 9	5/-
12	Telesm[atic] Images and Adonai	May 27	5/-
13	Secrecy and Hermetic (Love)	June 1	3/6
14	Talismans and Flashing Tablets	June 15	3/6
15	Man and God	July 26	4/-

16	Fama Fraternitatis	Aug. 24	3/6
17	Vault Sides	Aug. 29	3/-
18	Progress	Aug. 30	2/-
19	Aims and Means	Sept. 15	4/6
20	Elementary View of Man	Sept. 23	2/3
21	Know Thyself	Sept. 26	4/6 (5/-)*
22	Quaestor on Free Will [i.e. Quaestor Lucis = Oswald Murray]	Oct. 8	3/9
23	[Regulations for Exams. Oct. 16: erased] Tatwa Visions		2/3
24	Horary Figure by Resurg[am] [i.e. Dr Berridge]	Jan. 12, [18] 94	1/6
25	[Notice re Stamping Letters, 27/1/94: erased] S.S. on Clairvoyance [i.e. Sub Spe = J.W. Brodie-Innes]		3/-
26	Re Planets to Tatwas — a Supplementto XII		
27	Bullock on Theurgia	June 1894	3/-
28	Use of Implements in Divination — N.O.M. & D.D.C.F. [i.e. Non Omnis Moriar = Westcott, and Deo Duce Comite Ferro = Mathers.]	Nov. 3, 1894	
29	Order by D.D.C.F. as to 4 Lieutenants — declared June 18, '94 issued Nov. 8		
30	Tatwas and Skrying & Hierophant's making 0=0 signs		
32	[Originally numbered 31] Theban Letters		1/-
34	[Originally numbered 32] An Exorcism by S.S. [i.e. Sub Spe]		

287

33	[New Regulations: erased]	5/6
	Enoch Visions	
31	Ethiopic Letters	2/6
35	Notes on the Z Exordiums	1/-

Number 36 is not included as this was not issued until late in 1897, by which time Westcott had resigned from office in the Order.

*The revised prices are given in brackets.

R. A. Gilbert